MASTER

Agatha Christie was the most ... and remains popular. Numerous movies and television shows have been inspired by her work. Hercule Poirot and Jane Marple are her two best known detectives.

Josephine Bell wrote mysteries and historical romances prolifically for many years. Her medical background is apparent in many of her novels. Although Dr. David Wintringham is the detective in several early books, she soon abandoned him and wrote standalone mysteries from that point forward.

Managansett Press

MASTERS OF DETECTION

Don D'Ammassa is the author of:

Horror
Blood Beast
Servant of Chaos
Caverns of Chaos
Wings over Manhattan
Twisted Images
The Gargoyle
That Way Madness Lies
Little Evils
Passing Death
Date with the Dark
The Devil Is in the Details
Living Things
Shadows Over R'Lyeh
More Shadows Over R'Lyeh
Still More Shadows Over R'Lyeh
Dark Mistress (as Paula Sheffield)
Dark Muse (as Paula Sheffield)
Night Rules (as Paul Alan Sheffield)

Science Fiction
Scarab
Haven
Narcissus
Translation Station
The Sinking Island
Alien & Otherwise
Wormdance
Sandcastles
Carbon Copies
Phantom of the Space Opera
The Retro Collection
Translation Station & Other Stories

Mysteries
Murder in Silverplate
Dead of Winter
Death at the Art Gallery
Death on the Mountain
Death on Black Island
Death in Black and White
Death in the Neighborhood

Fantasy
The Kaleidoscope
Elaborate Lies
The Maltese Gargoyle
Perilous Pursuits
Multiplicity
The Hippogriff of the Baskervilles
Ten Little Homunculi
The 39 Adepts

Nonfiction
The Encyclopedia of Science Fiction
The Encyclopedia of Fantasy & Horror
The Encyclopedia of Adventure Fiction
Masters of Detection Vol 1 - 9
Architects of Tomorrow Vol 1-9
Masters of Adventure Vol 1-4
Masters of Horror Vol 1-4
Masters of Fantasy Vol 1-3
Not Exactly a Memoir

MASTERS OF DETECTION VOL IX

MASTERS OF DETECTION

Copyright ©2024 by Don D'Ammassa. All rights reserved. If you would like to use material from this book other than brief excerpts for review purposes, prior written permission must be received by contacting the author at dondammassa@cox.net.

.

Managansett Press First Edition 2024

MASTERS OF DETECTION VOL IX

MASTERS OF DETECTION

CONTENTS

Josephine Bell   7
Agatha Christie   65

JOSEPHINE BELL

Josephine Bell (1897-1987) was the pseudonym of Doris Bell Ball (birthname Collier). Bell was a prolific writer of mystery novels, although her later work was more properly suspense. She also wrote a number of historical adventures. Several of her early novels are so rare that they are essentially inaccessible, including some of the David Wintringham series. Her early career was in medicine and that provides background in several of her novels. The novels which unfortunately are not covered here are *Murder in Hospital* (1937), which introduced Dr. David Wintringham, *Death on the Borough Council* (1937), *From Natural Causes* (1939), *All Is Vanity* (1940), and *Trouble on Wrekin Farm* (1942

Bell's third novel, *Fall Over Cliff* (1938) features Wintringham. He and his wife Jill, toddler son Nicholas, and a nanny are vacationing on the sea coast when he is asked to help solve a murder that turns out to be the tip of an iceberg of crime and violence. Lillian Medlicott is on her deathbed, and her estate is likely to be divided chiefly between two nephews, Keith Warwick and Bernard Scott. Warwick is a wastrel and philanderer. Scott hopes to marry but is impoverished and with few hopes.

Warwick has been flirting with young Annie Hoad, despite the objections of her violence prone father Ted. He is walking along the cliffs one night, awaiting an unidentified second party, when he trips and falls to his death. It was not an accident because a tripwire is discovered the following morning, although the police believe it was a rabbit snare and investigate no further. Bernard Scott is also a suspect because he has no alibi and possesses some of the distinctive writing materials used to compose the note that arranged the meeting. The note was found in Warwick's pocket. The paper is common at the scout camp where both cousins were working for a man named Robertson.

Warwick's aunt, Julia Kershaw, also lives in the area, but the reader is given a glimpse of her thoughts and she is not the killer. Medlicott dies, clearly before Warwick, and Scott now inherits everything, but he is the one who asks Wintringham to look into the matter after the police lose interest. Wintringham is immediately disturbed to hear that several other members of the family have died under odd circumstances – a drowning, a sudden illness, a riding accident, etc.

Wintringham manages to meet a relative by marriage whose husband died of a sudden chill and diabetes while both Scott and Warwick were staying with them. Warwick emerges as a charmer who was constantly borrowing money which he never repaid. Scott was an introvert whom no one seemed to like. Both men had ample opportunity to tamper with the dead man's insulin.

Although Scott is the obvious suspect, he asks Wintringham to continue his investigation. The riding accident is also puzzling – a pony bolted for no apparent reason – and both cousins were in the area at the time of this death as well. Wintringham finds evidence that the harness was sabotaged and that this was also a successful murder. He also talks to Frew, who tells him that Scott has been noticeably depressed. He also ascertains that the drowned cousin was probably also the victim of an arranged accident, as a warning sign about a dangerous current had been removed.

Scott confides in Kershaw. He did in fact set up an appointment with Warwick on the cliff, but because a clock stopped at the local inn, he was much too late to keep it. He has not told anyone else about this, including Wintringham. Kershaw recommends that he ask Wintringham to end his investigation, but Scott does not want to get married while there is still the possibility that he might be suspected of murder. This pretty clearly suggests that he is innocent despite the growing body of circumstantial evidence.

Wintringham is almost drowned in the same manner as the cousin, and Scott has just arrived and was perfectly capable of engineering the attempt. Wintringham is ambivalent about turning over his findings to Scotland Yard, but decides to do so when Scott marries his fiancé, Eunice Fothergill. Unfortunately, there are holes in his theory and he has doubts once he has laid it out. The timing of events does not conform to his expectations.

The solution is that the earlier murders were committed by Warwick, who also planned to eliminate Scott. The note in his pocket was one of two versions he had written. The other had been given to Scott in order to lure him to the cliff where he could be murdered. Warwick, notoriously clumsy, fell into his own trap and died.

MASTERS OF DETECTION

The Port of London Murders (1938) spends considerable time creating a fairly large cast of interlocking characters, all living in the dock area. A man named Holman runs an import/export office to which no customers ever pay a visit, and it is obvious early on that he is involved in some kind of smuggling operation. He is friendly with Martha Kemp, who runs an expensive clothing shop for women. Her notable employees include Gordon Longford and June Harvey.

Longford is a drug distributor, and one of his clients is Pamela Merston, a wealthy young woman whose recent irritable outbursts have startled her friends. Longford is interested in June Harvey, but she rebuffs his advances. June's father is a tugboat captain. Her younger brother Leslie almost drowned recently and was saved with the assistance of Harry Reed, who has a dinghy. Reed and June begin a flirtation. Reed is a friend of Jim Sawyer, who works on the docks and seems to have more money than he could possibly have earned.

Residents in the area include two impoverished families, the Dunwoodys and the Popes. Their neighbor is the elderly Mrs. Bowerman, a compulsive drinker whose health is failing. There is also a boarder, Mary Holland. Holland is a drug addict and was Kemp's predecessor managing the store. She blackmails Longford who sends her to Dr. Ellis, also an addict and an involuntary distributor.

Because of a heavy fog and some carelessness, two barges being towed by Captain Harvey break loose in the estuary. They are recovered with only some minor damage, but Sawyer discovers that some of the cargo includes smuggled women's wear from the continent. Presumably the latest drug consignment was endangered as well, but apparently it was recovered without incident. Holman and Longford are friends and presumably work together to distribute the drugs.

Holland is found dead in her room, an apparent suicide. Her drug paraphernalia has been taken away. The detective, Chandler, who is investigating has his doubts. She had ingested a particularly painful poison, although there is no indication that she was forced to do so. She had recently consulted Dr. Ellis, who seems unusually uncomfortable when he is interviewed. His car was parked near the house earlier in the day, although apparently it was moved before the woman died.

Chandler mysteriously disappears. His superior is Inspector Mitchell, who appears in some of the Wintringham stories, and when Mitchell reviews Chandler's reports, he feels the same suspicion about Ellis. A group of boys find a box in the water that fell off a barge, and there is more contraband clothing concealed inside. The police quickly connect the smuggling with Holman.

Mitchell suspects that Ellis killed Holland by disguising the poison as cold tea, then returned and removed the drug paraphernalia. Chandler's body is eventually found in a condemned house. Ellis writes out a full confession and commits suicide, but part of the confession is removed before his body is discovered. He substituted poison for the cold tea left for Holland, and then removed the incriminating evidence.

Longford is driven into a rage by revelations that he has been publicly linked to Holland. He strangles Merton but manages to elude the police, who have by now figured that he and Holman were concealing drugs inside the hems of the smuggled dresses. He takes too many chances while escaping, however, and drowns. Holman and Kemp are arrested.

Curtain Call for a Corpse (1938, aka *Death at Half-Term*) brought back David Wintringham. Charles Redesdale is headmaster of a private school and is married to Judith, sister of Wintringham's wife Jill. The Wintringham's nephew Alastair is one of the students, son of Hugh and Margaret Wintringham. Through a combination of circumstances, the planned school play meant to entertain the parents during a summer get together has been replaced by a production offered by a small professional troupe of actors.

The actors include Robert Fenton, Edward Gash, Hilary Stockton, Joan Carson, Lionel Bassett, and Nigel Trent. Fenton and Gash are constantly arguing with each other. The stage manager is George Lemming and the general manager is Cyril Dewhurst. The troupe has been troubled by several acts of petty thievery and Bassett is considered the most likely to be the culprit. Fenton's wife Sonia is also a member and he notices that she seems to have been briefly shocked, as though she had encountered someone alarming after arriving at the school.

The school staff includes Ruth Fawcett, undermatron, Schofield, who is there temporarily to replace a man on medical leave, and

Cranston, who teaches Latin and who finds a mutilated playbill with scratches through the picture of the Fentons. Fawcett is engaged to a teacher named John Hill, but their plans seem to have been put on hold. Sonia Fenton is spotted flirting with Trent, who is not responsive.

Cranston encounters Schofield, who virulently refuses to watch the play and seems quite disturbed. The performance ends but Fenton does not appear for the curtain calls and he is found unconscious, possibly having suffered a stroke. While they are waiting for the ambulance, a pay envelope falls out of Fenton's pocket, and it belongs to Lemming. A closer examination reveals that he has been bludgeoned, the wound concealed by his costume.

Gash reports that his pay envelope has also disappeared. The post mortem confirms that it was murder. It appears that anyone in the troupe could have attacked Fenton. His widow is prostrate, but apparently from fear rather than grief. Dewhurst had been away from the area at the time of the murder, but mystery fans will find this alibi suspicious.

Mitchell arrives to take over the case and promptly finds Schofield in the room where the murder was committed, despite the fact that it was locked. He insists that he was looking for a pair of clubs he uses for exercise, but only one of them is there. The man who startled Sonia when they arrived was Schofield, who has remained out of sight of the actors ever since. Some cash is stolen from one of the teachers.

Mitchell makes a serious error when he discovers that the boys have been looking for the murder weapon. He tells them to stop and that no further possible clues should be brought to him. This is unfortunate because one of the boys, Bruce Pritchard, has in fact found the weapon, which is currently in his locker.

Part of the mystery is revealed. Schofield was once married to Sonia, although they have not met for several years. He was the one who defaced the handbill. He also moved his car at a time that means he could have removed the murder weapon from the scene, although we already know that is not the case. Bassett attempts to slip away during the night but is caught and arrested. Some of the stolen money is found in his wallet but neither Wintringham nor Mitchell believe that he is the thief.

Pritchard and Alastair attempt to find Wintringham since they have been forbidden to approach the police, but circumstances delay their meeting for a considerable time. When they finally speak, the weapon – one of the exercise clubs – is positively identified and turned over to Mitchell. It had been hidden in a cistern. Gash has a bad bruise on one arm that he claims to have gotten recently, but Trent saw it shortly after Fenton was found.

Various possibilities are discussed, the most interesting of which is that Fenton recovered from the eventually mortal blow, was very confused, and performed the last act of the play while already hemorrhaging. He then collapsed. This means that all of the previously determined alibis are potentially worthless. Schofield and Gash appear to be the two most likely suspects, but Wintringham suspects that Gash found the prostrate Fenton and collapsed himself, incurring the injury. This latter turns out to be true. Fenton seemed to be all right and Gash felt guilty later for not saying anything.

The experienced reader will know that Dewhurst is the killer. We have only his word to support his alibi. He had driven off, but he could easily have returned. He is the thief as well. Fenton caught him in the act, which led to the fatal attack. Dewhurst attempts to escape when confronted and is killed in a car crash.

Death at the Medical Board (1944) is a wartime novel. Dr. Rachel Williams is a member of a board that reviews the physical fitness of women volunteering for non-military service. She is surprised while sitting in a restaurant when a new waitress glares at a couple at a nearby table. The couple consists of Ursula Frinton and her new husband, Alan Duncan. Ursula's cousin Reginald is also in the restaurant, as is her old Nanny.

Ursula appears before the board. Although she was seriously ill as a child, she has a statement from a specialist that her heart is sound. This conflicts with the statement of Dr. Maurice Colman, who insists that she is unfit for service. The police suspect Colman, who is away on vacation, of providing bogus exemptions for men unwilling to serve in the army.

Ursula collapses in the dressing room and dies. The cause of death was poison administered by placing a hypodermic needle in a lipstick. It appears that someone had substituted the rigged lipstick for her own. A mysterious woman was present at the time, pretending to be an employee. She was not the waitress. The dead woman had written the letters "PH" before dying, which is the code for a known spy ring, so when Williams asked Dr. David Wintringham to investigate, the government gives him permission to do so.

Wintringham decides to confront the waitress, Phyllis Hilton, who admits that she hated the couple and that she moved Ursula's handbag. She had considered herself engaged to Duncan before he met Ursula. The restaurant uses the same poison in its garden. A visit to the board facility convinces Wintringham that the mystery woman was actually a man, and he finds discarded makeup supplies supporting his argument. It also seems clear to him that the murder went awry, that she was supposed to die before she ever reached the medical board.

Ursula was raised by her Uncle Hubert, Reginald's father. Hubert believed her to be in frail health but accepted her engagement to Duncan, who took an immediate dislike to Reginald. Ursula actually owns the family fortune, and Hubert and Reginald lived there on sufferance. Duncan mentions that Ursula's occasional flareups of heart trouble only happened when she was with her family.

There is some mystery about the various lipsticks connected to the case. Reginald acts forthcoming but Wintringham believes he is holding something back. Hubert is also lying, for no apparent reason, about his knowledge of Ursula's romance. Duncan is now, of course, owner of the estate which also makes him a suspect. Duncan gives Wintringham a cigarette, but it is poisoned and Wintringham collapses briefly. His first suspicion is that he has frightened someone into attempting another murder, but then he realizes that the cigarette might have been planted on Duncan to kill him and restore the estate to the family – although it is not clear that this would be the result. Sure enough, Duncan collapses while driving and has a fatal crash.

Things develop slowly for a while – Hubert had tried to marry Ursula's mother but had been turned down in favor of his brother. Nanny appears to be lying outrageously about her age. But then the situation heats up when someone, Reginald apparently, takes a couple of rifle shots at the Wintringhams while they are walking near the estate. He later admits to it but insists it was an accident. Colman appears to have been avoiding people for a long time.

Hubert invites Wintringham for a conference that accomplishes little, then sends him on a shortcut where he almost falls into a deathtrap, an uncovered well concealed in the darkness. His flashlight had been previously disabled. Nanny may have been responsible. Ursula's will leaves everything to the government but provides a life interest for Hubert, Reginald, and her husband. Her relatives were not aware of this.

"PH" could refer to the criminal, or to Phyllis Hilton, but it is also possible that they are reversed and actually point to Hubert, the "P" actually an "F." Ursula had sent some cough medicine to be analyzed and knew that someone was trying to poison her. Colman is suspected of having committed a murder in Canada, but in fact it is Colman who was killed and the supposed victim is impersonating him. Hubert was blackmailing him into undercutting Ursula's health status and was also poisoning her, with the help of Nanny, who had raised him. She had switched him with his twin brother shortly after they were born and feels guilty that she deprived him of his birthright. Hubert is accidentally killed when he attacks the fake Colman at the climax. The mysterious intruder is a complete red herring, a prank unrelated to the murder.

Death in Clairvoyance (1949) is a Wintringham story – he now has four children – and also includes a genuine psychic. Odette Hamilton just finished serving a brief prison sentence for fraud connected to her operation as a medium. She is in fact genuinely clairvoyant, or precognitive, the distinctions are blurred here. While recovering from her imprisonment, she and a friend – Lucy Travers – are attending a costume party. The hotel has six identical clown costumes available for rental.

Hamilton is alone on a balcony when two of the clowns emerge from a doorway. Moments later, she sees one of them fall over the rail with a knife in his neck. There is no body below and she realizes that the murder probably has not yet occurred. The two women try to account for all of the clowns, but it is impossible.

An hour later the murder is committed and the body is found. It apparently never occurred to the women to return to the balcony and wait. The dead man's papers say that his name is Faulkener, but when his mask is removed Hamilton recognizes him as her ex-husband. Detective Inspector Redbourne is skeptical of her claim about a psychic vision but interested because she knows so much detail about the attack, not to mention their sundered relationship.

There is a bit of a flaw here. Although the police do not credit the clairvoyance, they spend a lot of time trying to track down the other five costumes. A tourist named Parsons and a local man named Cecil Black each rented one. Mark Stone, the clerk who was handling them, is either incompetent of lying. He insists that one man forgot to leave his name, that one went missing unaccountably, and that one remained in his possession. A discarded costume is found in the building, but Parsons still has his.

The man whose name was missed turns out to be David Wintringham. Redbourne is satisfied with his story, confirmed by Hugh Parsons. Together they discover that the murder was committed in the room directly above the place where Hamilton was sitting, and probably just as she had her vision. The room's tenants had gone away unexpectedly, so it had been empty at the time. The chambermaid admits that she loaned her master key to Black, who also admits this is the case. Black is under investigation by Scotland Yard for his possible involvement with black market tire sales.

Two of Wintringham's children decide to do some investigating of their own. They heard that Black was known to keep company with Mirabelle Carter, an entertainer who works at the hotel where the murder was committed. They rather clumsily follow her around but do not learn anything of particular interest, although Black spots them and is indignant.

More connections are revealed. The empty rooms at the hotel are kept by a couple named Finch, who have attended Hamilton's seances, although without having revealed their names. Faulkener/Hamilton visited Marjorie Parsons while her husband was away, but on only one occasion. Black also appears to have paid her a visit.

The unidentified man is tracked down. His name is Frank Gunnell and he is clearly a red herring, although this does help the police to chart the courses of the other five clowns. The costume that was missing was "borrowed" by the town's mayor and returned when no one was around. He is another red herring, which leaves only Black and Parsons as potential killers.

The children witnessed Black's visit to Marjorie Parsons and he spotted them. Wintringham orders them to stop interfering, although in this case it was not their fault that they happened to see something. Wintringham's wife Jill decides to look in on the woman, who suffers from a degenerative disease, and finds her lying dead. There is a partially written note that appears to indicate she had planned to kill herself because of information she received in a private séance with Hamilton, compounded by Black's visit. Hamilton is never conscious of what she says during a séance so can not help. The dead woman kept notes about the séance but they have been destroyed.

The post mortem indicates that the cause of death was a broken neck, but this could have been an accident given the state of her health. A simple fall could have done it. Wintringham learns that Parsons' official duties include monitoring the sale of tires, but there is no indication that he has done anything wrong or that he knew Faulkener. Faulkener was almost certainly blackmailing Black and may have intended to do the same with Parsons.

The children are lured into a cave on the sea coast and a mysterious explosion traps them for several hours. There was a boat in the area just before that, and Wintringham discovers that it belongs to the mayor, although it was obviously taken without his permission. He now knows who the killer is so he convinces the police to organize a séance which all the surviving characters will attend. Black bolts when it is clear that the police know of his black marketing activities, and Parsons is revealed to be the killer. He disposed of Faulkener – who had borrowed the key to the room from Black – to avoid paying blackmail. He was a bigamist, although he had believed his first wife to be dead when he married Marjorie. He has also sent poisoned candies to his actual wife, although she survives. Marjorie had to be killed because she had learned the truth at the séance.

The Summer School Mystery (1950) takes place at a summer music school in the country. Brenda Cooper and Jean Summers are two friends who are the first to arrive and meet Miss Bristow, who manages the facility. The music director is Basil Hanington. Other students include Godfrey Farre, Nancy Knox, John Deal, Derek Fox, and Belinda Power, the last two of whom are a couple. Fox and Power were seen arriving in town but do not appear at the school on time. Fox arrives the next morning, alone.

Cyril Woodhurst, a member of the staff, quite obviously disapproves of Power. Farre is asked to play Power's kettle drums in her absence, but it malfunctions and investigation reveals her dead body concealed inside. The police arrive and quickly determine that she was killed before any of the students arrived at the school, and may have been inside the drum when the instruments were delivered. She had been strangled.

Fox tells Inspector Fitch that he had not seen Power for two days and had not helped pack the drums for shipment. He seems to be somewhat evasive. The drums were prepared for shipment at a music school in London the day before. A door at the site which was normally kept locked was found open. Most of the students were there at the time, as was Woodhurst, who was reportedly ill. He still seemed troubled and had fainted at the time the body was found.

Another student, Bruce Holesworth, tells the police that he saw Fox and Power together at the train station the day before her body was found, which would mean that she was not killed in London. Fox denies having seen her. The condition of the body confirms that she was already dead by then. Deal mentions that Woodhurst had been increasingly hostile to Power recently and had threatened her. Woodhurst disappears.

Fox goes to see David Wintringham. Their conversation takes place off stage, but he is afraid of something other than the police inquiries and has hired Wintringham to investigate. Woodhurst has been ailing for at least two months and the symptoms suggest a cerebral tumor. Wintringham interviews Power's roommate, Brenda Pearce, and inspector Mitchell talks to her aunt Helen, who raised her following the deaths of her parents and who is currently staying with a friend, Mrs. Lowe. Pearce tells him that some of Power's things were taken away the night before she was found but that she was not at home at the time and did not see her. This is not surprising because Power was already dead at that time.

Hanington had been visiting Power recently, although he was considerably older. Fox did not appear to be jealous. Woodhurst is found at a hospital where he is suffering from partial amnesia. Hanington admits that he proposed to Power the night during which she was murdered and that she had rejected him. Wintringham also discovers that a young woman named Smith who worked in the canteen in London was almost Power's twin, that she has recently disappeared, and her identification was fake.

Fox is arrested and Power turns up and announces that she and Fox are married. The dead woman is obviously Smith. She was hiding because she assumed Smith was mistakenly murdered in her place, but in fact she turns out to have been a petty criminal probably eliminated by someone in her gang. Wintringham has suspected the body had been misidentified for some time because her underwear was not the kind Power wore, which means that her aunt must have known that it was not her niece when she identified the body in the morgue.

Although Helen Power provides a reasonable explanation for her mistake, Wingtringham – and the reader – know that she and Lowe have been conspiring. Someone attempts to gas Belinda in her apartment, but Pearce arrives in time to save her. She reports having seen an unknown man on the fire escape. The gang motive for Smith's death is now implausible. Wintringham has a new suspect when he finds remnants of Smith's handbag and jewelry in Lowe's incinerator and a nearby pool.

That night, someone attacks Wintringham in his hotel room and makes off with some of his newfound evidence, but not all of it. With Mitchell's help, he tricks the two women into revealing themselves. Helen Power was the killer but Lowe had tried to cover up for her. Ironically, Power wanted her niece's money so that she could be free of Lowe. Power commits suicide and Lowe is killed accidentally while trying to stop her.

Stranger on a Cliff (1952, aka *To Let: Furnished*) is a variant of the woman in jeopardy plot. Rosamund Townsend is looking for a place to rent for three months while her children are at school and her husband is on assignment at the US embassy. She spots a house – much too large for her – in a remote village and decides to take it despite the high price, and the fact that other than her very efficient chauffeur, Peck, she will be living there alone.

The house is Wentforth Grange, which sounds vaguely familiar to her. This turns out to be the result of a not very credible psychological condition from which she suffers because her first husband, who died at sea shortly after the wedding, lived there for a time. The coincidence of her happening upon it is also rather a stretch of plausibility.

The present owner is Bruce Patterson, who is now abroad recuperating from injuries caused by driving his car over a cliff. Patterson's wife Constance had died of a heart attack a few months earlier, and she was the brother of Jeremy Arkwright, Townsend's first husband. Constance had a secretary, Claire Bates, who was assumed to be having an affair with Bruce. Bates died in the accident.

Townsend settles in well. A Mrs. Spring does the daily housework and Mrs. Godsen, wife of the gardener, does some cooking. The Godsens have taken Peck as a boarder. She also meets the vicar, Caldicott, although she is not really a church goer. The early marriage was in Australia and Townsend had been underage, so his family challenged the legality of the marriage and she had never met any of them. The family is now extinct except for a spinster aunt, Gertrude. Gertrude did not like Constance, but it is obvious that she shares the local suspicion that Patterson murdered her.

Ruth Caldicott, one of the vicar's daughters, was Constance's nurse. She is clearly in love with Bruce but also believes that he killed his wife. She asks Townsend to retrieve a personal diary she left in the house, but Townsend pretends not to find it so that she can read it herself. It implies murder so she takes it to the doctor who was handling Constance's case at the time. He points out that the comments are ambiguous at best.

Townsend finds a cache of family pictures which lead to a stunning revelation. The man she had married was not Jeremy Arkwright. She had married Bruce Patterson, who had stolen his cousin's name for that purpose. And Patterson was not only still alive, but he had just returned from the continent and was planning to stay at the local hotel until her lease ran out in a few weeks. If the marriage is Australia was legal, then Patterson's marriage to Constance was bigamy, as was her own marriage to Simon Townsend.

Patterson comes to look at the gardens and it is clear that he does not recognize Townsend. He makes a tentative effort to flirt which she rebuffs. As time passes, she suspects that he has realized the truth. They eventually have a confrontation and he suggests they renew their original marriage, much to her disgust. She now knows that he murdered Bates. Ruth Caldicott provides additional evidence proving he murdered Constance. Patterson is about to kill her, but Peck intervenes and Patterson suffers a fatal heart attack.

Bones in the Barrow (1953) is one of Bell's best mysteries. Terry Byrnes is taking a train on a night so foggy that the schedules are all disrupted and there are frequent stops. At one of these, he glances at the window of a house nearby just in time to see a woman murdered. The train immediately moves off and circumstances are such that he does not report to the police until the following day. The detective he speaks to believes that something serious may well have happened, but he is unable to determine even a location where the house might have been.

Weeks later, a workman finds bones on a roof that turn out to be from a human hand, probably that of a woman. A painstaking police investigation reveals that a man calling himself Harold Rust rented a room from about the time of the presumed murder until two months later. He had rented a refrigerator and had told his landlady that he sold cat food from a wheelbarrow, although there is no evidence that he ever did so. He was also known to feed stray cats, much to the annoyance of the neighbors. Rust moved out secretly and no one knows where he went. Blood stains are found on his windowsill.

Elsewhere, Janet Capthorn is concerned because her friend Felicity Hilton has stopped answering letters. Felicity has been away from home for months, apparently having her third known affair, this time with a man named Peter, whom no one has ever seen. Her husband, Alastair, has been making transparent excuses about her absence and is uncooperative when the police make inquiries. They are particularly interested because the letters stopped around the time of the murder. Alastair was providing her an allowance through a bank, but the money was withdrawn by means of a messenger. Despite objections from her husband Jack, Felicity goes to Scotland Yard.

Alastair is an amateur archaeologist and he spends a day digging in an old barrow. There he finds some pottery and some bones, the latter of which are clearly ancient. But the police also do some digging and unearth arm bones that match the ones found on the rooftop. Alastair could have buried them while he was digging, but another man – unidentified – had also taken a backpack to the site around the same time.

Byrnes tells his story to a friend who knows David Wintringham and who interests him in the case. He confronts Alastair who breaks down completely when he is told about the bones. Wintringham is quite certain that he did not kill his wife, despite appearances. He learns that a married acquaintance named Basil Sims had occasionally flirted with Felicity, but both Alastair and Sims' wife insist that it was harmless. Wintringham is understandably skeptical and pursues his inquiries.

Hilton calls Wintringham and tells him that his house has been burglarized, though only an old hat is missing. By chance Wintringham finds an abandoned cart near an empty house, and a quick look inside that building makes him even more suspicious. It seems likely that part of the body – the head - was hidden in the chimney. He also finds the man who rented the cart to a man he describes as prosperous looking.

Hilton decides to spend another free day digging, despite a deterioration in his health. The police plan to surreptitiously watch because they believe he will plant more of his wife's bones. Wintringham wants to watch as well, because he believes the real killer has been watching Hilton and using his excursions to plant evidence. The same man who shadowed Hilton on his last trip arrives as well and is recognized by the hotel barman.

The stranger reaches the site after dark, but is alarmed and escapes, leaving behind the severed head. The police conclude that Hilton returned but that makes no sense since they know that the man with the head had a motorcycle, which Hilton did not. They persist in attempting to arrest him even when two people insist that he never left the hotel that evening, and despite having found the motorcycle. The barman shows up and his information finally turns the tide.

The Wintringhams and Janet Lapthorn are on a train when she sees a woman – later identified as Shirley Gardiner – wearing a distinctive piece of jewelry that had belonged to Felicity. The police begin to watch her clandestinely, but news of the murder leaks to the press and becomes widely known. Gardiner says that the jewelry was a present from her new boyfriend, Eric Ford, about whom she knows almost nothing.

Felicity's luggage shows up, having been abandoned in a rooming house. Almost by chance, Wintringham notices that the first letters of each word on a sign at a newsstand spell out Peter. The attendant realizes that he is in danger and tries to kill Wintringham, but is instead arrested and subsequently identified as "Eric Ford" and "Harold Rust."

Fires at Fairlawn (1954) is a non-series mystery. Tom and

Margaret Seeley are planning to buy a house larger than they need so that they can subdivide and rent out the second floor. With the assistance of an uncle, they purchase Fairlawn and begin the renovations. The former owner, Laura Osgood, left the house following the death of her mother.

They meet their closest neighbor, Commander Bill Howard and his wife Buffy. Howard provides advice about the overgrown garden. They also hire a daily woman named Holbrook to help out. They are mildly disturbed to learn that Mrs. Osgood burned to death in a kind of modified wheelchair in one of the rooms. The workmen indicate that the woman was generally disliked because of her mean disposition. The vicar mentions that a former boarder there had supposedly concealed gold somewhere in the house, and that it is generally believed to be somewhere near the main staircase, which is to be demolished. Osgood tells her that Buffy spends money profligately.

They have a prowler who unscrews one of the posts on the staircase, revealing a hollow interior. They doubt the legendary gold was there because this was investigated years earlier, but it is still upsetting to have a break-in. They also learn more about the fire. They were outside with Laura when it broke out and Mrs. Osgood began screaming, and all rushed in together. The actual cause of death was shock.

The construction workers find that one of the basement windows has been recently sabotaged to allow access to the house. They repair it but another attempt is made soon after. Margaret learns that Laura Osgood has a cousin Christopher, wo he has spent time in prison but no one knows where he is at present.

Uncle George comes to visit and finds a will that was concealed in the staircase and then the basement. Under its provisions, it is not certain that Laura actually owned the house when she sold it. It also seems likely that she hid the document rather than forward it to the family lawyer. George takes possession of the will so that he can consult a lawyer, but his briefcase is stolen on the train. It is recovered but the will is gone.

Christopher Osgood comes to stay with his cousin. Buffy Howard suddenly becomes flush with cash. Through the vicar and thanks to an anonymous donor, the church purchases the staircase, which is to be relocated. The fire that killed Mrs. Osgood becomes more of a mystery because she was not using the gas heater that supposedly started the fire. The vicar had visited her shortly before the fire and the doctor who responded had noticed cigarette butts in the room.

The vicar knew about the new will, had witnessed its signing, and he had assumed that the daughter destroyed it. With no proof to offer, he had decided to say nothing. There were two signed copies, however, and Margaret speculates that Buffy found one of them and is blackmailing Laura.

Someone starts a fire in the loft. Christopher is found badly burned and he dies on the way to the hospital. The post mortem determines that it was a dose of drugs and alcohol that killed him, not the mostly superficial burns. A copy of the will is found in his pocket. It appears that Christopher was using it to blackmail Laura, even though he knew the will was not valid. Mrs. Osgood technically never owned the house – it was in a trust for Laura.

Laura Osgood is found hanged, but it was no suicide. There is some cheating here because the police know that Bill Howard is a career criminal, not a retired officer. He was doing the blackmailing and he killed Christopher to prevent him from telling the police. Laura had to be eliminated because she also knew the truth. But it was Laura who murdered her mother. She rubbed a substance she used in the garden into the invalid's clothing. When dried, it became highly flammable and the victim smoked.

Death in Retirement (1956) begins with some family tension. Gillian Clayton is annoyed when her aunt, Olive Clayton – a retired doctor – expresses misgivings about her engagement to Max Russell, an attorney and junior partner. Dr. Clayton spent most of her career in India. Russell lived with his parents in Canada for a while, but he had been born in England and decided to return. Gillian's parents had been killed in a car crash a few years earlier. She had been living with her aunt and sharing expenses and Olive is concerned that she will be alone and with diminishing savings if Gillian marries.

Gillian, formerly a teacher, now works as a tutor and adviser for an educational organization. She suggests that after marrying they should move in with Olive, but the doctor considers this inappropriate. Instead she proposes an agreement with a married couple, although the terms are such that it seems unlikely that anyone would agree. Nevertheless, the Weavers answer the advertisement and with a few minor adjustments, accept the terms. Gillian is mildly disturbed that Russell did not mention to her that he was the one who found the Weavers, Muriel and Sidney.

The first few weeks with the Weavers resident turn out well, although the couple own a dog whom the day help, a gardener and a housekeeper, do not like. Gillian begins to have doubts about the Weavers although Olive appears to have warmed to them. She and Russell set the date for their wedding.

The situation takes a sinister turn when a biscuit meant for Olive is fed to the dog, who immediately dies. When Olive is gone, Sidney accuses his wife of trying to poison him and Olive. An analysis proves there is nothing wrong with the biscuits, but the dog succumbed to rat poison. The gardener feels as though he is being quietly accused and quits in a huff. The housekeeper follows suit a few days later.

Muriel receives a painful shock from a sabotaged light switch and blames her husband, despite his denial. He also tells her that he saw her swap the biscuits before they were sent for analysis, but she insists that she believes he tampered with them and she was trying to protect him. Convinced that Sidney is trying to kill her, Muriel announces her intention to leave immediately, but instead reveals her fears to Olive.

The reader is kept in the dark about the next few events. Muriel leaves the house. Sidney sneaks out and sees her encounter another, unidentified person. After a while he sneaks back into the house, but is concerned about some "horror" in the garden, which the reader will assume is the body of his wife. Sidney has been struck in the head by a thrown stone. Gillian and Max have gone for a drive. When they return, the house is full of gas. Sidney is dead but Olive is only slightly affected.

Both of the Weavers had ingested a fatal dose of poison, although in neither case was that the cause of death. The appearance is a murder/suicide although the detective in charge is unconvinced. The Weavers had previously lived with another woman, who died under suspicious circumstances, as did her first husband. Sidney had served jail sentences for fraud. Muriel was drawing a pension from the government to which she was not entitled. By the terms of their agreement, Olive receives the earnings of their savings for the length of the contract, after which the balance goes to their heirs.

MASTERS OF DETECTION

Two children, brother and sister, have appeared occasionally and now become the focus of the plot. The boy has been having nightmares and his slingshot is found on the property. He admits that he fired the stone that wounded Sidney. His sister is convinced that Olive strangled Muriel, however.

A journalist becomes interested in doing a story, but is suspicious of Olive and steals a photograph from her collection. He takes this to the headquarters of the mission for which she worked and discovers that she is an impostor. The real Olive Clayton died on the voyage home and a nurse named Philips took over her identity. It is likely she contributed to Clayton's death.

The police are notified and they confront Clayton. Gillian and Max are away on their honeymoon. As yet the police do not suspect – as the reader surely does – that Clayton murdered both of the Weavers. Her lawyer, Polder, puts two and two together and confronts her. He offers to keep the secret if she goes away and never tries to see the newlyweds again. Philips/Clayton tries to poison him as well, but inadvertently drinks the tainted cup of tea herself and dies.

Murder on the Merry-Go-Round (1956, aka *The China Roundabout*) is a Wintringham mystery. Eileen Forrestall and her mother, Mildred, temporarily move to the rooming house left to them by her Uncle Monty Beresford. The family had not been close and she and her mother barely get along. They learn that Monty changed lawyers recently and that his will is currently being held by a man named Digby.

Eileen meets one of the tenants, Mrs. Rosenberg, and suspects that she has been exploring her uncle's rooms. Another tenant is Amanda Powell, who is much younger. A friend of Powell named Lewis MacKenzie warns them that Rosenberg, who lives with an adult daughter Sarah, is a thief. Mildred is annoyed because an elaborate to merry-go-round, or roundabout, is missing. It is a family heirloom which she insists has sentimental value only. The remaining apartment is tenanted by the Pickards, but he is a salesman and is currently on the road.

Rosenberg tells them that the roundabout was damaged, but repaired by a man named Meyer and she has not seen it since then. It turns up in a safety deposit box and is in good condition. The various tenants all seem unusually interested in it. Eileen is disturbed one night by prowlers at her window. She reads in her grandfather's diary about how he acquired it but some pages have been torn out and the story is incomplete. She does discover that the eyes of the horses were originally precious gems, although they are now simply glass.

Mildred's friend, Amy Henderson, comes to visit for a few days and Eileen returns to her own apartment, which is nearby. MacKenzie turns out to be a dealer in gems. A few days later, one of the horse heads is broken off and disappears. It is possible that the cleaning lady was responsible, but she denies it heatedly and quits her job. The missing piece is found in a trash bin.

Rosenberg is caught trying to steal the roundabout. After an ugly scene, she makes plans to move out. Powell also gives notice that she is leaving. Eileen agrees to take the roundabout to her apartment but someone had made a frantic search of her rooms before she arrives. Digby is also strangely interested in the toy. She moves it to a friend's place, then returns to the boarding house where she finds her mother dead.

Eileen's boyfriend is a doctor. He recognizes almost immediately that the dead woman had been bound and gagged and he calls his friend, Dr. David Wintringham. The key to the roundabout appears to be missing, but Mildred had actually swallowed it to prevent it from being taken. The police tell Wintringham that Digby, the Rosenbergs, Mrs. Pickard, and MacKenzie are all involved in criminal activities, but there is not enough evidence.

Eileen had given the roundabout to her boyfriend for safe keeping, but it is not in its box. The theft may have occurred while she had been storing it in a locker in the hospital where she works. Digby is found dead of a drug overdose and there are suspicions that his physician, Dr. Flood, was his supplier. It also seems likely that Digby had been blackmailing Beresford. Meyer and Flood have visits from the same two unidentified men, and records indicate that Beresford and MacKenzie traveled to the continent together on more than one occasion. Mrs. Pickard's real name is Flora Munning and she is a jewel thief. The Picards were introduced to Beresford by Harcourt, a bank manager.

Digby had the missing diary pages, which reveal that there is a secret compartment filled with diamonds in the roundabout. Beresford had apparently been selling them outside the country. A salesman attempts to extract something from Eileen, but fails to take the key to the roundabout, although he may have taken a wax impression. He turns out to be George Pickard, who has insured his wife's life rather highly and who has not, contrary to his statements, insured her valuable jewelry. It appears that he can now manufacture a key but that some other party has the roundabout.

Impulsively, Eileen pays a visit to the now mostly empty house. She hears the roundabout and finds it in Powell's now empty apartment. Eileen takes the roundabout and escapes from Meyer and an unidentified man, but when she finds a police officer and returns, they find Meyer stabbed to death. The diamonds are missing, of course, and an examination reveals that the secret compartment was used to smuggle drugs.

Wintringham confronts Flood, who collapses in a now dated and inaccurate scene involving marijuana. The only suspect who does not have an alibi for Meyer's murder is Harcourt. Harcourt, Wintringham, Eileen, and her fiancé Sunderland go to confront Pickard, who is employed as a purser on a boat. Harcourt is acting strangely. Powell and MacKenzie are also there.

Harcourt and Pickard go overboard. Harcourt has minor injuries but Pickard has been stabbed to death. Mrs. Pickard admits that Harcourt is her son, not her nephew. Beresford was misguidedly trying to investigate the drug ring on his own. There turn out to be two George Pickards, brothers, and the second returns to Beresford's house, where his wife has just died of an overdose. Harcourt killed Meyer for the drugs, and later murdered his own brother. Flood dies in the hospital. The second Pickard is arrested.

Double Doom (1957) begins with a puzzle. Hugh and Hilary Strongitharm are twin brothers. Dr. William Goddard and his wife Fiona read their obituaries in the newspaper, which claims they both died unexpectedly on the same day. Goddard knows this is nonsense because Hilary is his patient and, although hospitalized, is doing quite well.

He is still improving the following morning but Goddard refuses to let the family lawyer, Lionel Pusey, or the step-sister, Joyce Morley, visit him. Hugh was killed when gas backed up into a greenhouse where he was gardening. The brothers and their half-sister lived with their elderly common mother.

Hilary had been on anti-coagulants, but the doctors discover that someone had replaced them with aspirin, which may have caused his current medical problem. Hilary dies moments after they make this discovery, apparently from a heart attack. Morley may have entered the room undetected. She is both emotionally and intellectually challenged. The body has been moved, the pillow turned upside down, and a newspaper is found on the bed opened to the bogus obituary, despite a prohibition against allowing the patient to see the news.

Morley knows that Hugh was murdered because she found the blocked flue responsible for his death and knew that it was deliberate. She had destroyed the evidence. She was also convinced that Hilary had been murdered, but rather than feel alarm, she was elated. It was she who had sent the two death notices to the newspapers, and she had planned to show them to Hilary in the hospital, hoping it would provoke a heart attack. This part had not gone according to her plan.

Diana Fawcett visits Mrs. Strongitharm to help with correspondence and she is identified as Pusey's occasional lover. Mabel is a live-in nurse who takes care of mother and daughter. Pusey is dismayed when he is told that a younger brother will be asked to become Morley's guardian when her mother dies. He had hoped to take that position himself and it is clear that he has embezzled funds from the estate.

Hilary was obviously suffocated, which means that he was murdered. The police suspect that Morley brought the newspaper, although they think her motive might have been innocent. They are also certain that Hugh was murdered. They determine that Morley sent the death notices and they are confident that she is the one who destroyed the evidence at the greenhouse. Fiona Goddard meets Morley, who admits that she has a special friend. Fawcett hints that she is preparing to end her affair and Pusey reacts by threatening to kill her. Mabel, who hates Fawcett, is also opposed to the apparent good relations between Morley and Fiona.

Morley's uncle Humphrey arrives, and several people remark that he looks younger now than he did several years earlier, presumably the result of his recent marriage. Morley does not like him at all and insists that Pusey should be her guardian instead. Humphrey suggests to the family doctor, Matthews, that Joyce should be institutionalized, and muses that she should have been euthanized as a child.

Pusey is to become guardian after all, but the situation changes again when a fire drives Mrs. Strongitharm out of her bedroom. She falls, or is pushed, off the balcony. Humphrey accuses Morley, but she in turns accuses Mabel, although she subsequently changes her mind. Nurse Barker, meanwhile, has been completely cleared. None of the new wills have been signed so Morley inherits everything and has no guardian.

Morley goes to see Pusey, tells him they should get married, and suggests that he killed the twins. Pusey and Fawcett have a final argument and break off their affair. The police call everyone together and reveal the solution. Fawcett is actually Humphrey's wife, and Humphrey was the killer in all three cases, impersonating the nurse, blocking the chimney, and strangling his sister. Pusey is forced to admit his embezzlements when Morley is finally declared incompetent but is accidentally killed before there are any consequences. Morley drowns trying to run away.

The Seeing Eye (1958) was David Wintringham's final appearance. He and his wife are attending an art exhibit when they meet Oswald Burke - an unpopular critic, a disgruntled art student named Tom Drummond, and James Symington-Cole, an eye surgeon. Drummond is a rather bitter young man. He has a friend, fellow artist Christopher Felton, who is seeing a psychiatrist, Hugh Lampton.

Burke's body is found buried in a part of the gallery that was under construction. His neck was broken and it is believed to have been a murder. His wife had not reported him missing. Symington-Coles, who was a friend, had been willed his corneas for transplantation but the body was not found quickly enough for this to matter.

Drummond's girlfriend is Pauline Manners, who does not get along with Felton or his doting mother. Drummond had sketched a number of people who had attended the exhibit, and the police recognize one of them as Bert Lewis, a professional burglar. Lewis had been working with the construction company under an assumed name, but had left their employ before the exhibit. He had no reason to be there after hours, in work clothes, and in fact there was a burglary that night. Lewis had Burke's cigarette case in his possession, but when he is arrested, he insists that he found it on a staircase.

There is a fire in the studio used by Drummond and Felton. Drummond is offered a temporary room with the Wintringhams, while Felton goes to stay with Lampton. Drummond's new artwork begins to display a darker atmosphere. Wintringham tracks down two more of the attendees, who tell him they saw Lampton waiting outside the building.

Felton is found unconscious, a drug overdose, although he survives and insists that he was not suicidal. Lampton lost his standing as a general physician following a sex related scandal, after which he changed his name. The woman involved was Burke's sister, who is mentally disturbed and who now uses the name Tufnel. She had a son who is quite obviously Felton.

Drummond finally admits that he found the body in the stairwell and moved it because he feared that Felton was responsible. Tufnel abducts her son and attacks Manners, planning to kill Drummond, whom she thinks tried to kill her son. Wintringham believes that Lampton killed Burke to avoid a second exposure, and that Tufnel is responsible for the death of the woman Lampton was currently involved with. He is wrong. Burke's wife confesses that she killed them both, that she was in love with Lampton. Felton's supposed mother was actually a nurse who genuinely loved him and had been taking care of him since his mother had her breakdown. The conclusion this time is rather chaotic and insufficiently explained, particularly in terms of motive.

The House Above the River (1959) drifts from traditional mystery to simple suspense. Giles Armitage is aboard his small yacht along with his friends, Tony and Philippa Marshall, sailing off the coast of France. Because of a heavy fog, they anchor near a private dock. The Marshalls go ashore to find fresh food and meet Susan Brockley, whose cousin Henry Davenport owns the landing and adjacent manor house. Much to Armitage's chagrin, Davenport's wife Miriam is the woman who broke off her engagement to him eight years earlier.

They act as though they do not know each other, but the Marshalls realize that they do. They all find Henry daunting and a bit sinister. Miriam secretly tells Giles that she is frightened and needs help, but says no more immediately. Later she insists that Henry is planning to kill her and is actually in love with Brockley. Giles does not believe her. A storm makes it necessary for them to remain for at least two days.

It is Brockley who nearly dies, however. While walking in the woods with Giles, she falls into a concealed chasm and barely escapes death. Henry, who knew about the pitfall, apparently refrained from helping even though he knew what had happened. There was supposed to be a covering over it. The area, however, is one that Miriam often visited and the trap may have been meant for her. Tony nearly falls into a second, similar trap.

The three visitors decide to leave once the weather clears. Brockley and Giles have become more than friends and he wants to take her with them, but she declines. It seems likely that Miriam is mentally ill, although Henry is disturbing as well. Their plans are disrupted when they discover that their anchor chain has been sabotaged, and when the return to the manor, Henry has disappeared.

Miriam insists that the trap was laid for her, but Giles points out that she would have noticed that the safety cover was removed. If anything, the trap was designed to kill him, not Miriam. He tells Miriam that he is in love with Brockley. The boat is repaired and sets off at last.

Giles finds Henry in the hospital, seriously ill and registered under another name. He vehemently denies being responsible for the sabotage. A few days later he receives a letter from Brockley. Miriam has gone to Paris after telling the police she believes that Brockley murdered her husband, who is still missing as far as they are concerned. The police know that Henry is still hospitalized. Miriam returns and now claims that Henry must have committed suicide.

The police believe Miriam was poisoning her husband. Brockley and Giles announce their engagement. The boat is about to leave when a frantic Miriam appears, running recklessly toward them. She is seriously injured when she upsets some equipment that falls on her. Henry returns and tells the police they cannot arrest her because she has committed no crime, no matter what she might have contemplated. She is in any case now in serious danger of dying of her injuries.

Giles finds evidence that Henry rigged the equipment to fall and kill his wife, who is now paralyzed and in bed. A few days later he learns that she is expected to live at least for a while but never walk again, and also that Henry is now showing symptoms of having been poisoned. Both could die at any moment. She lasts several months and Henry recovers. It is clear that he killed her, but that he will escape punishment.

Easy Prey (1959) opens with the description of a domestic arrangement. Reg and Mavis Holmes have purchased a large house of their own. They have one child, an infant named Joy. They have also rented a spare room to Helen Trubb, a middle aged woman who works as a stenographer. Trubb is kindly, babysits for free, and they like her even though they know little about her family or even where she works. One evening they return and smell gas in the house, but it is not at a dangerous level. Trubb is acting strangely, however. The family spends the night with a sick friend, and when they return in the morning, the gas is stronger than ever and Trubb is unconscious in her bed.

The assumption is attempted suicide. Reg finds an envelope in his briefcase with a note asking him to deliver it to Frances Meadows and provides an address. The police reveal that Meadows is Trubb's sister. Her real name is Helen Clements and she served fifteen years in prison for murder of a child.

After the shock has passed, the Holmes couple refuses to believe that Trubb actually committed infanticide. They talk to the sister who tells them the story. Unmarried, Helen had become pregnant, although she tried to keep it secret. She was later observed with an infant, who was subsequently suffocated in his crib, obviously deliberately. Helen offered no explanation and even claimed that the child was not hers, that she was caring for it as a favor to a friend. She did not identify the friend and would not talk about the child's death.

Trubb is released from the hospital but does not return to the house. Reg is particularly interested in pursuing his investigation, and is furious when an anonymous note threatens to harm Joy if he does not stop. The police dismiss it as a hoax. Reg believes that the gas was attempted murder, not suicide, and that Trubb intended to disappear, not die. The ventilation from the house was plugged from the outside and the note was torn and part of the message missing.

Reg suspects that Frances was really the mother of the dead child. She married less than a year after the boy was born. Trubb's employer liked her and is sorry that she seems to have disappeared following her release from the hospital. She then has herself voluntarily committed to a sanitarium. They allow her to leave the premises during the day, however, and when Joy disappears, she is the one who brings the child back, telling them that they are in danger.

Trubb's lawyer is interested now and looks up the sister's boyfriends. One of them, Roger Thorne, is unpleasant and very defensive about his whereabouts on the day of the incident with the gas. Another former lover, Leslie Coke, has a tainted reputation as an accountant. Frances' husband Colin tries to convince Reg to drop his inquiries and he makes a very bad impression on the couple.

Reg and Mavis are on their way to visit another old friend of the Clements family named Breadley, but their map is inadequate and they nearly drive off the edge of a ruined bridge. There is a dead man and a crashed motorcycle at the scene, and Reg is puzzled because the man's injuries seem to be on the wrong side of his body. He looks in his pockets and discovers that the dead man is Leslie Coke. The danger sign had been removed, but now it is back in place.

Bradley insists that the map they received is not the one that he mailed to them. Colin Meadows appears to be the only person who could have substituted a new map in the letter from the Bradleys as he had taken it to the post office. Coke's death was clearly murder. A long out of touch midwife is located and confirms that it was Frances and not Helen who had the baby. Coke – who was the father – knew and had been blackmailing her.

Helen believes that Frances killed the child. Thorne disappears. His body turns up in a field. Helen leaves the sanitarium and returns to her job. The solution moves quickly, but not entirely convincingly. The family lawyer had been embezzling from the Clements family and killed the child to frame Helen and prevent her from discovering the truth. He was being blackmailed by Coke and also worried that Thorne would spill the beans, so he murdered both of them as well. His motives are rather convoluted and Helen's motives for not telling the truth are implausible.

A Well-Known Face (1960) brings back Claude Warrington-Reeve, an attorney who was a minor character in *Easy Prey*. Jane Fuller, whose husband Andrew is a doctor and a friend of Warrington-Reeve, tells him that she wants a divorce. Fuller lost his license to practice when he was accused of having an improper relationship with a patient, Millicent Prentice. That, combined with the Fullers' inability to have a child, led to him going to South America to practice and leaving her behind. He has never answered her letters and she wants to use desertion as grounds for the divorce.

Jane faints when the attorney tells her that earlier that same day her husband had been found dead by her gardener, inside the house where she has been living. The police clearly believe that she killed him by slipping barbiturates into his drink. She is constrained in her answers because she does not want to reveal the identity of her lover, Dr. Martin Seymour, who spent the night with her.

The dead man was seen arriving on a train the night before his body was found. Dr. Gerald Lovell is a friend who expresses his support. He was Andrew's partner before the scandal and Andrew had come to see him the day before his death. Dick Prentice, Millicent's husband, reports that Andrew called his house looking for him, but that they had not spoken.

Disparate facts emerge. Lovell drove Andrew to his former home but did not wait because he expected an argument when Martin was found there. Millicent Prentice appears to have invented the story of her affair with Andrew. Jane Fuller's lawyer, Hugh Manning, is not particularly helpful. Lovell reportedly is smitten with Jane. Some minor physical evidence links Jane to the crime, but there are plausible explanations. Nevertheless, the police detective involved is quite certain she killed her husband.

Millicent Prentice is found dead. It appears that she threw herself in front of a train. She habitually placed bets on horses and usually lost, but her bookie suspects she was acting for someone else and had no interest herself. The police case weakens when another witness comes forward and claims to have seen Andrew return to the medical facility after Lovell had driven him to his house. Martin now suspects Lovell.

The bookie is stabbed at the race track and both Lovell and Seymour were present at the time. He dies without speaking. Jane has doubts about Seymour's commitment to her. Millicent Prentice had been drugged prior to her death. Andrew had been working as a ship's doctor and Seymour had done so previously, so it is possible that the former was investigating the latter's past. Seymour had been a compulsive gambler and had acquired a great deal of money from a rich passenger under questionable circumstances.

It was Seymour who was having an affair with Millicent, not Andrew. The story about his disgrace at sea turns out to be false. It is Lovell who was the compulsive gambler and he used Millicent as his agent. Lovell killed all three of them to protect his secret. He falls down a staircase and breaks his neck while trying to escape from the police.

New People at the Hollies (1961) is set in a small village. The Hollies is a sprawling white elephant of a house that has been empty for years. When Tony and Roy North, brothers, return from a vacation with their parents, they are surprised to learn that the property has finally been purchased and is undergoing renovations. The boys had disguised a connection between their bomb shelter and the one at the Hollies, so no one else knew that they had a secret way into the property or that they had been clandestinely visiting the house.

The Hollies is to become a nursing home for the elderly, administered by Tindall, assisted by Joyce Hunt. Tindall is unwelcoming when approached by the boys' mother, and the brothers are watching when one of the supposedly elderly women patients turns out to be a man and not elderly at all. A visit by a local health official finds nothing out of the ordinary, but the reader knows that something is wrong.

They decide to use a local physician, Dr. Jennifer Mount, as a consultant. They accept an elderly male applicant named Alfred Coltman, who will prove to have a significant impact. He provides misleading details about his past. Other residents include the Dents, a married couple, and an irritating complainer, Miss Dacre. Several of the permanent residents are puzzled by the "temporaries," patients who come and go in a matter of hours, but who are never seen by a doctor, or the residents for that matter.

Another resident, Mrs. Marsh, is a kleptomaniac and is caught by Dacre. A dementia patient named Shorter wanders at night and sees a body being carried to the medical station. Tindall gets her back to bed and she dies during the night – her heart was bad. Mount sees nothing suspicious but notices that there are spots of blood on her nightgown. Coltman spots Hilda, the cook, rummaging through one of the resident's belongings and realizes she is a thief.

Coltman meets the brothers and learns about the secret entrance.

A valuable broach is stolen – by Hilda – and there is pressure to inform the police. Coltman makes a clandestine effort to report the situation, but the officer on duty is a dolt and Tindall arrives and convinces him that Coltman is delusional. Fortunately an inspector overhears part of the conversation and makes a few quiet inquiries. As it happens, there have been reports that fugitive criminals may have been seen in the area, at least one of whom was injured.

Another member of the staff has a man in her room and is overheard. Dacre has a serious accident and falls down a staircase. Tindall drugs Coltman and convinces Mount that he is senile and paranoid. The police identify the cook's fingerprints – she has a police record – and connect her to an attempt to dispose of stolen goods. She promptly disappears.

Coltman tries to use the brothers to summon help. A fire breaks out and both Tindall and Dacre are killed in the conflagration. The illegal operation is ended, of course, but without the authorities ever learning the truth.

The story is unconvincing – one of Bell's rare complete failures. There is no mystery because we know from the outset what is going on. Even worse, the police, the health inspector, and doctors are all criminally unprofessional and stupid, ignoring obvious problems, and refusing to believe people who have supporting evidence for their claims simply because they are elderly.

Adventure with Crime (1962) was set in the United States. Frances Aldridge lost her husband in a freak accident and accepts an invitation to visit two friends, Mollie and Dan, who live in New York. She decides to take a bus to Colorado and visit friends there, and she observes and is observed by some of her fellow passengers. She spends the first night at a hotel in Cleveland, inexplicably fails to lock her door, and some of her cash is missing in the morning.

The only fellow passenger whose name she knows is a man named Jim Field, who seems pleasant. He also stayed at the hotel. Aldridge is a bit startled to read in the newspapers that a woman was strangled at the hotel that same night. She had seen the woman talking with Field. She considers talking to the police, but Field gets off the bus and she decides not to do so.

At another stop, two passengers board. One looks very much like Field and the other is another woman who had been seen with him earlier. She also meets a man named Terry Gruber, whom she immediately likes, although she rebuffs his attempt at intimacy. When they reach Colorado, Gruber has already connected with another young woman.

Nick and Louise Harmon welcome Aldridge. At first she is comfortable, but then she goes for a walk and finds the dead body of a woman she believes was Gruber's mother. She returns to the hotel to report it and finds Field there. This is rather like piling one coincidence upon two others. Then she runs into Gruber, compounding the error, and stupidly allows him to dissuade her from notifying the police right away. Instead he attempts to kill her "accidentally" and she still does not suspect him.

When she finally reaches the police, they are unbelievably unprofessional and are convinced she is an accomplice to the murders. Not surprisingly, she eventually realizes that Gruber is the killer and that she is in love with Field. The red herrings are so badly done that no one could possibly have been surprised and the plot is poorly and lazily constructed.

Room for a Body (1963, aka *Fiasco in Fulham*, aka *A Flat Tire in Fulham*) begins with a bank robbery gone wrong. The driver of the getaway car is delayed by a flat tire and abandons it and two of the four thieves are captured. The abandoned car had been stolen from a man who is out of the country, and therefore has not reported its theft, and it is found parked in front of a cottage.

A constable eventually inquires about the car, but the owner of the house, Mrs. Wilton, is both rude and uninformative. The thieves who are still at liberty, O'Hara, Burt, and Corri, are infuriated because of the non-appearance of the driver, Len. Burt was the mastermind and he has a heated argument with the other two.

The owner of the car is Sir John Drewson, currently attending a conference on public welfare on the continent. He has a niece named Belinda Tollett and his secretary is Mrs. Wood. Tollett had been meant to retrieve the car from the airport and move it to a safe place, but through a mix-up, she thought other arrangements had been made through a friend. She assumed that the friend, Hugh Mellanby, might have taken the car to visit another acquaintance, a man named Jeremy Ditchling. Mellanby works for Warrington-Reeve, the attorney who has appeared in previous books.

Mellanby is a college friend of Ditchling, a failed law student who has some associates with dubious reputations. Ditchling is also known to Drewson, visited him the night before he left on his trip, and he appears to have gone missing the day the car was stolen. This provides a dead end for the police, but one of the arrested men finally talks and names the other gang members, although some of them may be assumed identities. Len Smithson, however, is well known to the police.

Arrangements are finally made to change the flat tire at the police impound lot, but when the trunk is opened, the body of Ditchling is discovered inside. Mellanby identifies the body and is evasive when Tollett asks why he spent so much effort searching for Ditchling before he was found. Mellanby had taken a photograph of a man and a woman from Ditchling's rooms and he conceals it from the police.

Smithson is still at liberty. He knew Ditchling as Jimmy Dice, a fellow criminal. Ditchling had been drugged and suffocated. Burt – who is actually an insurance executive named Simpkins – owned the cottage where Ditchling had been living. He searched it after the body was found and locked the doors, which puzzles the police because Mellanby had found it open.

Drewson returns and explains that Ditchling had spoken to him about wanting to marry a girl from a nearby reform school, but is otherwise unable to help. He did not open the trunk on the morning of his flight. The girl Ditchling was supposedly interested in, Mavis Henning, disappears from the school. Two days later she is found drugged and drowned not far away.

Mellanby admits that he burgled Ditchling's cottage to secure a photograph that was being used to blackmail a friend of his. The police attempt to trace the ownership of the cottage. They already suspect that Burt is connected to the insurance industry. Wood confesses to Warrington-Reeve her suspicion that Henning had seduced Drewson, which suggests that he was the killer. The police believe correctly that Simpkins is Burt.

Warrington-Reeve allows Henning's mother to believe he is Burt, so she gives him a package she withheld from the police. It contains film and prints proving that Drewson was involved with the underaged Mavis. He shows them to Tollett and Mellanby. Tollett storms off in a fit of rage.

Burt confronts Drewson with his partner, who unexpectedly is Wood. They poison his tea and attempt to steal a sizable amount of cash, but they are caught by a roadblock. Drewson survives. Contrary to what seems to be Drewson's obvious guilt, it was Burt who killed Ditchling for double crossing him and with Wood's assistance he later killed Henning as well.

The Hunter and the Trapped (1963) is a suspense novel set against a college backdrop. Simon Fawcett is brilliant and popular with his students, but he is highly conceited and not liked by his colleagues. One young woman, Penelope Dane, is obsessed with him. She is dismayed when he explains that he is in love with a married woman who will not consider divorce.

Dane met him at a party hosted by Bill and Diana Allingham. Diana is having an affair with Fawcett and is presumably the woman he loved. Fawcett's only male friend is George Clark, to whom he spins a story about rejecting advances from an unnamed gay man. Penelope's father, Hubert, consults Bill Allingham about his daughter's infatuation with Fawcett. A male student recently committed suicide after Fawcett rejected him. Penelope accepts a proposal from Richard Carrington.

Penelope was also being wooed by John Allingham, but she tells him she is breaking off the engagement and going away with Fawcett. There is a great deal of time spent on reactions from various parties, as well as an open quarrel between Diana and Penelope. Penelope also has a heated argument with Fawcett, who refuses to marry her and even borrows some of her money. He is being blackmailed by his housekeeper, although it is not clear what she could have revealed.

John Allingham confronts Fawcett about his treatment of Penelope, and disarms him when Fawcett attacks him with a knife. Hubert Dane hires private investigators to look into Fawcett's background. The housekeeper returns for more money and Fawcett strangles her, but she recovers. Ten days later, her body is found in a dumpster.

The police discover that the housekeeper, Morris, was dealing in drugs as well as blackmailing some of her employers. Fawcett denies that he was one of them. Penelope had written a check to loan Fawcett money, and he had given it to Morris as a blackmail payment. It was found in her handbag by the police, who questioned her. Confused, she goes to John Allingham for advice.

A check of Fawcett's background reveals no lies, although some of his statements were misleading. He was visiting a small town when a young boy was drowned, apparently a murder. Fawcett was ill for a long time. Officially it was asthma but it appears to have been a nervous breakdown. The doctor who was supplying Morris with drugs commits suicide.

All of the main characters come together for a confrontation. Fawcett confesses to having killed Morris, becomes violent, and is subdued. Diana reveals her infatuation in front of her husband. He frees himself and jumps from a window to his death, almost taking Diana with him.

The Upfold Witch (1964) has an ominous prologue. Two men are hunting a rogue dog one night when they see a man named Farnham bring home Celia Wainwright, who lives alone in a cottage. Something seems wrong so they investigate further and find Wainwright dead in her bed. She had obviously died hours earlier. She was rumored to have been a witch. The reader is not immediately told the outcome of their discovery and the story leaps forward ten years to the new occupants of the cottage.

Dr. Henry Frost and his wife Jean are an older couple and he is looking forward to a quiet retirement. They are first greeted by the neighboring Snowthornes, who are evasive when asked about the cottage's former owners. There are hints that someone had entered the cottage during their absence, but they assume it was curious local children.

Jean meets a local woman, Mrs. Graveney, whom she does not like. Graveney tells them that Celia Wainwright was much younger than her husband. Celia disappeared and was reported dead by her husband, who moved away. She had been noticeably friendly with Julian Farnham, the author. The vicar, Maurice Shalford, mentions her mysterious disappearance and the fact that she was widely hated locally. The Frosts hire a cleaning lady named Thompson, whose son committed suicide, supposedly because Celia bewitched him.

The Frosts' daughter Judy comes to spend a week and meets some of the local people, including Farnham. She learns that the villagers blamed Celia when the local butcher's son drowned in the adjacent river. Farnham takes Judy to lunch and expresses intense dislike for Celia, without being specific.

Frost has been gardening and eventually uncovers some human bones. This sequence is rather implausible. He digs up the entire skeleton – the head is missing – and takes it into his study. He is lackadaisical about contacting the police, does not mention it to his wife, and when the local constable suggests that it is a hoax, he appears to accept that position without question. He does withhold some of the bones because some of them are in fact from a specimen skeleton. They were substituted after he dug them up and before the constable arrived.

Frost takes his bones to a specialist who confirms that it was a young woman who died ten years earlier, obviously Celia Wainwright. A local farmer, Cutler, was one of the two men who found Celia's body during the prologue. His brother is a doctor who owns a specimen skeleton. This skeleton is missing, except for the skull, which means that the supposed prankster knew that there was no buried skull. The skeleton belonging to the local doctor, Marshall, is also missing.

During Judy's next visit, a woman named Mabel Snell makes a social call designed to warn her away from Farnham. Farnham is stunned when he learns of the bones. Judy and Farnham profess their love for each other – a week after they meet – but he later accuses her of suspecting him of Celia's murder. Scotland Yard finally gets involved, but Inspector Falk is not amiable and ruffles feathers.

Two men, Pauley and Cutfield, admit to having found the body and buried it, after cutting off the head and driving a stake through the heart. It also appears that she was pregnant at the time of her death, presumably by Farnham. Their testimony suggests that she had taken an overdose of sleeping pills and committed suicide. Snell tells the police that Celia was at Farnham's house on the night she died.

Farnham tells Judy that Celia died in his bed and that he panicked and brought her home. An analysis of some surviving medication reveals that poison had been substituted and Celia was in fact murdered. An elderly local woman admits that John Wainwright referred to his wife as a witch and that she made some poisoned capsules for him. Her daughter is found murdered and it is evident that she had been attempting to blackmail Wainwright. The marriage was bigamous – he had a wife in Canada. Frost confronts him and he disappears, apparently having committed suicide.

No Escape (1965) returns to the medical world. Dr. Timothy Long is overworked and his social life has not taken the direction for which he had hoped. The nurses he admires are not interested in him. Jane Wheelan annoys him with her lack of seriousness in a case of some missing paperwork. Long rescues Sheila Burgess from drowning in a river, but it appears that she may have attempted suicide. She is recognized at the hospital by Wheelan.

Burgess refuses to say where she lives or why she was in the river, but eventually tells Wheelan where her apartment is so that she can pick up some clothes. While there, Wheelan notes that Burgess posed for a number of nude photographs, not pornographic, taken by someone named Ronald Bream. There is a roll of film which she takes as well. As she is leaving, she meets Gerald Stone, who says that he is a friend of the Burgess family. He gives her a ride back to the hospital where he meets Long briefly. Long does not particularly like him.

Burgess is to go home the next day. Stone shows up again and asks Wheelan questions about Burgess, and suggests that she is mentally unstable. He also knows Bream, for whom Burgess worked. Although she has some reservations about him, Wheelan agrees to accompany him to a party to meet Bream. Bream is there, along with his partner Giles. Several people at the party react strangely when Burgess is mentioned and one man suggests that she should not travel alone. A woman named Toni is quietly hostile for no discernible reason.

Burgess leaves the hospital before Wheelan can give her the roll of film. She is accosted on the train by a thug who has been sent to retrieve it. In the scuffle, she falls out of the train, and her dead body is found a short time later. The consensus is that she committed suicide.

Long and Wheelan look at the film, which contains some very illegal pornographic scenes. They speculate that this led to her murder. Rather unbelievably they defer notifying the police even though they acknowledge the necessity to do so, and even more unbelievably, Wheelan is not alarmed when Stone persistently tries to meet with her. There is something peculiar about the spool and there is mention of espionage and microfilm. After consulting with Long's boss, the evidence is finally turned over to Scotland Yard.

There is microfilm, but it is in cipher. Wheelan has finally begun to suspect Stone. The police want her to see him again and promise that someone will be watching out for her. The beads Burgess was wearing turn out to contain dangerous drugs. Long snoops and is nearly killed by Bream and his partner. Stone tries to murder Wheelan at the hospital, but the police prevent him from doing so and he is electrocuted by the trap he set for her.

The Catalyst (1966) is once again more of a suspense novel than a mystery. Hugh Wilmot and his wife Florence decide to vacation in Greece with her sister, Beatrice Shaw, who lives with them. Hugh almost married Beatrice before switching to the sister. All three of them hate the other two despite their pretense of affection. They are to be gone three weeks and they have barely arrived before bickering replaces pleasure.

They meet Rosamund Oakley, a noted actress traveling incognito, who is quite friendly. Hugh is immediately attracted to her. There is an incident in which Florence either falls from a balcony or is pushed by her sister. Florence later recants on her claim that she was attacked but it is not clear to anyone that she is sincere. They also meet Peter Elworthy and his girlfriend, Jennifer, who are in the country doing research into folk music.

Tensions build steadily. Hugh wanders out onto some dangerous rocks. Beatrice follows and falls, suffering some minor injuries, and Hugh has to rescue her before the tide comes in. He briefly considers allowing her to drown. The following day Beatrice makes a ridiculous scene in a local shop, after which she becomes lost in a crowd and is stabbed, though not seriously. Hugh speculates that it was a self inflicted wound. The weapon is found nearby and he throw it into the sea. The police are told nothing.

Oakley, although drawn to Hugh, is confused about the trio because they so often contradict themselves and each other. She is still trying to understand their dynamics when Beatrice falls or is pushed down a long flight of steps, and this time she dies. The police conclude that it was an accident, lacking any evidence of wrongdoing. Hugh's romance with Oakley ends quickly.

The closing chapters are a bit confusing. Hugh seems murderously inclined toward his wife, whom he apparently believes killed her sister. A woman wearing Florence's distinctive shawl goes on deck one night and is never seen again. Hugh leaves the ship alone, and what we see of his thoughts suggests that he murdered Florence, and possibly Beatrice as well. He goes home and almost immediately commits suicide. But Florence is still alive. She loaned the shawl to someone else, and she murdered Beatrice. But she has now become completely irrational and is taken to an asylum.

Death on the Reserve (1966) brought back Dr. Frost from *The Upfold Witch*. Frost and his wife Jeannie are visiting their daughter Judy and her husband, Julian Farnham, who are living in a secluded nature preserve. The reserve is administered by a warden named Arthur Budd. They arrive in time to hear that a young couple who had been bird watching seem to have disappeared.

The preserve area adjoins a quarry, a small sea port, a lighthouse, and some local residences. Ted Stone, one of the preserve workers, was formerly dating Shirley Anderson, the missing woman, until he was replaced by Wilfred Potter, who has also disappeared. The quarry is owned by Edgar Trouncey, whose brother Colin owns the factory where Wilfred was employed. The Grey Goose tavern is run by the Stones, Ted's parents, who also own a nearby farm.

Budd finds Anderson's bicycle in some bushes. Divers begin searching nearby ponds. Potter's bicycle is found by the divers, but there is no body. Anderson turns up, having gone to visit a relative without telling anyone, so they were not together. Shortly after a pointless confrontation with Edgar Trouncey, someone tries to run over Frost with a truck. Oddly, he does not see fit to notify the police.

A gang of Potter's friends beat up Ted Stone and commit various acts of vandalism. There have been hints of smuggling, arranged by one or both of the Trounceys. Someone shoots and kills Ted's father while he is driving his car. Wilfred turns out to be a bastard whose real father's identity was unknown. Edgar bolts and eventually admits that he caused Wilfred's death, although inadvertently. Neither of the Trounceys is his father – who turns out to be an irrelevant, unnamed character. The body was hidden at sea. Edgar is eventually captured. Colin killed Ted's father, who was threatening to expose the lucrative smuggling operation. Colin also flees, but during a violent storm and he is killed.

Death of a Con Man (1968) begins with a car crash. The only serious injury is to Fred Holmes, a professional swindler, who was driving one of the vehicles. Evidence at the scene suggests that there was a woman in the car, but she has vanished. Holmes is in bad shape, possibly exacerbated by a stab wound. A bloody knife is found near the wreck. Holmes is rushed to a nearby hospital where he is treated by Dr. Ahmed Patel.

Patel is told that the patient's blood group is listed in his diary and decides to save time by not having it tested. Colin Frost is the hospital registrar. The diary disappears, the blood group was incorrect, and Holmes dies. At the inquest, a man named Amos Gregson testifies that Holmes stole the car and drove off with Clarice Field as his passenger. The diary is later found, but it appears that the blood group has now been cleverly altered.

Frost is curious and finds evidence, but no proof, that Holmes was actually the last of the Stowden family, supposedly lost during the war. This leads him to the dead man's uncle, the retired Brigadier Stowden. The police meanwhile are unable to find Field. Frost extends his inquiries. Stowden was thrown out of the army for embezzlement. He had married, under another name, the daughter of an attorney, now retired, who describes his daughter's disillusionment when she discovered his dishonesty. Frost also identifies one of Stowden's criminal friends, Roy Waters.

Frost compares notes with the police, and both agree that someone altered the diary. A journalist, Barry Summers, has also taken an interest in the case. Frost does not like him, but he has more details about Stowden's criminal career. At least one of his victims, Gertrude Short, committed suicide and her sister blamed him for the death. Another woman lost most of her retirement money because of one of his schemes.

The police find one of Field's boyfriends, Bob Trueman, and follow him to a bar where they subsequently spot Field. They also notice that Gregson is there and is watching her. Summers also knows Field and takes Frost along to speak to her. She tells them that another man, Alec Hilton, was also in the car when it crashed. Hilton was the boss of a criminal gang and Stowden was trying to quit and go straight.

Hilton bolts and becomes a fugitive, then is arrested when he tries to stab Field, who is being protected by Trueman, who turns out to be her brother. Hilton and Stowden had fought over the knife in the car, which is what had precipitated the accident.

Summers and Frost turn their attention to Waters. Summers is nearly run down by an automobile and Frost almost succumbs to a contrived accident. Frost finally figures out that Waters, under another name, was the ambulance attendant who brought in Stowden and had the opportunity to change the blood group in the diary.

The Fennister Affair (1969) is a sea cruise mystery whose protagonist is Sally Combes. A woman disappeared from the ship the night before it arrived to pick up passengers for Bermuda, where Combes boards, and the circumstances surrounding that event are mysterious. Her husband has disembarked while inquiries are conducted but the ship is to continue onward. Their name is Fennister.

The first person Combes meets is Agnes Fairbrother, an affable older woman who is traveling alone. The only other new passenger is a young man, Tim Rogers. Combes discovers that she is in the cabin formerly occupied by the Fennisters. In a book from the ship's library, she finds part of a note in which Felicity Fennister announces her intention to stage a disappearance in view of the fact that someone, presumably her husband Mario, has found another person to love.

Captain Crowthorne seems unusually interested in having the note in his possession, but Combes decides to hold onto it. She meets several other passengers, including a pair of missionaries, and learns that the Fennisters were famous acrobats who were using a false name to avoid being recognized. She also overhears a small group of passengers who apparently are involved in something shady, and who misinterpret her visit to the captain, suggesting that she is an official but undercover investigator.

Rogers tells Combes confidentially that he is following a woman, currently working as a stewardess, who claims to be married to Mario Fennister, actually Fenestri. Another passenger, Ann Longford, is a close friend of the captain and was also Felicity's sister, although she does not appear to be much affected by her presumed death and certain disappearance. Rogers speculates that it was murder. Combes meets a young officer named Richard Groves who is smitten with her.

Combes learns that Mario lied. He was on deck when his wife disappeared and he was seen there. The stewardess, Conchita, was also in the area. Conchita claims that she married Mario a decade earlier and that his marriage to Felicity was therefore bigamous. She wanted Mario back, but did not want to break up his act with Felicity, which earned considerably more than Mario could have managed alone. This suggests that neither she nor Mario would have a good motive to have thrown his wife over the side and is an argument against it being murder.

Conchita quits at the next stop and goes ashore, obviously expecting Mario to be there. He is not and she hastily returns. Rogers also left the ship, but he does not reboard before it sails and has to fly to the next island to rejoin them there. Conchita goes ashore again, but there is still no Mario and she hastily goes back onto the ship. Combes shows the supposed suicide note to Longford, who destroys it.

Rogers is poisoned and nearly dies. He initially suspects that Sir John Meadows was responsible because he swapped drinks, supposedly inadvertently. When he recovers, he realizes that this is unlikely and that Meadows was probably the target. He confronts Meadows with this information and learns that the four bridge players aboard the ship – they are never named – are a gang of confidence men and blackmailers, and that they threatened to expose the fact that Meadows' daughter had recently been arrested for drug use.

Conchita is distraught and tells Combes that she saw Mario throw Felicity over the side. Rogers finds out there were some odd marks on the rail, and most readers will assume at this point that there was something going on that involved the acrobatic talents of the Fennisters. Meadows talks to the captain who radios ashore, and a police contingent meets the ship to arrest the blackmailers. One is killed, one arrested, and one escapes by jumping overboard and being rescued by friends in a small boat. The fourth man is assumed to be hiding on the ship,

Rogers has several revelations. Conchita was married to another man before she met Mario, so that later marriage was invalid and the one to Felicity was legal. He also stakes out Combes' cabin and captures the fourth man, who for some reason decides to murder Combes. Conchita's real husband takes her away and we learn later that he has killed her and then committed suicide. The ship reaches Bermuda where Felicity suddenly reappears. Longford, Mario, the captain, and several crew members were hiding her so that the blackmailers could not pressure Mario, although it is unclear what leverage they had and why they lost it by her disappearance. They staged her "murder," which is an unnecessary complication and also implausible since they had no way of knowing that they would be seen.

The Wilberforce Legacy (1969) is also set in the Caribbean, in a fictional island nation, and it is also unfortunately badly plotted. Benedict Wilberforce has been living in a rundown hotel managed by Luigi and Maria Mancini. A subplot of no particular relevance has Luigi insuring Wilberforce's life – he is elderly and in poor health – so that he can collect the proceeds after arranging for Wilberforce to have a fatal accident. Mancini has no insurable interest in Wilberforce and no insurance company would have issued the policy.

Wilberforce retired from the army after his brother George was revealed to be a professional criminal. George emigrated to the United States and has since died, leaving a son, George Junior. Wilberforce also has a sister, Lucy Maclean, who is widowed and has an adult daughter, Allison. There were rumors that he had a large amount of stolen cash provided by his brother. He also owns a small coffee plantation whose location is something of a mystery.

The employees at the hotel include Paula, a rude and mildly suspicious character. The cook is Therese, whose husband Jim is very fond of Wilberforce, and vice versa. Jim helps him take a nightly swim in the hotel's swimming pool. Wilberforce receives two telegrams and a letter, all on the same day. The two telegrams appear to be from George Junior, but they come from two different countries and obviously cannot both be genuine. The letter is from his sister, announcing that Allison is on her way to visit and will arrive in a few days. Wilberforce's lawyer is Henry Gopal.

The first George to arrive is a supercilious cad who tries to extort money from Wilberforce, threatening to reveal his connection to his criminal brother and demanding that all of the assets be signed over to him immediately. Wilberforce, who worked as a Nazi war criminal hunter, recognizes him as Manfred Stein, son of a wanted man, and rejects his claim. This subplot also makes little sense. Even if Stein could have convinced Wilberforce, the transfer of ownership would be to George Junior by name, so he could not have profited from it.

The second George arrives a short time later. Although he is the real one, he is just as obnoxious as Stein and is also refused. Wilberforce arranges to provide a new will to Gopal – which names Allison's mother as heir. That evening, a body is found drowned in the pool, but is not reported until morning. It is initially identified as Wilberforce, but it turns out to be Stein wearing a life mask of the older man. We later learn that Wilberforce used the mask as a kind of dummy so that anyone looking in his window would see what appeared to be him asleep in his bed. But Bell never explains why he resorted to this subterfuge. Stein died of a broken neck.

Stein was related to Dr. Stone, who works at the local hospital. Stone is a radiologist who fakes x-rays so that Wilberforce will believe that he is closer to death than is actually the case. This is another subplot that seems to have no purpose, as it does not affect Wilberforce's actions in any way.

Allison arrives and hears the story. Her uncle is missing, of course, and apparently so is Gopal. Peter Grant, the Maclean family lawyer and Allison's romantic interest, arrives to help find Wilberforce. Three mysterious tourists register at the hotel and show an odd interest in the location of Wilberforce's plantation. Grant notices this right away, but he disappears immediately when a fourth man joins them. This is George Junior, using another name, and Grant had met him once.

There is another terrible plot error here. George applies pressure to Allison to sign over her uncle's property to him, and attempts to kill her when she refuses. He has already killed Gopal and plans to burn the body so that it will be mistaken for Wilberforce. But if Allison is dead, she cannot inherit, and in any case her mother is the beneficiary. There is no progression through which he could acquire title to the property. There is a secondary problem as well. The plantation is rumored to have a substantial amount of bauxite. The three new tourists make up a team that wants to purchase the land for that reason. They are, for some reason, accompanied by a CIA agent. They tentatively sign a contract without ever visiting the site, and when they do, they discover the bauxite vein is negligible. No company would have made the offer without a preliminary survey.

It is never clear why George killed Gopal, although possibly to acquire the will. But it appears that he did not know about the will, and it had already been locked in a bank vault. His attempt to kill Allison is similarly inexplicable. She is rescued by Hulbert and Grant, but they and the authorities pretend that the dead man is Wilberforce – it is wearing the life mask which was somehow stolen from the police – in order to set a trap to catch George. No one could possibly believe that the autopsy would not notice the body was wearing a mask.

Wilberforce shows up at his own funeral. George bolts and later drowns while trying to escape. The company tries to back out of the purchase, but the CIA agent somehow forces them to comply because Wilberforce has turned over to him extensive files about German war criminals. There is no explanation for why he held them until this point, or belatedly provided them to the government. Paula, who was working for George, tries to murder Allison with a poisoned knife and dies herself. There is no explanation for the attack. The plot is overall a complete mess. And why did George murder Stein?

A Hydra with Six Heads (1970) has another doctor as protagonist. Roy Cartwright has accepted a four week stint substituting for a partner in a suburban practice. Dr. Markson is away on vacation and Cartwright is waiting for a permanent position to open for him. An unpleasant woman named Muriel Southport claims that Cartwright assaulted her, and her husband backs her up. Lillian -spelling alternates with "Lilian" - Barlett, the secretary, tells Cartwright confidentially that the same thing happened when she saw Dr. Markson. He suspects that the second senior physician, Dr. Phillips, is in collusion with the couple. And he knows that the most senior, Dr. Williams, is an alcoholic. Barnett, his niece, lives with him.

Cartwright discovers that his predecessor on his new job was Markson, which contradicts the story that he had been in the other partnership for two years. The housekeeper at the practice, Mrs. Gladstone, tells him that Markson is not on vacation, that he is working at another site – the one where Cartwright is supposed to start in a few days.

The practice handles a number of hardcore drug addicts, two of whom attack Cartwright after hours, although he suspects they did so at the direction of Phillips. The drug treatment program is a sham and probably illegal. Cartwright is happy to take his leave, and almost immediately learns that Markson has been found dead, murdered, though this is not immediately obvious. Williams rages at Barlett when she asks questions about the matter.

Through a relative, Cartwright has a connection to Scotland Yard. In fact we later learn that the Yard manipulated him into taking this job because they were suspicious of both practices. Barlett tries to investigate on her own. Markson was drowned but there is evidence that he was murdered and his father insists he would never have committed suicide.

It appears that Markson had uncovered some evidence that some of the various doctors were involved in some kind of international conspiracy, illegal immigration or smuggling or both. Cartwright is suspicious of his new bosses and spies on them when they make a mysterious journey by boat and meet Phillips as well as the thugs who had attacked him. He takes photographs. Barlett was with him, but when she arrives home she finds her uncle dead. Cartwright discovers he has been a pawn and is upset.

Barlett realizes that the suicide note left by the body was a forgery, but Phillips is there so she pretends to accept it. Her uncle had given her a letter to be opened only after his death and it reveals where he kept records of the crime ring, which was smuggling people into the country, but sometimes dropping them off to die at sea. She is closely watched and one of the gang pretends to be a police detective and questions her, to determine whether or not she has been fooled. She plays along and later escapes and consults a lawyer and then the police.

Barlett is briefly kidnapped but the police have been watching and she is subsequently rescued unharmed. The members of the gang are all arrested, including one named Pullen who had been masquerading as Markson's father in order to find out how much was known.,

A Hole in the Ground (1971) takes place initially shortly after the end of World War II. Martin Filton is a college student vacationing by hiking the moors of Cornwall. He sees a woman driving a jeep with a bloody rag in plain view. Evidently she had been shooting squirrels. He later finds more blood at the opening of a ventilation shaft of an abandoned mind. Although suspicious, he does not pursue the matter.

Twenty years later Filton, now a surgeon, returns to the area for the first time He remembers the incident and walks to the ventilation shaft in time to help a young couple, John Penmore and Drina Polesden, who were caught in barbed wire when the edge of the shaft collapsed. He is invited to lunch by Drina's mother Marian after the emergency is dealt with, learns something of the family history, and then meets Rita Gates, Drina's aunt, whom he recognizes as the woman who was driving the jeep. When he mentions the encounter, Drina's mother nearly faints.

Filton subsequently learns that Mrs. Polesden could not have children. Drina was presumed to be the daughter of a refugee whom Gates brought to the house and who subsequently disappeared, apparently with Marian's husband. Marian then adopted the infant. Drina evades her bossy aunt and goes off with two friends, supposedly to let her damaged ankle heal. She has asked Filton to help find out the truth about her parents. Gates is furious. Gates nearly hits Filton with her car, not entirely accidentally.

Filton returns to London but begins investigating Vicki Orchinska, the woman supposed to have been Drina's mother. He is startled to discover that while Orchinska was indeed pregnant at the right time, her baby was reportedly stillborn. So neither of Drina's parents have been identified.

Penmore is part of a caving club, so Filton corresponds with its organizer expressing his interest in visiting the abandoned mine if such an expedition is under consideration. A small party does explore the mine and Filton finds the skeleton of a woman who was obviously shot in the chest. He manages to gather some of the bones before someone begins shooting at the party and a cave-in traps them.

Everyone is rescued and Filton brings the incriminating bones with him, although some of them are promptly stolen. For some reason never adequately explained, Filton conceals the existence of the bullet wound for a time. When he finally tells the police what he knows, they are justifiably annoyed by his meddling. He pursues his own investigation regardless and learns that the missing Colin Polesden proposed to Rita before Marian, but was turned down. He also hears of a young man named Leslie North who was a friend of the sisters.

Rita believed that she had shot and killed Orchinska because she was blackmailing her, but she had missed. She did hide the body in the well, but it was actually Colin who had murdered her. Filton and the police track down an old family servant, only to discover that she has just died of a mysterious overdose of sleeping pills. Marian attempts to kill Rita, though not before witnesses. Leslie North turns out to be a woman who was involved with Robert Gates, who died in the war. They were Drina's parents and had planned to marry. North also died of natural causes a short time after Gates.

Colin was poisoned by another servant, who is also dead. Filton, Drina, and a police officer are investigating a shed on the property and find two buried suitcases. Marian shows up, locks them inside, and sets fire to the building, but they are able to break free. The two sisters kill each other in the midst of a major landslide caused by the collapse of the mine. Their concern about Drina was because she was heir to the estate, not the two of them.

Death of a Poison-Tongue (1972) begins when Althea Swinford takes a train to the small town where she is to study foreign languages at a local college. On the train she meets Dorothea Golden, an older woman, who tells her the town is plagued by someone who spreads false rumors, including about her hosts, Bill and Violet Chambers. Chambers in fact expresses dislike of Golden almost immediately. Swinford is oddly sleepy on the train and does not overhear the conversation between Golden and an unidentified man, except one small snatch which suggests they are speaking in Turkish. She never suspects, though the reader does, that her sleepiness is the result of having been drugged by Golden, who is the head of a quasi-Christian cult.

Chambers is the local vicar. The rumor monger is Harriet Smith. The latest victim of the smear attacks is Jason Court, a local artist, who supposedly is having an affair with a local woman. He is concerned that someone will vandalize the paintings he is preparing for a show, so they are moved clandestinely to the vicarage. Swindon does not care for him and there seems to be unusual affection between him and Violet. Swindon meets several people at the college, including Bren Marston, a young man who shares her scholastic interests.

Swindon then meets Judy Downs and her sister Gwen. Judy has been connected by rumor to Court, Violet to a local farmer, and Golden to a visiting professor at the college named Englefield. When Swindon meets Englefield, she realizes that he was the mystery man on the train. She also meets Smith, who is a repellent and abusive invalid. Golden persistently tries to get her to visit. She does attend one of her meetings, where Golden speaks in tongues, but she remains unconvinced.

Court invites her to a sketching session on the coast, where they observe two reclusive men who routinely visit over the weekend and seem to be connected to Golden. He becomes inexplicably angry and she becomes frightened and arranges another way of getting home. She suspects that he might have wanted to have her fall over a cliff at one point, notes that his sketches are not remotely talented, which underscores her feeling that he is not really an artist. He also expressed unusual interest in a specific boat, upon which the two weekenders – who are a gay couple – arrive.

Englefield and Golden meet clandestinely. They are aware that Court is a fraud and that he was inordinately interested in the arrival of the gay couple. Court's thoughts are also revealed. He wished to injure Swindon, not kill her, in order to get her hospitalized and out of his way. The vicar visits Smith and finds her strangled in her wheelchair.

Marston tells Swindon that the gay couple is probably providing drugs to some of the students at the college. Like most of her contemporaries, Bell did not understand much about addiction, marijuana, or LSD, but pretended to do so. The police exercise search warrants and find evidence of drugs in the cottage rented by the gay couple, but nothing at Golden's house or anywhere else that they search.

Swindon agrees to see Court alone, which seems rather implausible given their previous meeting. He admits that he is not an artist and that he is spying on Golden, although he does not explain whom he works for. She believes she is in love with him, but when she walks in on him examining some smuggled art objects and he attacks her – fortunately aborted when Chambers shows up – she also notices some unusual cordage which matches the kind used to strangle Smith. She tells the police everything, including about the candy which she now thinks was drugged.

The police had been planning to arrest the gang and Swindon's adventures disrupt that effort. Nevertheless, Englefield and Golden are taken into custody. Court has disappeared. Golden was peripherally involved with smuggling drugs. Court escapes to France but is arrested there. Smith was actually murdered by a minor character, a neighbor whom she had been blackmailing, in a side plot almost unrelated to the main story,.

A Pigeon Among the Cats (1974) follows Rose Lawler, a retired school teacher, who is off for a tour of Italy. The younger woman sitting next to her on the bus introduces herself as Gwen Chilton and explains that she and her husband are not happily married and she has just left him without notice and run off with their savings. At their first stop, a man with a disfigured face offers to guide them to a cathedral they wish to visit. Lawler finds him a bit strange but not menacing. It turns out that he is staying at the same hotel and he later introduces himself as Owen Strong.

Another tourist notices that Chilton's passport is not British, as she had claimed, and that there was a different name on it. She also mysteriously acquires some cash in a town although the banks are supposedly not open yet. There is a married couple named Banks whose daughter Peggy is obnoxious and troublesome. They reach Rome and Lawler, purely by chance, spots Chilton meeting with Strong.

Chilton was actually Roy Chilton's mistress using a false name. Strong recognizes her and is trying to figure out if she absconded with some of her lover's money – he is wealthy. She now has a new passport made out to her assumed name. Chilton tells Lawler that Strong is trying to get her to see him socially and that she is afraid of him.

Strong continues to shadow the tour group. He is now certain that Chilton has access to a considerable amount of money and he wants to take it from her. Peggy Banks smokes some pot and has to be hospitalized – Bell still harbored misconceptions about drugs – but that does not seem to have been her real ailment. Strong openly rejoins the tour and is outwardly amicable. Chilton tells him she did not steal the money but was only serving as a courier. Someone pushes Lawler down a staircase and she suspects it was Strong.

Chilton steals Lawler's room key and is caught rummaging through her suitcases. Peggy leaves the tour group. Another man begins hanging around and Chilton is sure he is some kind of crook. Strong claims that someone has stolen his wallet. His competition kidnaps Chilton and Lawler and keeps them on a boat. They throw Lawler overboard and try to run her down, but she is a skilled swimmer, fakes her drowning, and swims to shore.

Strong, Chilton, and Lawler are briefly on the run. The gang shoots Chilton, but she survives. The police arrest Lawler after Strong does finally kill Chilton and steals something she is carrying. The other crooks are killed in a car crash, although at least one of them was shot by Strong. Strong apparently escapes.

Victim (1975) is essentially a woman in jeopardy suspense novel. Laura Mellanby is getting on in years and has decided that living alone in an oversized house is no longer appropriate or practical. She welcomes an offer from a developer that would allow her to move to a smaller house elsewhere, but is warned that her neighbors will likely object to the change. Several of them are in fact openly hostile to the idea of a housing development or apartments, even though most of the houses in the area have already been converted to accommodate tenants.

Mellanby's next door neighbor, Florence Short, is in a similar situation and is also considering selling. Short's daily help finds her dead in bed a few days later and her doctor discovers that her sleeping pills are gone. The autopsy confirms that she died of an overdose. Mellanby had visited and was possibly the last person to see her alive. Another neighbor, a retired military man named Streeter, detested Short, as did his wife. He had once served under Short's deceased husband.

Another neighbor named Clarke has a private entrance to Short's property, but the police cannot find him and he has not taken in his milk delivery for two days. He is spotted in another village, but moves on before the police can interview him. Clarke is elsewhere, and is temporarily stranded by a mysterious cab driver who tricks him into leaving the car on a lonely beach. The car is obviously abandoned and turns out to be a rental, although the man who paid for it is nowhere to be found.

Village politics prevail for a while. Short was on the planning board and has to be replaced. Another neighbor suddenly recalls seeing a man named Redfern arrive at Short's house just as Mellanby was leaving. Redfern was vehemently opposed to any kind of local development. The man who stranded Clarke is found dead on a remote beach.

The planning council disapproves Mellanby's application for developing her property and selling it. The police follow Clarke's trail, but he reportedly is now somewhere on the continent. The dead driver, King, is a small time thug who was apparently hired to dispose of Clarke. Another developer sends a proposal, but Mellanby is temporarily sidelined by illness.

A friend of Mellanby overhears a violent argument between

Redfern and an unidentified woman, although he does not hear enough to know what the disagreement concerned. The new member of the planning council, Tims, is generally disliked by those who know him. He is also believed to be accepting bribes and is suspected of attempting to molest a child.

Redfern and Tims argue – and it is obvious that Redfern had bribed him and was not happy how events were unfolding. Redfern also turns out to have connections in the construction industry and had a personal, though concealed, interest in how the area was developed and by whom. Tims resigns and tells the police he is afraid of Redfern. Clarke returns to the village. The police speculate that Redfern was trying to finesse the property away from Clarke, Short, and Mellanby for a private development project for his own profit.

Redfern tries to force Mellanby to sell, but is interrupted by Clarke. The two men go off together and Redfern is found shot to death, apparently a suicide. Clarke then tries to pressure Mellanby to sell because he owns the second developer. She surreptitiously calls the police but Clarke – who murdered Short and Redfern – has a heart attack and dies before he can be arrested.

The Trouble in Hunter Ward (1976) has a hospital setting. Enid Hallett is retired from the nursing position at a hospital where she has just been admitted. The hospital is in the throes of a labor dispute. She immediately has words with a porter, Joe Wells. Hallett was notorious for her bad temper and tendency to slander patients and staff. Her internal disorder is probably inoperable.

Sister Baker is a nurse who ignores Hallett's manner. Mrs. Mitchell is another patient who tries unsuccessfully to be sociable, The non-medical staff votes to stop work in this particular ward because they disagree with what is seen as special treatment for some patients. Zia Camplin, another patient who had minor facial surgery, is just as disagreeable as Hallett. Daphne Parker has appendicitis and tends to be hysterical. Adams is a teacher who was badly beaten by one of her students. Fred Gates is a disagreeable union official with lung cancer. Guy Harper and Ian Campbell, both staff members, endeavor to keep the patients satisfied despite the work stoppage.

Years earlier, Hallett had accused a nurse named Wheeler of having an inappropriate affair with a Dr. David Thompson, who still works at the hospital. Wheeler had been fired and later committed suicide. Thompson has been very friendly with Dr. Joan Fisher and is dismayed that she might believe Hallett's slander. Hallett accuses Nurse Wilson of using drugs.

Hallett has exploratory surgery and dies unexpectedly while recovering. She died because of a narcotic introduced into her system. Her last injection was performed by Wilson, and another patient quietly tells the doctors that he believes she is an addict. An investigation indicates no irregularities with the drugs that could have led to Hallett's death, but it is now an open secret that Wilson is a drug user. Wilson has been buying drugs outside the hospital with money provided by Camplin. Faced with disgrace, Wilson takes an overdose and dies the following day, leaving behind a sealed suicide note for the coroner. Camplin, who has had several mildly mysterious visitors, is discharged.

A drug sniffing dog alerts in the room Camplin vacated, which arouses the interest of the police. Parker develops a puzzling swelling in one arm. Camplin seems to have disappeared and is thought to have quietly left the country. Parker has a recurring "dream" of seeing someone menacing in the ward at night. Mitchell tells the police that the night prowler is Mrs. Norris, a part time aide who has barely been mentioned earlier.

Gates knows something and sends a letter to the police, but almost dies when someone sets fire to his oxygen tent. The police quietly tell him that they lack sufficient evidence for an arrest and are assigning an undercover man disguised as a maintenance worker. Nurse Biggs is attacked from behind in the parking lot. Gates also names Norris as the killer, and this is confirmed moments later when Norris unsuccessfully attacks another nurse with a knife before fleeing the hospital.

Inexplicably, the police interview Norris without mentioning the knife attack. Her testimony and some evidence suggest that she is telling the truth about her time in the hospital, which would mean she is innocent. The solution is that she has a sister who looks very much like her, but whose mental age is that of a child. Norris brought her sister to the hospital at times and while she killed Hallett, the sister was responsible for the other incidents.

Despite a strong first half, this is a rather dreadful novel. Norris is barely mentioned until the closing chapters and there is no hint of a motive. Her sister is not mentioned at all. At least two of the patients actually know who the killer is. One never tells the police, although she mentions it to someone else who does. The other eventually tells the authorities, but only by writing a letter rather than during his interview. The detective does not act against Norris strongly even though there were multiple witnesses to the attempted stabbing of a nurse.

Stroke of Death (1977, aka *Such a Nice Client*) is another traditional mystery novel. Lucy Sommers is a physiotherapist assigned to work with the elderly Lawrence. Lawrence suffered a stroke and is partly paralyzed. He cannot speak. He is living with his son and daughter-in-law in a remote house. When Sommers first arrives, she notices that Lawrence is noticeably hungry, stealing a crust of bread from some birds. He is clearly being starved and is terrified of Dorothy Lawrence

She reports her suspicions to Dr. Geoff Harris. The visiting nurse notices that Dorothy is upset when she insists on helping Lawrence with a meal, but there is still nothing overt upon which any official action can be initiated. Various steps are taken, but no one cares very much and their efforts to investigate are easily derailed. This is a bit of a strain on credibility because the interference is quite obvious although none of the people sent to look into the matter seem to notice.

Harris visits and Lawrence manages to speak a single word. This development obviously terrifies Dorothy. Her husband Jim is out of the country on an extended trip. Their marriage is obviously not a happy one and Jim is aware of the plan to starve his father to death. Nothing significant is done until it is too late. Lawrence "accidentally" runs his wheelchair over a cliff and is killed. The son does not return for the inquest.

Dorothy wants to sell the house, but cannot do so until her husband is back in the country. His continued absence is considered suspicious. He quietly returns and the reader is shown that the two of them hate each other intensely. There is also some uncertainty about where or not he really is the dead man's son. The real son shows up and identifies Dorothy as the dead man's wife, not his daughter-in-law.

The two conspirators disappear and despite committing another murder to cover their tracks, they are located and brought to justice.

The story is oddly unengaging and is more about the dysfunctions in the British welfare services than it is about the murder and its ultimate solution.

Treachery in Type (1978, aka *A Swan-Song Betrayed*) involves the publishing industry. An elderly widow named Grosshouse was once a successful writer as Anita Armstrong. As her finances become strained, she decides to resurrect her writing career with a new historical novel. She talks to George Carr at her publishing house, who is cautious and clearly not enthusiastic, and also mentions it to her friend, Mervyn Haston.

Grosshouse hires Judy Smith to type up the manuscript in process from her handwritten drafts. Judy is not very bright and Grosshouse is not the most patient person in the world, so there is some tension between them. Judy's boyfriend is Chris Trotter. They are friends with Leonard and Claire Stockley. Leonard is also a publisher.

In a not very convincing sequence, Leonard is intrigued enough by Smith's description that he encourages her to steal a copy of the finished chapters so that he can read them. Several of these chapters have already been provided to Grosshouse's publishers, who are much more enthusiastic than they had been. As the manuscript nears completion, Grosshouse decides to take an extended vacation on the continent where she can write the final portions of the novel.

Smith and Trotter have no idea that the book hass already been sold. They steal a copy of the manuscript and Smith makes superficial changes as she retypes the novel under her own name. This is not very plausible given that she struggled to understand many of the words in the manuscript when she first saw them. Nor is she portrayed as particularly literate.

The stolen book is published and garners considerable attention, and money. Grosshouse's publishers become aware of it and inform her of the plagiarism. Trotter is found drowned but there is no evidence of foul play. A legal battle begins with Smith insisting that it was all Trotter and Stockley and that she was just a pawn. Stockley's boss and financier, Sir Edgar Seven, is outraged, leading to a physical confrontation with Stockley.

Stockley suspects that Sir Edgar arranged to have Trotter killed. Smith is invited by Sir Edgar to a party where she is nearly targeted for violence, though she runs away. The police have by now found a connection between Sir Edgar and Trotter. Smith goes out on a boat with the Stockleys and is attacked again. This time she escapes by jumping overboard.

The boat sinks and Clare Stockley's drowned body is found in the wreckage. The wreck is raised and Leonard's body is inside, but there is also evidence that it was sunk by an unlikely explosion. By accident, the police learn that drugs were being smuggled in marked copies of the plagiarized book, which is rather too elaborate a project to be convincing. Sir Edgar is arrested.

Wolf! Wolf! (1999) was the first of two novels to feature Amy Tupper. Tupper is a cross between Miss Seeton and Jane Marple. She is elderly and is having a brief hospital stay when she notices two men having a clandestine meeting in a storage room. She recognizes one of them as a recently released serial killer named Tilsett, but when she writes to her niece and nephew, Phyl and Tom, and mentions the incident, they decide that she is imagining things. That perception changes when the body of a strangled nurse is found at the hospital.

The police interview Tupper but are skeptical of her account, even when she says that Tilsett knew he had been recognized. They suspect a pharmacist in part because he is foreign and mostly because he was dating the dead nurse and had recently quarreled with her. He also went home sick at about the time of the murder and admits that he found the body but was afraid to tell anyone. Interviews with the other nurses suggest that the victim was a blackmailer.

Although the police arrest the pharmacist, a new development troubles them. The keys to the storage room had been loaned to a construction company that was planning some renovations, and the head of the company is named Tilsett. He and an architect did visit the room on the day in question. Tupper is asked to meet the two men and it is Victor Crawthorne whom Tupper thought was the famous killer, although she now realizes that he is far too young. Tilsett had a son, however, and Crawthorne is the right age.

Elsewhere, an official notices that Tilsett's construction company has been receiving quite a large share of government work recently. The police still believe the pharmacist is the killer, but Tupper's story is bothersome. Crawthorne is belligerent when the police interview him but admits that he is the son of the famous murderer.

He does not mention that Ray Tilsett, who runs the construction company has just advised him that their business affairs are being investigated.

Two men break into Tupper's home, tie her up, and search the premises without telling her what they are looking for. She is released by her niece and the police understandably do not believe it was a random burglary. Tilsett, the killer, died of cancer months prior to the murder of the nurse. The investigator looking into Ray Tilsett's business is nearly killed by a sabotaged hedge trimmer and the police know that it was attempted murder.

Both Crawthorne and Tilsett tell the police that they were being blackmailed by the dead nurse, but they are cagey about revealing what she knew about them. While recovering from the attack, Tupper discovers that one of the nuns has been dating Crawthorne. The nurse tries to kill Tupper but fails and is arrested for the earlier murder. The solution is a bit disappointing because there had been no hint of her involvement with Crawthorne until the end.

A Question of Inheritance (1980) was the second Tupper novel. Florence Bennet is an unsuccessful actress trapped in a bad marriage. When their infant son dies of crib death, she flees England and her husband. She had threatened to leave him but has no money and no real friends, although she knows Amy Tupper slightly. She is the only one who knows the child has died, so she secretly buries him and flees the country under her original name, Maisie Atkins.

She arrives in France after an encounter with a thoughtful worker at a long term car park. Bennet has friends there and they help her look for work. She meets Paula Luccini, who has married into a family of acrobats. She has an infant son and she is terrified that he will take up the family tradition and be killed., When Bennet learns that her husband died in a car crash less than a week after her flight, she pays Luccini a bribe and promises to bring up her son in safety and comfort. The trip back to England is uneventful and she retrieves her car. The attendant notices her again but doubts she is involved in smuggling or anything else illegal.

No one questions the child's identity and twenty years pass. Tupper arrives in answer to a frantic but vague letter from Bennet, only to find that she has been attacked during the night and eventually dies without regaining consciousness. She had had an unidentified late night visitor, a man, and he is presumed to be the attacker. Her letter to Tupper suggests she is in danger connected to the time when her husband died.

Percy Bennet had a sister who married into the Thornton family and emigrated to Canada. Florence hinted that there was a bit of a family feud because her son Philip had inherited the bulk of the estate, but that it was not expressed openly. The Thorntons were planning to come to England to visit and might already be in the country. In fact they have arrived and are consulting a lawyer about contesting Percy's will. A former servant named Somerton claims now that Percy fathered her son Reg before Philip was born. Reg has a long record of petty crimes.

The police are interested in the six days in which Florence was missing, suspecting it may have something to do with the murder. This is a bit of a reach because twenty years had passed and there was nothing to suggest it was significant. More importantly, Philip mentions having dug up a buried cat when he was very young and he digs it up again for Tupper. She recognizes it immediately as the body of an infant.

There are some clumsy plot elements at this point. Philip has inherited a fondness for acrobatics, which is nonsense. The infant is found in a very contrived sequence. Tupper remembers a not particularly distinctive baby's toy that was buried with the body. The garage attendant remembers Bennet's encounter after twenty years even though nothing unusual happened at the time. He even recalls that she was not wearing a wedding ring. It is possible, however, that he has been blackmailing her ever since.

Someone sets fire to the house and Philip is nearly killed along with some of the servants. They all escape, though with some injuries. Medical records and blood types prove that Philip is not related to Percy or Florence, which means the estate must go to the Thorntons.

Tupper goes to France and Italy and finds out where Tupper spent the missing time. Philip loses his teaching job along with his fortune, but his girlfriend remains loyal even after learning about his false identity. The girlfriend's mother is Italian and she tracks down a report that Paula Luccini died with her child, both drowned, although the infant was never found and suicide was suspected. Her husband vowed to kill whoever had driven Paula to kill herself.

The climax is dreadfully melodramatic. Philip attends a circus performance and sees his father get into trouble on the high wire – although he does not yet suspect they are related. With no formal training he mounts the apparatus himself to save the older man. They both realize the truth when they are safe. The garage attendant finally admits that he was blackmailing Florence, but insists that she was already dead when he arrived that night. The killer is a minor servant who regarded the original Philip almost as her own child, and she was in league with the Thornton's son.

A Deadly Place to Stay (1982, aka *The Innocent*) was Bell's final novel. Lesley is a homeless young woman who is not above thievery to improve her situation. She takes shelter with a cult managed by the Ruler, determined to use it as a base from which to find a job and get a real life in London. The cult is pretty much what readers will expect, strict rules, domination by the leader, odd inhibitions.

Lesly tries to break free but the cult is well organized. It is also concealing the fact that it illegally punishes its own members, and eventually that leads to an actual murder, Lesley is even more desperate after that and eventually she is able to escape and the Ruler is arrested. A very disappointing final novel with a thoroughly awful protagonist.

MASTERS OF DETECTION

AGATHA CHRISTIE

Agatha Christie (1890-1976) was a British mystery writer, probably the best known contributor to that genre of all time. Her main protagonists were the Belgian detective Hercule Poirot and the British Miss Jane Marple. Numerous movies have been made adapting her works and the long running Hercule Poirot television series was a major project.

Christie's first novel was *The Mysterious Affair at Styles* (1921), which introduced Poirot. The story is narrated by Hastings, who serves as a kind of Watson for Poirot. He is on leave from the army when he runs into an old friend, John Cavendish, who invites him to visit the family estate, Styles Court. John's stepmother, Emily, who is seventy, has recently remarried. When John's father died, he left the bulk of his estate to his wife, although she has been generous to John and his brother Lawrence.

Evie Howard serves as Mrs. Cavendish's assistant and she is vaguely related to Alfred Inglethorp, originally her employer's secretary, now her much younger husband. Lawrence is attempting to make a career as a writer, without much success. John is technically a lawyer, but is no longer practicing and lives at Styles with his mother, brother, and his own wife, Mary. Cynthia Murdock is Mrs. Cavendish's protégé. She dispenses medicines at a nearby clinic.

On the first day of Hastings' visit, Howard tries to warn Emily that her husband is unfaithful and only wants her money. The quarrel is so heated that Howard moves out of the house. Dr. Bauerstein, an expert on poisons and a friend of Mary Cavendish, is staying in the nearby village. Hastings take an immediate dislike to both Bauerstein and Inglethorp.

By chance, Hastings runs into Poirot, who is one of several Belgian refugees from the war who are living in the village thanks to the largess of Mrs. Cavendish/Inglethorp. Poirot was at one time a prominent member of the Belgian police force. Shortly after that encounter, Hastings learns that there has been a major row between the Inglethorps and a lesser one between the older woman and her daughter-in-law Mary.

That night, Mrs. Inglethorp takes coffee up to her bedroom, but several people have had access to it, including Bauerstein, who had somehow fallen into a nearby pond. That night, Mrs. Inglethorp goes into convulsion in her locked bedroom – it appears that she engaged the locks herself. The household is aroused, and it is discovered that her husband is not in the house and has not slept in the bed. Shortly after the door is forced, she has a final convulsion and dies. Bauerstein suspects poison. Inglethorp returns in the morning, stating that he was so late in conducting a business deal with a man named Denby that he spent the balance of the night in the other man's guest room. Inglethorp is also rumored to be having an affair with a local woman named Raikes.

Hastings convinces the brothers to allow him to enlist the aid of Poirot. Poirot immediately makes the observation that too much time passed between the drinking of the coffee and the onset of the attack, which appears to eliminate the coffee as the source of the poison. The cup has been smashed and ground to powder, which appears to have been a deliberate act, either to conceal the fact that is was poisoned, or to conceal the fact that it was not.

Poirot finds a variety of potential clues in the dead woman's bedroom including a splash of candle grease, a small piece of fabric, and a fragment of a will that has been burnt in the fireplace. An interview with the maid who overheard the first quarrel casts some doubt as to whether or not Inglethorp was one of the parties. Further questioning of the servants reveals that a cup of cocoa was always placed in the bedroom, and that it might be heated and consumed at any point during the night. There were also granules on the tray which could have been strychnine.

Poirot continues his investigation, providing enigmatic hints about what is important and what is not. He cites the unusually hot weather, the fact that Murdock does not take sugar in her coffee, and Inglethorp's long beard as relevant details. He does not, however, necessarily believe – as does virtually everyone else – that Inglethorp is the killer.

At the inquest, the local chemist testifies that Inglethorp purchased strychnine on the day preceding his wife's death. Inglethorp denies this – and the fact that he has a long beard suggests the obvious possibility of an imposter. There is considerable confusion about the disposition of the estate – the marriage having invalidated the previously existing will under English law. There was clearly a more recent one, witnessed by the gardeners a few hours before her death, but it has been destroyed. Inglethorpe denies arguing with his wife, and no one actually saw them together. Inspector Japp from Scotland Yard arrives to investigate what is clearly murder. They are determined to arrest Inglethorp until Poirot explains that at the time he supposedly purchased the poison, he was accompanying Mrs. Raikes, in front of several witnesses.

John inherits the house and enough money to maintain it. Inglethorpe gets the bulk of the money, and moves to a hotel while trying to develop his future plans. Japp arrests John for the murder. Two months pass before the trial. Poirot appears to believe that John is guilty but that he will be acquitted, even though it is now known that he was the one who quarreled with his stepmother, not Inglethorp.

It was in fact John who was having an affair with Raikes. His lawyer attempts to demonstrate that Lawrence had equal opportunity and motive. The trial is still underway when Poirot has a brainstorm and calls the others together. Mary Cavendish lied about where she was on the night of the murder. The piece of fabric caught in one of the bolts was from her clothing. She was searching for a document which she erroneously thought referred to her husband's infidelity when Mrs. Inglethorp went into convulsions and she hastily escaped through a connecting door, after dropping her candle – hence the grease. The document actually impugned Inglethorp, which is why she burned the will favoring him.

The dead woman burned the will herself, which explains why she had a fire set in her room despite the hot weather. Mary had drugged both Murdock and Mrs. Inglethorp in order to search safely. The sleeping pill retarded the effect of the strychnine, which means that it could have been administered in the coffee after all. But Poirot dismisses this as well because the stain on the rug suggests that she spilled her coffee and did not drink it. Nor was the cocoa poisoned. Her medicine had been rigged so that she would receive an overdose, but for various reasons, she did not take a dose on the night which was intended to be her last. The actual killer is Inglethorp after all, and Howard was his co-conspirator.

The novel is an excellent debut mystery with only some minor cheating. Despite being touted as presenting the reader with all of the necessary facts to solve the crime, it actually does not do so. Unless the reader is already aware that a sleeping potion retards the effect of strychnine, it is impossible to reach the correct conclusion from the facts as presented.

The Secret Adversary (1922) introduced the team of Prudence "Tuppence" Cowley and Tommy Beresford. They meet following a prologue in which a man gives important papers to an American woman aboard the sinking Lusitania, insisting that they are important to the Allies. Tommy served in the army and was twice wounded and they originally met in a hospital. They are both young and broke. The war is over, now, however, so years have passed since the prologue.

The two of them decide to advertise themselves as freelance adventurers, and are overheard by Edward Whittington, who asks her to come for an interview. He wants Tuppence to accompany him to France for three months and pose as his ward. There is no suggestion of anything involving sex, but she distrusts him instinctively and gives her name as Jane Finn, whose name Tommy had mentioned hearing and which had struck him as unusual. To her surprise, Whittington reacts violently to the name and accuses her of knowing all about his business. He gives her some money and they agree to further discussion later.

Tuppence convinces Tommy to follow Whittington, since he is unlikely to be recognized. They are forestalled when they discover that Whittington has closed his business and disappeared. Still curious, they place an ad looking for information about Jane Finn, to which they receive two replies. The first is from "A. Carter," who turns out to be a pseudonym for a government intelligence official whom Tommy recognizes.

Carter offers to hire them. He explains that the courier carrying a draft treaty was killed when the Lusitania sank, but that it was believed he may have passed the documents on to an American woman, Jane Finn. Finn was listed among the survivors, but had completely disappeared. The treaty would now be political dynamite. A mysterious man known as Brown is the head of a group of communist infiltrators who are also searching for Finn. He warns them that the government will disavow them if they get into trouble, a common ploy in espionage stories.

The second response was from Julius Hersheimmer. He is an

American, claims to be Finn's long lost cousin, and explains that he is in England to find her. He has been working with Inspector Japp, but another man had come earlier that day to take the only known picture of Finn. The inspector gave his name as Brown and is, of course, a fake.

There are some absurd elements in the story, which is implausible as a whole. Whittington mentioned the name Rita, so Tuppence decides that the courier must have been followed by an enemy agent, and that this agent was almost certainly a woman, and that the woman is probably Rita. She also considers standing in Piccadilly Square on the off chance that Whittington would pass by. There is a list of Lusitania survivors, but many lack the first name of the women involved, so they decide to visit each unidentified family and look for a Rita. They find the home of Rita Vandemeyer and immediately spot Whittington and another man leaving the premises.

Tommy follows them and learns that the other man is named Boris. Brown is mentioned, and the name Flossie, but most of their conversation is inaudible. Tommy is able to arrange for Hersheimmer to follow Whittington when the two men part and he follows Boris. By a bluff, he is able to hear part of a secret meeting of subversives before being discovered and knocked unconscious. Elsewhere Tuppence learns of an opening for a maid in the hotel where the Vandemeyers live so she takes the job.

She does not like Rita Vendemeyer at all. Almost immediately Boris – actually Count Stepanov – pays a visit. He and Rita are careless about being overheard and mention Brown. Tommy is still missing and Hergesheimmer has some minor adventures following Whittington to a nursing home. Tuppence is also well disposed toward Sir James Edgerton, who had warned against working for Rita.

Rita figures out that Tuppence is spying on her and attempts to drug her. Tuppence gets the upper hand just before Edgerton and Hersheimmer arrive. Rita had indicated she might be willing to talk for a cash award, but she collapses before saying anything. The other three mount guard during the night but the woman is dead in bed in the morning.

Tommy meanwhile has been questioned extensively to no effect, and manages to escape. Hersheimmer proposes to Tuppence, who demurs and goes off on her own, thus is unaware that Tommy has resurfaced. Edgerton sends Tommy a telegram indicating that he has found Finn. He tells them that Finn was in a motor accident and is currently staying with a doctor friend while she recovers. They visit, but Finn had had recurring problems with amnesia and is of limited help.

With the information she does provide, Tommy recovers a packet of papers, but they are not the ones he is looking for. They are in fact a derisive message from Brown. Tuppence is now missing. She and Finn, are being held prisoner by Brown's minions. One of Brown's men is actually Hersheimmer –the real Hersheimmer was killed and the fake took his place before he arrived in England. Edgerton is actually Brown, who gets thwarted in the end.

The novel is inoffensive but confusing and forgettable. The political events outlined early in the book are uninformed. The possibility that the intelligence service would hire two young people with no experience to track down Finn approaches zero. Carter puts information into letters that no intelligence officer would ever mail to an employee.

Murder on the Links (1923) takes Poirot and Hastings to France in response to a letter from P.T. Renauld, an English businessman who made his money in Chile and who believes that his life is in danger, although he provides no details. After a brief prologue in which Hastings meets a charming but unidentified young woman on a train and the reader is advised that Hastings and Poirot now share lodgings and that the latter has established himself as a private detective, the two head for the continent.

They arrive only to discover that Renauld died sometime in the early morning hours of the previous night. His wife Eloise reports that two masked men who spoke some Spanish tied and gagged her and led her husband away at knifepoint. It appears that this was the same knife with which he was stabbed in the back. His body was found beside a freshly dug grave on a golf course under construction just outside the manor grounds..

One of the French investigators is Lucien Bex, who knows Poirot and invites him to help them find the killer. Interviews with the house staff indicate that Renauld was frequently visited by Madame Daubreuil, although it is not clear that there was any intimacy involved. The housekeeper says that Daubreuil was present the previous evening but had left shortly after ten o'clock. One of the maids confirms the times but indicates that the visitor was another woman whose name she does not know.

There are other potential clues. A wristwatch is smashed but still running, but is two hours off the actual time. A love letter is found from someone named Bella. The dead man's will leaves everything to his wife. He had an adult son, who is believed to be on a ship headed for Chile, and a secretary, Stonor, who is on vacation. They also employed a chauffeur, but Renauld had sent him on a sudden leave, which is strange because he was supposed to have sent a car to meet Poirot. There is also a fragment of a check made out to someone named Duveen. The masked men mentioned some unspecified secret that Renauld supposedly possessed. Poirot finds some footprints in one of the gardens which Bex dismisses as irrelevant.

The famous Inspector Giraud arrives and it is clear that he resents the presence of Poirot. He also disparages Poirot's interest in a piece of old pipe found at the murder scene. A visit to Daubreuil and her adult daughter Marthe elicits no new information. Hastings runs into the mystery girl from the train and unwisely agrees to show her the murder scene. Quite implausibly he shows her the body, at which point she pretends to faint and he runs off to get her some water. He escorts her home and only then remembers to relock the door.

Renauld had recently had a violent quarrel with his son Jack. Giraud finds a match and cigarette which originated in South America. Poirot considers this discovery rather overly convenient and clearly suspects that the connections to Chile are spurious. The footprints match the gardener's boots, but that does not mean he was wearing them.

Gabriel Stonor arrives and tells them that Renauld had been very upset recently. He also believes that Daubreuil was blackmailing him and that Renauld was completely loyal to his wife. Jack Renauld also appears. His ship did not leave due to engine trouble and he returned when he heard of the murder. He admits arguing with his father because he was in love with Marthe Daubreuil and his father objected. He does not know why his father sent him a telegram insisting that he go to Chile. The murder weapon has disappeared, and obviously the mystery girl stole it.

Poirot explains that the wristwatch was altered to confuse the estimated time of the murder. He is convinced that Eloise is lying, at least about that fact. Further, he believes Chile is irrelevant and that the match was planted. The masked men do not exist. Poirot goes off on a mysterious mission to Paris and while he is gone, a stranger is found murdered on the grounds, stabbed to death with the same knife.

No one recognizes the dead man, who was obviously murdered elsewhere. An additional puzzle is that the man has been dead for at least two days, since before the dagger was stolen. Hastings discovers that Jack was in town on the night of the murder, despite his insistence to the contrary. Poirot returns. Poirot is initially shocked by news of the second death, but then recovers and, after examining the body, asserts that the man died of natural causes and that the knife was used well after he was already dead.

Poirot has identified Daubreuil as the former Madama Beroldy, who was involved in another murder case. She had been cheating on her husband with several men, including an American named Hiram Trapp. One day a servant arrived to find her bound and gagged, while her husband had been stabbed to death in the same room. Her story involved two masked men, Russians, who had been trying to get her husband to reveal some secret. She had been arrested and accused of a conspiracy with another lover, Georges Conneau, who had disappeared. She convinced the jury that Conneau acted alone, that she feared for her life, and she was acquitted. Conneau was never found.

Giraud arrests Jack for his father's murder. Marthe remembers seeing Renauld senior talking to a tramp, and she suspects the tramp is the second dead man, now dressed respectably. Poirot also surmises that the letter from Bella was sent to Jack, not his father, that her name is Bella Duveen, and that Renauld tried to buy her off with a check. She was the woman who visited on the night that he died. Further, he points out the lack of background about Renault and concludes that he is the missing Georges Conneau.

Poirot reconstructs the situation. Conneau/Renault was being blackmailed by Daubreuil. He decided to fake his own death and substitute a body – source unknown. The changed will would allow his wife, who knew what was going on, to control the funds and meet him elsewhere under a new identity. The tramp had a fatal attack and his body would have made their project easier. Jack and the chauffeur had to be sent away because they would recognize the body – which Eloise would identify as that of her husband.

Conneau would bury the body in a conspicuous place so that it would be found immediately. Duveen's arrival upset his timetable, but after she left, he tied up Eloise. The piece of pipe was used to smash the tramp's face so that he would be less recognizable. Finally he reveals what he found in Jack's room – a photograph of Duveen. And Hastings recognizes her as his mystery woman.

Duveen and her sisters have a stage act and they are tracked down by Poirot and Hastings. Hastings decides he is in love with her despite believing that she impulsively killed Renauld. Only later does he discover that the sisters look very much alike, and Bella is the one he has not met. She turns up in France and confesses to killing Renauld in a burst of temper.

Jack's mother disowns him, blaming him for creating the circumstances that led to his father's death. It appears that he had happened upon the scene and knew that Bella was the killer, and shielded her because of his feelings of guilt about dropping her in favor of Marthe. But this is a somewhat clumsy red herring. Marthe was the actual killer and Bella only confessed to save Jack. She attempts to murder Eloise as well, there is a struggle, and Marthe is accidentally killed. Both Jack and Bella arrived after the crime and each believed the other was responsible. Hastings ends up with the sister, whose real name is Dulcie.

This was a very fine mystery puzzle, despite the fact that Hastings is even less astute than Dr. Watson and his function is solely to prompt Poirot by asking questions which are designed to further confuse the reader. At one point Poirot claims to have told Hastings everything that he knows – and presumably the reader – but as in his first case, this is untrue. We know that he found something while searching Jack's room and its nature is not revealed.

The Man in the Brown Suit (1924) was a standalone novel. Nadina Grey is a successful dancer who also works for Colonel Race, a criminal mastermind who has announced that he is retiring. She tells a fellow member of the gang, who calls himself Count Sergius Paulovitch, that she has information with which she can blackmail the colonel, despite his careful career and his generosity to his subordinates.

The story switches to first person narrative, with Anne

Beddingfeld as the protagonist. When her father dies, leaving her virtually penniless, she goes to London to seek employment and adventure. She is in the subway station one day when a man – later identified as Carton, a South African – takes sudden alarm at something and inadvertently falls to his death onto the live rail. A man claiming to be a doctor examines him, then hurries off. Carton had a note in his pocket authorizing him to inspect a house owned by Sir Eustace Pedler, which was to be rented.

The mystery deepens when the police find a body in Pedler's house, a young woman who has been strangled. Pedler has been in France for some time and is not a suspect. The caretaker reports that the woman had also obtained permission to view the house – using a false name – and had been given the keys. A man in a brown suit had arrived a few minutes later, had explained that he was with the woman, and returned the keys a short time later, indicating that it was unsuitable. He looked upset at the time.

Beddingfeld approaches Scotland Yard and explains that she worked in a hospital for a time and the doctor at the subway accident was not in fact a doctor at all. She believes he stole the dead man's wallet. She retrieved a piece of paper that the "doctor" dropped, which contained only the name Kilmorden Castle and some numbers. The police are uninterested so she makes use of a ruse to see Lord Nasby, who owns a newspaper. Nasby is impressed, but not enough to hire her as an investigator.

There does not appear to be any such place as Kilmorden Castle, so she decides to pose as a prospective tenant and visit the house where the unidentified woman was strangled. The description of the mystery man believed to have murdered her matches that of the false doctor. She finds a roll of photographic film, but it has never been used. Through chance, she discovers that the Kilmorden Castle is a cruise ship and she impulsively buys a ticket for the date she has constructed from the numbers.

The story jumps to Pedler's diary and describes his reaction to the murder and his decision to return to England with his secretary, Guy Pagett. Coincidentally, the government wants Pedler to undertake a secret courier job to South Africa by way of the Kilmorden Castle. Pagett, however, is taken ill suddenly and a man calling himself Harry Rayburn tells Pedler that the government wants him to go along in place of Pagett. Pedler does not confirm this assertion but agrees.

Beddingfeld's first three days on the ship are unpleasant as she has acute seasickness. She begins to recover and meets Suzanne Blair, a well known society woman, who is accompanied by Colonel Race. She also sees Pedler but not Rayburn. Pagett has recovered and is also aboard. Since there are a number of empty cabins, she tries to move into number 17, only to find that Pedler has tried to reserve it as an office and Reverend Edward Chichester also stakes a claim. There is no obvious reason why it should be so popular.

Beddingfeld appeals to the purser, who installs her. A short time later, something that smells obnoxious is spilled in her cabin in an attempt to drive her out. It is only then that she remembers one of the numbers on the slip of paper was 17. That evening a man she has never seen before bursts into her cabin and asks to be hidden. A steward seems to be searching for him. The man has been stabbed but refuses treatment and rudely leaves once the danger is past.

The following day she decides that she like Blair, is wary of Race, and suspicious that Chichester is not actually a clergyman at all. Pagett is evasive about his recent visit to Florence. Someone has searched her cabin, and it appears to have been Chichester. The various characters exchange stories during the trip. Race mentions the theft of some diamonds, which was blamed on a man named John Eardsley, who later died in the war, and a second man, Lucas. This was the robbery which Grey had alluded to when she spoke about blackmail. Rayburn appears and he is the man who was stabbed.

Beddingfeld decides to confide in Blair. They conclude that cabin 17 was not the one intended, that the note refers to cabin 71. That is Blair's cabin, but she was switched into it when another prospective passenger failed to show up. That person was Nadina Grey. She suspects that Rayburn was the doctor and the man in the brown suit, but she does not believe he killed Grey and admits she has fallen in love with him.

Beddingfeld tricks Pagett into revealing his trip to Florence was a fake, and later tricks Rayburn into admitting that he is Lucas. Pagett tries to throw her overboard but Rayburn/Lucas intervenes. They decide not to accuse Pagett openly. Pedler has a private car on the train to Rhodesia and has invited Race and Blair to accompany him. The document he was supposed to deliver has, however, been stolen, and a cable confirms that no one sent Rayburn – who disappeared as soon as they came ashore in South Africa - to act as his second secretary. Since Pagett is recovering from the beating administered during his attack, Pedler tries to hire Beddingfeld on a temporary basis.

A fake invitation lures Beddingfeld to a house where she is held captive overnight, but she manages to get away in the morning. While she was there, she saw Chichester talking to her captors. She pretends to be parting from the Rhodesia bound party, but doubles back. Unfortunately, she realizes that a strange man has been following her. She later sees him talking to Pagett and narrowly escapes being arrested after a stolen wallet is planted in her bag. She evades the police and is able to board the train to Rhodesia just as it is pulling out.

The plot goes off the rails a bit at this point. Beddingfeld falls for another fake note and wanders into the jungle, where she is pushed over a cliff. She is unconscious – for a month! – but was rescued by Lucas, who lives on a nearby island. This entire episode strains credulity. Lucas explains that he and his friend had been framed for the robbery, that he had been reported missing during the war and had adopted a new identity as Harry Parker. A chance encounter with Carton had convinced him that he needed to clear his name.

Lucas had followed Carton and recognized Grey as one of the conspirators. He followed her to the house and found her dead. Pagett was supposed to have gone to Florence that week, but obviously he had not. Another implausible situation arises. They know that the head of the gang is known as the Colonel, but neither of them ever considers the possibility that Colonel Race is the man in question until quite late. And of course they are wrong when they do. Coincidentally, just as they finish comparing notes, several members of the gang land on the island and start a gun battle in the background.

Pagett finally admits that he was in England, not Florence, but only to visit the wife whose existence he had concealed from Pedler. Pedler is actually the Colonel, and he sneaked back to England and murdered Grey. Rayburn acquires the stolen diamonds and Pedler decides to trade Beddingfeld for them. Race is a government agent who is after Pedler, and Chichester is working for him. And finally we discover that Lucas is not Lucas after all. He is John Eardsley, who is no longer suspected of theft.

There are lots of unanswered questions. Why did Pagett attempt to murder Beddingfeld? Why did the government agents invade the island with blazing guns? How could a man successfully play three different characters without being detected within a small circle of people? Why were the diamonds still around years after the crime? There is also an unreliable narrator – there are excerpts from Pedler's diary which portray him as absentminded and incompetent – which would have served no purpose in his plans.

The Secret of Chimneys (1925) was the first book to feature Superintendent Battle. Anthony Cade is working as a tour guide in South Africa when he runs into an old friend, Jimmy McGrath. McGrath has received a manuscript from a recently deceased Balkan politician, Count Stylptitch, and needs someone to hand deliver it to a publisher in London. He offers the job to Cade, warning him it might be a hoax, and is unable to explain why the package was not sent to them directly, rather than by way of Africa. Stylptitch was also apparently targeted by King Victor, not nobility but a powerful crime boss.

McGrath also wants him to deliver some stolen love letters to Virginia Revel, who was being blackmailed until her tormentor died of a fever. The only thing known about Revel is that she was writing from Chimneys, a famous estate where, coincidentally, foreign dignitaries often gather to negotiate. Chimneys is owned by Lord Caterham. His daughter is Eileen Brent.

An unofficial gathering, disguised as a hunting party, is to facilitate the signing of an oil development agreement with Michael Obolovitch, representing the government of a fictional Balkan nation. Also present will be Herman Isaacstein and William Eversleigh. The government is concerned that Stylptitch's memoirs will contain a scandal that will undercut the deal, so they decide to invite Cade – who is traveling under McGrath's name – to the same conference where they can convince him to suppress them. Virginia Revel is, rather coincidentally, selected to attend as well and to influence him.

Eversleigh is in love with Revel, who is a young widow. Cade arrives a day earlier than expected because of a mix-up about his vessel, and he is approached by a Balkan aristocrat who tries to bribe him to destroy the memoirs. A short time later he overwhelms a gunman who sneaks into his room, and that night he fights off a knife wielding waiter who manages to steal Revel's letters, but not the memoirs.

The waiter attempts to blackmail Revel, unaware that her husband is dead. He is also ignorant of the fact that despite the signature, she did not write the letters. Inexplicably, she gives hm some money and tells him to return the next day for more. She finds the situation amusing. She is also invited to Chimneys, but her attitude exasperates the official who suggested that she be given an invitation.

Cade gives the manuscript to a man representing the publisher. He tries to track down the waiter, who has disappeared. He also declines the invitation to Chimneys. Someone fakes a telegram to lure all of Revel's servants away from her house. The waiter has come to see her while she was out, and she finds him shot to death in her study. She is dithering about calling the police when Cade arrives and she allows him to take over without even knowing his name. This scene is highly implausible.

The name Virginia is engraved on the murder weapon. Cade convinces her not to notify the police. He disposes of the body in a wooded area, then drives to Chimneys – to which Revel has already gone – in time to hear a shot from somewhere in the house. He tries to enter through a window but they are all locked. He decides it was probably a poacher and goes to the local inn.

Obolovitch was shot to death in the library, but no one in the house heard the shot. Superintendent Battle arrives the following day. Cade's footprints are matched to his boots, but he pre-emptively tells the entire story, leaving out only the first murder. He and Revel pretend to be old friends. He meets Hiram Fish, an American houseguest, and the others. Battle shows him the body and he recognizes it as the supposed representative from the publisher to whom he gave the manuscript.

The next in line is Prince Nicholas, who is inclined to grant oil concessions to America, not England. Cade finds a stranger on the grounds who claims to have gotten lost. He is also suspicious of Genevieve Brun, governess for Brent's two children, whose room showed a light at the time of the murder, but her references check out. The stranger is staying at the inn under the name Chelles. The waiter's body has been found.

MASTERS OF DETECTION

Revel and Eversleigh surprise a burglar searching the library, but he manages to escape. The burglar returns, is caught, and identifies himself as Lemoine from the French police, using the name Chelles. Lemoine contends that the current events are linked to the disappearance of a fabulous diamond during another diplomatic event, presumed to have been stolen by King Victor and concealed somewhere in Chimneys.

The missing letters were actually between King Victor and his mistress. He had also assumed the identity of Prince Nicholas – the real one died in Africa. The murder weapon is discovered hidden in Isaacstein's luggage. Cade spots some criminals and spies on them until he is apprehended by Fish. Lemoine tells Revel that Fish is an American detective trying to capture King Victor.

There is a shadowy transition. Revel receives a message from Cade and disappears. Everyone else gathers at Chimneys for various reasons and Cade reappears. Obolovsky's valet, who was very devoted, kills Brun – who was being impersonated by King Victor's mistress, who was believed to have died. Lemoine is King Victor, or actually he is impersonating Lemoine, who is being held captive until freed by Fish.

Cade is the real Prince Nicholas. He has married Revel off stage and they are going back to his home country to rule as king and queen. They will negotiate oil development with Isaacstein, who did not know that someone had put the murder weapon in his luggage. Cade has also figured out where the diamond was hidden. The memoirs are tame and were only being sought because it was possible they held a clue to the hiding place of the diamond. Cade still has the real memoirs. He was not taken in by the fake publishers' agent and gave him a package of blank paper.

The Murder of Roger Ackroyd (1926) firmly established Poirot as Christie's primary detective. It is narrated by Dr. James Sheppard, who lives with his sister Caroline. He had recently been attending to the aftermath of the death of Mrs. Ferrars, a possible suicide who was rumored to have poisoned her husband. Roger Ackroyd is a wealthy businessman who lives in the same village with his stepson, Ralph Paton, who is in his twenties. Paton has been away for several months, possibly the result of a quarrel with his stepfather. Ackroyd's wife died when Ralph was a child.

Ackroyd was believed to be courting the unfortunate Mrs.

Ferrars. Also present in his household is his widowed sister-in-law and her daughter Flora. Ackroyd's housekeeper, Miss Russell, does not get along with the widow. His secretary is Geoffrey Raymond and his butler is Parker. Paton returns to the village but stays at the inn rather at the house, and it is considered possible that he is courting Flora against his stepfather's wishes, although Ackroyd professes to be pleased.

Sheppard finally meets his new next door neighbor, Poirot, who is keeping a low profile and is supposedly retired from the detective business, though he misses it. Hastings has gone to South America. Sheppard then accepts a dinner invitation from Ackroyd, and meets Hector Blunt, an old friend of Ackroyd who visits from time to time and has a reputation as a big game hunter.

Ackroyd tells Sheppard that Ferrars confessed to him that she had murdered her husband, and adds that she has been blackmailed by someone ever since. He had no suspicion that she would commit suicide. Even as they are speaking, a letter arrives which the dead woman mailed just before taking the overdose that killed her. The letter probably contained the blackmailer's name, but he decides to read it later. Sheppard runs into a stranger who asks directions to the house but thinks nothing of it at the time.

Predictably, Ackroyd is murdered during the night and the letter is missing. Sheppard receives a telephone message, purportedly from Parker, who later denies making the call. The murder is only discovered when Sheppard raises a fuss. Ackroyd has been stabbed in the back in his study. The door is locked but a window is open. Raymond reports hearing Ackroyd talking to someone after Sheppard left. Flora spoke to him briefly after the unknown party was gone.

Parker knows that blackmail was involved and the police suspect that he is the killer. Then Paton disappears and he becomes the chief suspect, particularly since tracks outside the study window appear to have been made by his shoes. Flora asks Sheppard to help her convince Poirot to investigate. He keeps his own council but shows Sheppard a scrap of cloth that he found in an outbuilding. Poirot also notes that the ground under the window was wet even though the weather had been dry, possibly to ensure that the footprints would be detected. They are not an exact match to the shoes found in Paton's room.

Poirot recovers a wedding ring from a pond on the property. It has the initial "R" inscribed. Ackroyd's will leaves a large amount to Flora but the bulk of the estate goes to Paton. Ackroyd also kept cash in his room, and a substantial sum is missing. One of the maids, Ursula Bourne, gives notice. She has only been employed there for a year. She is the only member of the household who has no alibi for the time of the murder. Sheppard is sent to talk to her previous employer. The woman he talks to is clearly concealing something and provides no information.

Poirot tells Sheppard that the unidentified stranger had an American accent. Flora and her mother had been living in Canada until recently. He suggests that Paton asked his stepfather for money after Sheppard left, may or may not have received it, and departed through the window. There is evidence that two people met in the outbuilding, one of them the stranger, and the stranger could have climbed in through the open window and killed Ackroyd.

The stranger is identified as Charles Kent, who is uncooperative but who can prove that he left the area well before the murder took place. Flora admits that she lied and never saw her uncle, and she was the one who stole the money. Poirot recognizes that Blunt is in love with Flora, and that Flora does not love Paton. The engagement was arranged to please Ackroyd.

Russell admits that she met Kent in the outbuilding. He is her son and is addicted to drugs. Bourne and Paton have been secretly married for several months. Her former "employer" was actually her sister. The solution is a bit of a cheat. Ackroyd had looked into purchasing a dictating machine but had told Raymond that he had decided against purchasing one. Actually, he had acquired a machine and there was no one with him when he was heard talking in the study. In fact, he was already dead and the machine was playing back his voice.

Sheppard is also an unreliable narrator. He has known all along where Paton was hiding. Sheppard was the blackmailer and the murderer. He arranged for an innocent telephone call which he represented as having announced Ackroyd's murder. The book ends with Sheppard killing himself.

The Big Four (1927) begins with Hastings' return from South America. Poirot's retirement has been forgotten and he still has his office, although he is the process of shutting it down. He was about to sail for South America to do a lucrative investigation for Abe Ryland, and hoped to surprise Hastings there. His intention is never to return to Europe.

Poirot has heard rumors of the Big Four, some kind of criminal enterprise. Before he can leave, a man stumbles into the office, incoherent and in shock, and when that phrase is uttered, he replies "Li Chang Yen." He then gives a short speech in which he describes Li as the brains of the Big Four, and asserts that the other three consist of a rich American, a mysterious woman, and a man he calls the "destroyer". Although he still intends to sail, at the last minute Poirot abort his trip. He has realized it is all a ploy to get him out of the way.

The mystery man is murdered in their absence. Another man from an asylum shows up and insists that the dead man was insane and had been locked up for two years, but Inspector Japp recognizes him as a secret service operative named Mayerling, who had disappeared. A phone call proves that there has been no escape from any asylum.

Poirot consults with John Ingles, an expert on China, who tells him Li is possibly the most dangerous man in the world. The three of them decide to follow up a lead but their contact is murdered hours before they reach him. The murderer's identity appears to be obvious but Poirot proves him to be innocent.

The plot goes off the tracks a bit at this point. Christie was never good at international intrigue and adventure. A brilliant scientist disappears. Several American warships are sunk by a mysterious force – and an expert on magnetism has disappeared. Poirot and Hastings rescue him after Poirot survives an attempted murder. They are threatened by a man who escapes, and abducted by a woman from whom they escape.

Another wealthy man is murdered and Poirot investigates, with particular interest in the man's Chinese servant. After solving that crime and a puzzle involving a chess problem, Poirot eventually makes his way to the secret headquarters of the Big Four. There he pretends to be his own twin brother, promises to restore a dead child to life, and escapes an explosion that kills three of the Big Four. Li commits suicide in humiliation. Arguably Christie's worst novel.

The Mystery of the Blue Train (1928) begins with a mysterious transaction at night in which an American man purchases something valuable from two people using false names. An attempt to mug him is unsuccessful and is observed with amusement by a masked man who gives his name as Monsieur le Marquis when he subsequently visits an antiques dealer, Demetrius Papopolous. They clearly are interested in stealing from the American.

The American is Rufus Van Aldin, who is very rich. He returns to London and meets with his secretary, Richard Knighton. Van Aldin's daughter Ruth is married to Derek Kettering, but it is not a happy marriage. The items he purchased in France – a collection of fabulous rubies – are meant to be a gift to her. He wants her to divorce her husband, who has been openly seeing a dancer named Mirelle, but she is hesitant – presumably because she does not want it known that she has also been unfaithful. Her father soon learns that her lover is Armand de la Roche, whom he knows is a swindler and fortune seeker.

Katherine Grey was a companion to an elderly woman for ten years and has now inherited a sizable fortune, to the consternation of the woman's family. Rosalie Tamplin is a rich society icon working on her fourth marriage. Her daughter Lenox does not care for her mother's life style. Rosalie is Grey's cousin and invites her to come visit them in France. Grey knows that this is meant as a way to divest her of some of her money but accepts anyway. She is also a bit disturbed because it appears that she is being followed, although it is actually a coincidence. The man is Derek Kettering.

Van Aldin tries to buy Derek off, but Derek perversely turns down an amount that would have made him well off. Grey, Mirelle, and both Ketterings – traveling separately – are all on the same train across France. Ruth impulsively confides in Grey, who is quite embarrassed. Grey is then seated at a meal across from Hercule Poirot, and they get along well. Somewhat confusedly, Poirot is described this time as having been retired for some years.

During the night that follows, Ruth is murdered and her maid, Ada Mason, disappears. The conductor explains this as Ruth had told him that the maid would be disembarking at an earlier stop. Grey notices that a fancy jewel case is missing – which presumably held the rubies. Grey tells the police all she knows, but forgets that she saw Derek at the door to his wife's compartment late that night.

Ruth meets the Tamplins and settles in. Coincidentally they have invited Derek to visit, and since Grey does not know the dead woman's name, nor that of her husband, she is not prepared to run into him for the fourth time. He receives word of his wife's death – and is evidently completely surprised. Mason tells the police that Ruth met an unidentified man at one of the stations and told her to leave the train and wait in a hotel for further instructions. A note is found in Ruth's possessions written by de la Roche and he clearly knows that she was carrying the rubies with her.

Derek will inherit a considerable amount of money from his wife so he has a motive. De la Roche probably planned to steal the rubies, but Poirot doubts that he would have committed murder. He has an alibi, but a weak one. Derek insists that he had not spoken to his wife in weeks, but he lets slip that he knew about the rubies. He did not know that Mirelle was on the train and is unhappy to see her, particularly when she makes it clear she believes he killed Ruth. Derek tells her their affair is over and she angrily goes to see de la Roche in an attempt to convince him to help get Derek arrested.

De la Roche mails the rubies to a shop that holds parcels, but the police intercept them. They are fakes. Poirot notes that Papopolous has come from Paris – he is believed to deal in stolen property. He receives a veiled hint that Monsieur le Marquis has the real jewels. Mirelle tells the police a not entirely accurate story suggesting that Derek planned to murder his wife, but she also betrays the fact that she knew Ruth was dead well before her body was found.

Poirot destroys de la Roche's alibi and confronts Mirelle, who refuses to admit that she found Ruth dead and failed to tell anyone. Derek is arrested and Grey returns to England. Poirot arranges a trap and unmasks Knighton as the Marquis. Ada Mason is also a false name for an unscrupulous male impersonator. They worked together to commit both the murder and the theft and much of the evidence they provided was fictitious. Derek is freed and heads off to marry Grey.

The Seven Dials Mystery (1929) brought back Superintendent Battle from *The Secret of Chimneys*. Jimmy Thesiger is a guest at the country house of Sir Oswald and Lady Coote. The house is in fact Chimneys from the earlier book, which the Cootes have rented. Sir Oswald's secretary is Rupert Bateman. Also visiting are Thesiger's friends Bill Eversleigh – also from the previous book - and Ronny Devereux, plus three young women, Helen, Nancy, and Socks.

The last guest, Gerald Wade, is a notoriously late riser so the others decide to purchase a number of alarm clocks as a practical joke. That evening, multiple clocks are introduced to his room after he has fallen asleep. But he does not respond when they go off in the morning and he is found dead in his bed, apparently having taken an overdose of sleeping medication. The clocks have been moved and one of them is missing. It is later found on the ground outside the window.

Thesiger and Devereux inform the latter's sister Loraine of the situation. Thesiger has a crush on her. The inquest declares it an accidental death. The Cootes' rental ends and Lord Caterham and his daughter return to the house. The daughter, known as Bundle Brent, finds a letter that Wade had been writing to his sister on the day before he died, in which he mentions Seven Dials and hints at danger. Seven Dials is a vaguely disreputable part of London.

Brent goes for a drive and a man steps in front of her car. Although she thinks that she avoided hitting him, he collapses in the road. When she reaches him, he dies – but only after asking her to mention the Seven Dials to Thesiger. Although she feels responsible, the man died of a bullet wound and the car never struck him. The dead man is Ronald Devereux. She goes to Thesiger's home where she meets Loraine Wade, who is now convinced that her brother was murdered.

The three of them suspect that Wade somehow found out about the existence of a secret society connected to the Seven Dials area. The seven clocks left in Wade's room seem to support this. They decide to investigate. Brent has also learned that a politician named George Lomax received some sort of threatening letter postmarked in the Seven Dials. Thesiger believes that Wade was actually a secret service agent. Thesiger and Brent plan to acquire access to a party that Lomax is going to host, but Brent also secretly informs Battle of some of her suspicions. He suggests that she discuss the matter with Eversleigh.

Eversleigh plays dumb but admits the existence of the Seven Dials Club. Brent bullies him into taking her there without explaining why she is interested. One of the servants from Chimneys – Alfred - is working there, having been offered a better job. He was replaced by a footman named John Bauer shortly before Wade died. Brent bullies Alfred into showing her around the club, including the secret room where she presumes the secret society meets. She decides to conceal herself in the room and eavesdrop on their next gathering.

Six men show up for the meeting, all wearing masks resembling the faces of clocks. The seventh member is the leader and apparently never attends. Bauer is implicated in Wade's death. She reports everything to Thesiger and they both attend the party – one might wonder why the conspirators sent a warning but this is ultimately explained – and Brent gets chased and Thesiger is shot in the arm. Loraine Wade, who refuses to be completely sidelined, is with Battle when the shots are fired and they both hurry to the scene.

Thesiger was wounded by a presumed burglar, who manages to steal the secret formula for a new kind of steel. Since the guard was drugged, it was obviously an inside job. The formula is recovered but there is no luck capturing the intruder or unmasking his confederate. Brent is knocked unconscious once when she sticks her nose into the wrong place but the injury is not serious.

At the conclusion, Brent discovers that the conspirators are led by Battle himself, that they are actually an anti-espionage organization. The murderer is Thesiger. The nightclub is a front and Bauer is a government agent. Brent agrees to marry Eversleigh.

Murder at the Vicarage (1930) introduced Jane Marple. It is narrated by the vicar, Leonard Clement, whose household consists of his wife Griselda, nephew Dennis, and an incompetent maid/cook named Mary. Hawes is his curate, but has only held that position for a short time. Colonel Protheroe is churchwarden, an unpleasantly opinionated man who has many enemies.

Colonel Lucius Protheroe's second wife is Anne. His first, who is mother to Lettice, who resents her father's stinginess, ran off before he moved to the area. Protheroe is also feuding with Dr. Stone, an archaeologist who has permission to excavate on Protheroe's property, and with Hawes, whom he considers too wedded to ritual. He has forbidden Lawrence Redding, a painter, to enter his house because Lettice wishes to be painted in her bathing suit and he disapproves. Stone's secretary is Gladys Cram. Jane Marple is, of course, a member of the congregation.

Protheroe is pressing for an audit of church funds after an incident in which a portion of the day's offering may have disappeared. There are a couple of low key mysteries in the community. A reclusive Estelle Lestrange has just moved into the village, and there was a brief visit from a woman who claimed to be from a government agency, but who disappeared and was later found to have lied. Lestrange appears to know Dr. Haydock, who is the village physician.

Quite by chance, the vicar discovers that Redding is having an affair with Anne Protheroe. Her husband accuses a man named Archer of poaching on his property. Archer has been dating Mary. Redding decides to leave the area rather than cause a scandal. Both Hawes and Dennis seem to be oddly disturbed, though neither offers an explanation.

The vicar is lured away by a false message. When he returns, he encounters a distraught Redding, who runs off. He finds Protheroe in his study, shot through the head. The police arrive and an overturned clock agrees with the doctor's assessment of the time of death, but the clock was wrong by a considerable amount. It had to have been stopped earlier than the police believe, while Protheroe was still alive.

That evening, Redding turns himself in to the police and insists that he killed Protheroe. Marple tells the vicar that this proves he is innocent – presumably he believes that Anne was the murderer and is trying to protect her. Haydock insists that this is impossible because Protheroe had to have been dead before Redding arrived at the house. Anne confesses to the murder a short time later, but her story is also clearly fabricated, although she did actually visit the vicarage grounds shortly before the murder. Maple saw her there, as she also saw Redding, Cram, and Stone, at about the time of the murder.

Protheroe had been writing a message to the vicar when he was shot. For some reason, he had noted the time in the note. That leads to speculation that the time was added in by the killer, who also altered the clock. The murder weapon was Redding's pistol, but he never locked his doors, it was in plain sight, and anyone could have taken it. Griselda believes that the murder was designed to implicate Anne, which suggests either Lettice or her real mother. It is known that Lestrange made a brief visit to Protheroe on the day of his death.

The gunshot was heard by three people, all of whom believed it to be someone shooting in the nearby woods. Hawes tries to implicate Archer. Lestrange refuses to divulge the purpose of her visit with Protheroe.. One of the maids admits having overheard part of the conversation between Protheroe and Lestrange, which suggests that she was his first wife.

Lettice makes an excuse to visit the study. Stone goes to London and while he is away, the vicar learns that he is an imposter, not the real Dr. Stone. Cram is spotted carrying a suitcase into the woods and returning without it. Lettice makes an attempt to frame Anne but it fails miserably. The vicar finds the suitcase, which contains valuable items stolen from Protheroe – with fakes left in their place. Cram naturally denies any knowledge of the suitcase.

Haydock lets slip that he has known Lestrange and Protheroe for many years, and that Lestrange is terminally ill and only has weeks to live. The note Protheroe was supposedly writing turns out to be a forgery. The vicar finds Hawes drugged in his room, along with what appears to be the real note that Protheroe had prepared, which identifies Hawes as the embezzler at the church.

The police are satisfied that Hawes is the murderer, but Marple shows up and insists that the real killer is Anne, aided by Redding. The gunshot that people heard was a ruse – a silencer had been used during the actual murder. They trap Redding into bolting and both he and Anne are arrested. Lestrange is finally revealed to be Lettice's mother.

Marple is a formidable character, but is not always admirable. She loves to gossip, has an air of superiority, and is occasionally unkind. It may well be that she was not supposed to be a recurring character when she made her debut. There is very little background concerning her other than that she has a nephew, Raymond West, who is a popular writer.

Murder at Hazelmoor (1931, aka *The Sittaford Mystery*) begins with a mild puzzle. Mrs. Willett and her adult daughter Violet rent a house on the moor for the winter, offering a fee which its owner cannot turn down. There are six bungalows surrounding the property and a tiny village is nearby. Their neighbors include Major Burnaby and men named Ronald Garfield, Duke, and Rycroft.

One snowy afternoon, they all gather at the Willetts' and in due course play at having a séance. The owner of the house, Captain Trevelyan, is living in a nearby town. During the séance, the party receives a message to the effect that Trevelyan is dead, murdered. Everyone denies having influenced the choice of letters. Burrnaby is a close friend and he decides to walk to the town and check on his friend. There are no telephones in the village of Sittaford and the roads are impassable for cars.

Burnaby recruits the assistance of a policeman and they find Trevelyan bludgeoned to death in his study. The doctor's examination suggests that the murder occurred during the séance, which was six miles away. There is a broken window and the room appears to have been searched. But when Inspector Narracott arrives, he dismisses this as fake evidence. The window was not locked in the first place, and a burglar would have gone after valuables, not papers.

Trevelyan's only servant was Robert Evans, who lived next door with his wife. Evans had gone home about two hours before the murder and the snow had prevented him from going anywhere else. There is evidence that the killer came in through the window, but oddly it appears that the dead man had helped him to do so.

The local inn had one guest who was out at the time of the murder. James Pearson stayed one night and had already returned to London by train. Trevelyan's will left his estate essentially to his living sister Jennifer Gardner – from whom he was mildly estranged, and three children by a second sister who had died ten years earlier. The dead sister's married name was Pearson, so James Pearson was probably his nephew.

Narracott interviews Gardner, whose husband is an invalid. The dead sister's children are James, Brian, and Sylvia. James works in the insurance business. Sylvia is married to Martin Dering. Brian is in Australia. Sylvia's interview is uneventful, but James is in a panic. He admits having visited his uncle briefly around the time of the murder and rather clumsily lies about the time he left in a futile attempt to avert suspicion.

James' fiancé, Emily Trefusis, decides to investigate the murder herself and enlists the aid of a reporter, Charles Enderby. Trefusis thinks that there is something odd about the Willetts having rented the house in the middle of the winter and she has also heard about the mysterious séance. James has now been arrested. Narracott detects some evasion when he talks to Mrs. Willett and her daughter faints when he mentions James Pearson.

Trefusis talks to Burnaby and Rycroft, both of whom offer to help in any way they can but neither of whom has anything concrete to offer. Enderby suggests that someone at the séance knew that

Trevelyan was going to be murdered, and that is why his death was so mysteriously announced. She also learns that the last cottage is owned by Captain Wyatt, an invalid who discourages visitors. While she is conducting these interviews, a convict escapes from a nearby prison.

Garfield, who is broke, is visiting his aunt, Caroline Percehouse, who is elderly, wealthy, and in uncertain health. He clearly hopes to benefit from her will. Percehouse tells Trefusis that the Willetts claim to be from South Africa, but their slang and some other evidence suggests that they are actually from Australia. After briefly meeting Wyatt, she visits the Willetts but only sees Violet, who strikes her as suppressing considerable uneasiness. She also overhears the mother expressing dismay about something.

Through a stroke of luck, Enderby discovers that Dering's alibi – a formal dinner – is false. He did not attend. Gardner's invalid husband Robert is also suspect. His inability to walk is psychological rather than a physical disability, and he sent his nurse away on the afternoon of the murder. Enderby stakes out the Willett house and watches Violet rendezvous with a stranger, who turns out to be Brian Pearson.

Brian openly moves in with the Willetts and admit that he has been back in England for months. Narracott is no longer convinced that James is the killer. He decides to interview Dering and notices that he has a book with the name "Martha Rycroft" inscribed inside the cover. He also believes that Brian would have returned to Australia and claimed his legacy from there if Enderby had not spotted him. The convict has been recaptured.

Gardner and Garfield are spotted together in a tea room. Trefusis discovers that Robert Gardner had a secret female visitor. Dering's alibi is further disproven and he refuses to say where he really was at the time of the murder. The Willetts came from Australia under the name Johnson. It is implied that Duke has a criminal record but that the police believe that he has reformed. Dering had been married to Martha Rycroft. A pair of boots is missing from the murdered man's house.

In a mildly clumsy scene, Trefusis finds the missing boots wrapped in paper and stuck up inside the chimney. She decides that she knows who the killer is and goes to see Narracott. Rycroft reveals that he is Sylvia Dering's uncle. The Willetts decide to leave but host a final party.

Burnaby is the killer. Trevelyan was murdered well after the séance. Burnaby used skis to reach his house much more quickly than anyone thought possible. The motive is well masked. Trevelyan had submitted a contest entry using Burnaby's address and it had won a substantial amount of money. Burnaby was nearly broke and decided to kill his friend so that he could keep the prize.

Brian had been secretly trying to help the convict escape – because he was Violet's father. Gardner was Garfield's godmother. Trefusis decides to marry James despite her fondness for Enderby. Duke turns out to be a retired police official. The identity of Robert Gardner's girlfriend is not revealed. Dering probably was covering up an illicit affair but this not confirmed either.

Peril at End House (1932) is a Poirot novel. He is still retired and his friend Hastings has returned, although his wife Bella is apparently still managing their ranch in Argentina. They are vacationing when Poirot contrives a brief introduction to Magdala "Nick" Buckley, who lives in the crumbling mansion known as End House. She is accompanied by Commander George Challenger, of whom Poirot is immediately suspicious. She mentions in passing that she escaped three potentially serious accidents recently. This is significant because Poirot has observed that someone has just fired a gun at her, although from such a distance that no one but he noticed.

Buckley refuses to believe that she is in danger. Her confidence is shaken a bit when she discovers that her late father's revolver is missing. The estate is negligible because End House is heavily mortgaged. Her only living relative is a cousin, Charles Vyse, who is a lawyer. There is a lodge on the property which has been rented by the Crofts, who are Australian. The only servants are a married couple with a young son.

Her closest friends are Freddie Rice, who is estranged from her husband, and Jim Lazarus, an art dealer who has tried to purchase some of the Buckley family portraits. Buckley's will leaves the house to Vyse and the rest of her small estate to Rice. Rice supposedly just arrived the previous day, but she lies about where she has been.

Poirot meets the Crofts, who seem to be a nice older couple, but he has the impression that they are projecting an image. They tell him that both Vyse and Challenger are courting Buckley, but that neither is having much success. They also meet Vyse and learn that he was not in his office at the time of the shooting. Buckley's cousin Maggie is invited to stay with her as a safeguard, but she is rather incredulous about the possibility of murder. Buckley mentions that she met a man named Seton, who has disappeared during a round the world solo flight.

There is a large evening party at the house to watch fireworks. It turns cool and Buckley loans Maggie her shawl. This apparently confuses the killer, who shoots and kills Maggie. In the aftermath, Rice admits that she and Lazarus were having an affair and that this is why she misled people about her whereabouts. An expert assures Poirot that the painting Lazarus tried to buy is not worth half what he offered. Buckley finally admits that she has been withholding a secret – she was engaged to Seton, who has now been declared dead.

Poirot speculates that Seton's will leaves a substantial fortune to Buckley. Although the engagement was secret, Rice suspected the truth and Buckley had a habit of leaving papers in plain view, perhaps including love letters. If she had been shot instead of Maggie, the bulk of that inheritance would have gone to Rice. Poirot finds the love letters, which include mention of Seton's will, and he is sure that Ellen, the housekeeper, has read them. Ellen also may have lied about her movements when Maggie was shot, and she alludes to a secret panel that Buckley has never heard of.

Buckley's will is nowhere to be found. She insists that she mailed it to Vyse, who claims never to have received it. If she dies intestate, Vyse and not Rice would inherit. Poirot secures Croft's fingerprints, but the police have no record of him being involved in a crime. Lazarus' business is believed to be completely honest, but it is in financial difficulties.

Buckley is poisoned by chocolates supposedly sent by Poirot, but she survives. Poirot decides to pretend that Buckley has died this time. The following day Vyse receives a will in the mail, purportedly the one Buckley signed, in which she leaves her entire fortune to Mrs. Croft, supposedly for services rendered to her father. Buckley then makes a ghostly appearance that shocks everyone. Japp identifies Mrs. Croft as a well known forger.

Complicating matters, Rice's estranged husband shows up and tries to shoot her, but only manages to graze an arm. He promptly dies. The initial assumption is that he killed Maggie, but Japp had been watching the house and he saw Buckley remove the murder weapon from a secret compartment. She was the one who murdered Maggie – who was Seton's real fiancé and her will was in favor of Buckley. She commits suicide rather than be arrested.

Thirteen at Dinner (1933, aka *Lord Edgware Dies*) is a Poirot novel. He appears to be back in the private investigation business. Jane Wilkinson, an actress, is the estranged wife of Lord Edgware. Her name has been recently associated with that of Bryan Martin, another actor. They are dining with a stage performer, Carlotta Adams, when they encounter Poirot and Hastings. Adams does impersonations, including an effective copy of Wilkinson.

Wilkinson rather oddly asks Poirot for advice about getting rid of her husband. There are no grounds for divorce, which he opposes strenuously. She wishes to be free to marry the Duke of Merton, a man reputedly dominated utterly by his mother. Poirot agrees to talk to Edgware, primarily out of curiosity.

Martin comes to see Poirot and tells him that he is being followed. The discussion also includes his assessment of Wilkinson, whom he describes as cold-bloodedly self obsessed and capable of murder. The interview with Edgware is a surprise. He insists that he wrote to his wife months previously agreeing to a divorce. When Poirot reports this to Wilkinson, she seems quite surprised and denies having received any such letter.

Edgware is stabbed to death after a woman claiming to be his wife is closeted with him at his home. Inspector Japp arrests Wilkinson. Martin unwisely impugns her character in front of Japp, suggesting that she would not balk at murdering someone if it was to her advantage. She has an alibi, however. She was attending a party after she had told several people that should would not be there. Martin in particular is upset to hear this, and he is transparently trying to make her look more guilty.

Edgware's title passes to Ronald Marsh, his estranged nephew. Edgware's daughter is Geraldine, his secretary Carroll, and his butler Alton. Wilkinson received an anonymous call during the dinner party, but if it was from the murderer, her presence there would have clearly made the attempt to frame her unworkable. This suggests that there was someone else involved.

Adams is dead – an overdose of sleeping pills. A friend, Jenny Driver, suspects that she was taking drugs at night. Her maid's description of her clothes and movement the previous evening confirms that she impersonated Wilkinson. They talk to Geraldine, who hated her father, and then meet Ronald Marsh, who turns out to be the man who was with Adams when they first met. He seems genuinely shocked, however, when told that she is dead. The dinner party was shy one guest, a man as yet unidentified.

Alton disappears. Adams wrote to her sister that Ronald was paying her a princely sum to impersonate Wilkinson for a short period. Geraldine and Ronald had similar alibis – the opera – but it is discovered that they slipped away together and went to his uncle's house briefly, then returned. He has a plausible alternate explanation but is arrested.

Poirot is puzzled until he examines the letter from Adams and discovers that a portion of it is missing, and that means that Marsh may not be the person who arranged the impersonation. Donald Ross, who attended the dinner party, calls Poirot because he has remembered something that may be important, but he is stabbed to death before he can speak.

The rather favored murderer is now Martin, who hated Wilkinson for dropping him in favor of Edgware. He may have hoped to frame her for the murder. Poirot advances this theory – the story about being followed was a lie – only to declare this false as well. Wilkinson is the real killer. Adams impersonated her at the dinner, not at the murder scene. Ross had realized that the false Wilkinson had talked about erudite subjects at the dinner which Wilkinson could not possibly have done.

Murder on the Orient Express (1934, aka *Murder on the Calais Coach*) is one of Christie's two best known novels. Poirot has just wound up an investigation in Syria and has decided to play the tourist in Constantinople briefly before returning home. To this end he boards Taurus, a small train that can only accommodate about a dozen passengers. It is winter and there is some concern about the possibility of a heavy snowfall.

Poirot notices that the other two passengers, Mary Debenham – a governess – and Colonel Arbuthnot know each other even though they pretend to have just met, and that both of them are tense. A possible delay might cause them to miss their connection to the Orient Express, which greatly alarms Debenham, but fortunately the train is able to make up the lost time.

During the layover, Poirot sees a man named Ratchett, who strikes him as almost supernaturally repellent. Ratchett is accompanied by his secretary, Hector MacQueen. Eventually the entire cast of characters gathers on the Orient Express. Most of them seem to be strangers to one another, but Poirot notices some inconsistencies.

Ratchett approaches Poirot, having heard his name, and indicates that he wishes to hire him as a kind of bodyguard. He indicates that he has enemies, some of whom may be aboard the train. Poirot is so repelled by the man that he refuses quite rudely. Poirot briefly meets Mrs. Hubbard, a lively matron, and Gretta Ohlsson, a nurse and missionary who talks very little. The conductor points out Princess Dragomiroff, a wealthy aristocrat.

That evening they all retire to their compartments. Poirot is wakened by a hoarse cry from Ratchett and opens his door. The conductor knocks on Ratchett's door and is told that he is all right and does not need any help. The conductor leaves. There are more disturbances during the night, thuds, footsteps, and muffled conversations. Poirot sees Hubbard talking to the conductor, spots an unidentified woman in a kimono, and hears more noises from Ratchett's room.

In the morning, the train is at a standstill because of a wall of snow across the tracks. The railway official aboard the train takes Poirot aside and tells him that Ratchett was stabbed to death during the night. The conductor confirms that he talked to the dead man through his door but did not see him. His body was found by MacQueen early in the morning. The other passengers have not been told yet as they are already somewhat disturbed by being snowbound and possibly missing their connections. Poirot agrees to investigate.

MacQueen admits that he did not like Ratchett, but denies that there was any bad feeling between them. He last saw Ratchett at ten o'clock the previous evening when he arranged to have some letters written. Ratchett had received threatening letters and the one shown to Poirot is odd in that it was written by people with varying handwriting. There are a dozen stab wounds in the body, not all of which would have been fatal, and it appears that some but not all were inflicted by a left handed person. Poirot also believes that a glass of water beside the bed once contained some kind of drug.

There are some physical clues that were obviously fakes planted to mislead any investigator. The only one Poirot believes to be real is a fleck of ash and a used matchstick. The ash contains the name Daisy Armstrong, whom he knows was a young girl who was kidnapped and killed in America. The death led to suicides and the ruination of multiple lives, among servants of the Armstrongs and others. From this he concludes that Ratchett is actually Cassetti, the leader of the gang of criminals who were responsible. He escaped justice through a technicality, although it is generally known that he was the ringleader.

Poirot begins to interview the passengers and make note of their movements and what they saw, but shortly after he begins, Hubbard announces that there was an unidentified man in her compartment during the night. She produces a button she claims was dropped by the intruder. Poirot has asked several women if they own a silk kimono, but no one yet has admitted to having one. With few exceptions, they insist they have never previously met the other passengers. Arbuthnot is very protective of Debenham and Count Andrenyi even attempts to forestall an interview with his wife.

Poirot is quite sure that at least some of the passengers are lying to him. Each interview hints at another connection and he finally realizes the truth. All of the passengers were involved. They each had a connection to the Armstrong family – a chauffeur, a police officer, servants at the house, friends and relations. They organized things so that each of them would deliver a potentially fatal wound. Ratchett would die and they would all, technically, be guilty of his murder. Although it appalls Poirot to circumvent the law, he invents a story about a mysterious assailant, which will satisfy the police, but only after making them all aware of the fact that he knows the truth.

The Boomerang Clue (1934, aka *Why Didn't They Ask Evans?*) does not involve any of Christie's recurring detectives. Bobby Jones is the fourth son of a rather stodgy clergyman. He is playing golf with Dr. Thomas when they discover a dying man with a broken back, apparently having fallen from a cliff to a ledge below. Thomas goes for help while Jones remains with the man, who speaks only one sentence before dying. "Why didn't they ask Evans?"

A stranger to the area who identifies himself as Bassington-ffrench offers to guard the corpse so that Jones can tell his father what has happened. Jones had also noticed that the dead man carried a photograph of a woman later identified as his sister, Amelia Cayman. The dead man is Alex Pritchard. After the inquest, the Caymans – Leo and Amelia - ask Jones if there were any last words, and he says no, having forgotten the odd question. He recalls the phrase later and sends them a note.

Jones has two close friends. Frances Derwent is a childhood playmate but from a wealthier family. Badger Beadon is another friend who has failed in business several times and is trying again. He has opened a garage and hired Jones as his mechanic. Jones receives a mysterious job offer that would require him to move to South America, but he turns it down,

Someone puts drugs into Jones' beer, but he recovers. He is now convinced that Pritchard was pushed over the cliff. He also discovers that the picture of the woman found on his body was not the one he saw, so Bassington-ffrench must have switched them so that Pritchard would be falsely identified by the Caymans, who are clearly in league with Bassington-ffrench, whom Jones and Derwent decide to investigate. He had given his real name, but not his real purpose for being there.

Derwent fakes an automobile crash and injury so that she will be invited to convalesce at the home of Herny and Sylvia Bassington-ffrench. Henry's brother Richard is the man they suspect, although Derwent is favorably impressed when they first meet. Henry has become addicted to drugs. Their young son Tommy has recently survived two near fatal accidents.

Their friends are Jasper and Moira Nicholson. Jasper runs a rest home that specializes in drug recoveries. From her conversations with Sylvia Derwent he believes that the dead man is actually Alan Carstairs, who became oddly interested when he chanced to see a picture of the Nicholsons. At the same time, Jones runs into Moira, who tells him that she fears that her husband is planning to kill her. Moira is the woman whose picture Carstairs was carrying when he died. There are rumors of improprieties at the nursing home.

Henry's drug use becomes obvious enough that his wife wants him to enter the nursing home. Derwent and Jones now believe that Jasper in the killer and that he was also involved in the suicide of a rich man who died shortly after changing his will. Henry is found dead and it appears that he left a suicide note, but the note is forged and he was actually murdered. Jasper had been in the house at the time.

The surprise ending is that Jasper is completely innocent. Moira and Richard are the criminals. They killed the businessman, as well as Henry and Carstairs. Richard also tried to kill the boy, hoping to inherit Henry's money. Moira arranged the businessman's death so that a forged will would leave his fortune to the nursing home, i.e., her husband. Moira is captured when the story falls apart but Richard escapes to South America. Evans was a maid who had information that would reveal the plot, although she did not realize it.

Murder in Three Acts (1935, aka *Three Act Tragedy*) features Poirot. Sir Charles Cartwright is a famous but recently retired actor who owns a house set atop a cliff that overlooks the sea. His houseguest is the popular Mr. Satterthwaite, along with Sir Bartholomew Strange, a neurologist. Hermione Lytton Gore is helping Cartwright to learn how to manage a small pleasure boat. He is planning to host a dinner party as well and his housekeeper, Miss Milray, warns him that there will be thirteen for dinner, which is considered unlucky.

The guests include Angela Sutcliffe, another successful actor, and Freddie Dacres – whose past is supposed to contain a scandal connected to horse racing, and his wife, Cynthia, who runs a fashionable clothing store. Anthony Astor is a female playwright whose real name is Muriel Wills. Stephen Babbington is the local pastor and is accompanied by his wife. Gore is coming with her mother, Lady Mary. Oliver Manders is a journalist. And finally there is Hercule Poirot.

The party convenes and is just having cocktails when the pastor suddenly falls dead. An analysis of his drink finds nothing amiss and it is deemed to be natural causes. Even Poirot accepts that verdict. Satterthwaite is very observant and decides that Cartwright has fallen for the younger Gore, but that she is more interested in Manders despite her mother's disapproval. Cartwright comes to the same conclusion and announces that he is moving away immediately, at which point Gore admits that she is interested in him, not Manders.

Cartwright and Satterfield are in France when they receive word that Strange died at a dinner party he was hosting, in the same manner as had Babbington. The Gores were attending, as were the Dacres, Sutcliffe, Manders, Wills, and others. The cause of death was nicotine poisoning. The two men decide to return to England, and a chance encounter with Poirot stirs his interest as well.

There was no poison in the food or drink that remained. The butler, John Ellis, disappeared mysteriously within a few hours. Ellis was temporary, filling in for a vacationing butler, and there are hints that Strange had maneuvered things in order to have him in the house. Manders was apparently not invited but had an accident near the front gate on his motorcycle and had been offered a bed for the night.

Somewhat implausibly, Cartwright finds documents in Ellis' room which the police missed. They suggest that he knew who the killer was and had tried blackmail. He and Satterthwaite and the younger Gore decide to conduct an investigation, and they are later joined by Poirot, who admits that he was wrong to believe Babbington's death was not murder.

Gore uncovers rumors that Mrs. Dacres was having an affair, in which Strange intervened. She also discovers that Mr. Dacres is terrified of any kind of psychiatrist and is paranoid in general. There are also rumors that the dress business is in financial trouble. And Milray knew the Babbingtons from many years in the past. Babbington is exhumed and nicotine poison is found in the autopsy. Wills seems to know more than she is saying. Manders admits that his accident was staged, but claims that Dr. Strange asked him to do so.

Poirot demonstrates that both murders were committed in such a way that the poisoned glass could be replaced before anyone noticed. One of Strange's patients asks Poirot to come see her at the sanitarium, but when he arrives he learns that she has just been fatally poisoned. Wills disappears.

Cartwright is the killer. He was disguised as Ellis. The telegram from the patient was faked and she was poisoned only to distract attention from the truth. Babbington's death was a dress rehearsal. He was really after Strange, who had realized that Cartwright was on the verge of a complete mental collapse. When confronted, he flies into an impotent rage and is taken away.

Death in the Air (1935, aka *Death in the Clouds*) poses Poirot as one of the suspects in a murder case. Poirot is aboard an airplane which is to fly from France to Croydon in England. Jane Grey, who works in a beauty parlor and won a lottery that paid for a vacation on the continent, is the first of several viewpoint characters.

Lady Cicely Horbury is one of the other passengers, a rather snobbish woman whose maid is seated in a less luxurious part of the aircraft. She takes drugs and despite her friendly overtures to the woman next to her, Venetia Kerr, she actually dislikes the woman. Kerr reciprocates because they both coveted the same man and Horbury prevailed. Norman Gale is a young man who has his eye on Grey, and vice versa, although they had only met on one brief occasion.

Doctor Roger Bryant is an anxious man who seeks solace in music. Jean Dupont and his father, Armand, are both archaeologists. Daniel Clancy writes detective stories for a living and James Ryder is a businessman currently concerned about a cash shortage. Madame Giselle appears to be asleep when they approach their destination, but she is actually dead. And naturally Poirot is aboard as well.

The senior steward, Henry Mitchell, discovers that Giselle is not breathing and quietly asks Bryant to look at her. There is a noticeable mark on her neck. Poirot spots a blowgun dart on the floor nearby and it is obvious that this is murder. The plane lands but the passengers are not allowed to disperse. The police recognize Poirot and allow him to observe the interviews.

Giselle's real name is Marie Morisot. Poirot is also interested in the fact that a wasp was killed during the flight. The blowpipe is found stuck behind Poirot's seat. No one admits having known Morisot – who is a famous moneylender – except that Mitchell had seen her on at least one previous flight. The jury at the inquest is inclined to blame Poirot, but the coroner overrules them.

Morisot was also a blackmailer but her maid burned all of her confidential papers as soon as she heard of the death. The maid tells Poirot that Morisot's daughter had an English father, but she does not know the name. She also provides a small book with cryptic entries. An estranged daughter inherits everything. The various passengers are discussed at length. Poirot is puzzled that they found the blowgun because it could easily have been pushed out through a ventilation hole while they were still in the air.

Morisot's book has some interesting entries involving forged antiquities, attempted murder, a rich English woman and her husband, a doctor, and an embezzler, all of which could pertain to one or more of the passengers. The shopkeeper who sold the blowgun is certain that it was purchased by an American. A booking agent admits that he was bribed to arrange for Morisot to have a specific seat on a specific flight, also by an American, who identified himself as Silas Harper.

Cicely Horbury and her husband Stephen have separated, in large part because of her gambling debts. Poirot learns that there was an extra spoon in Morisot's coffee cup. He talks Gale into pretending to blackmail Cicely Horbury. Through a leap of logic, Poirot knows that she was having an affair with an actor named Barraclough and that she was heavily in debt to Morisot.

The police agree with Poirot that the blowgun was not used in the murder. Horbury, the Duponts and Bryant all had hollow tubes in their position which could have been used for that purpose. They are discussing this when Morisot's estranged daughter shows up to claim her legacy. She is genuine, but Poirot eventually realizes that he has seen her before – she was Horbury's maid who briefly attended her during the flight.

Poirot suddenly realizes that Anne is in danger, but he is too late. She is dead, apparently a suicide. But he knows the truth. Her husband is Gale and he is the killer. He dressed as a steward briefly and brought Morisot a spoon, then stabbed her with the dart. The wasp was released from a box as a distraction. He had not realized that his wife would be on the airplane and killed her, fearing that someone would recognize her when she claimed the estate. The murderer's plan is a big too complex but it makes a good story.

The A.B.C. Murders (1936) features Poirot again, assisted by Captain Hastings. Poirot receives a letter challenging his competence and although the police believe it to be a hoax, he is concerned. It was signed A.B.C. and we have briefly met a character named Alexander Bonaparte Cust. The skepticism of the police alters a bit when a shopkeeper, Alice Ascher, is murdered on the day and in the town which were mentioned in the letter.

The police suspect Ascher's estranged husband, but they have no evidence and the letter to Poirot is a disturbing factor. A copy of the A.B.C. travel guide is near the body, and Poirot does not believe it to be coincidental. Ascher was bludgeoned to death from behind. Poirot talks to the dead woman's niece, Mary Drower, who can offer no suggestions.

Poirot is stymied but, as expected, he receives a second letter after which a young woman named Bernard is strangled. Poirot and the police are helpless since the victims appear to have been chosen almost at random by a homicidal maniac. After the third letter, Sir Carmichael Clarke is found, also bludgeoned to death.

Previous investigations have shown that Ascher's husband was the only person with an apparent motive, but he was not smart enough to have written the letters, and that Bernard's lover was prone to violence, but is obviously shaken by her death. If the killer is truly insane, this may have been a waste of time, but Poirot is methodical and investigates Clarke's death in the same manner. He had one brother, Franklin, and was married, but childless. The wife is dying of cancer. His secretary is Thora Grey.

Franklin Clarke organizes the other survivors as a kind of labor pool for Poirot. Grey insists that she saw no strangers near the house on the day her employer was murdered, but she has been fired by the widow. Poirot visits Mrs. Clarke and she tells him that Grey lied, that she had been seen talking to a strange man in shabby clothing despite her denial.

Poirot finally finds a common element. A nondescript man had been selling stockings door to door in each case. Cust's landlady notes without taking alarm that he was near the site of three of the murders. The fourth letter arrives, indicating a town staring with "D" on a day when it is hosting a popular horse race and will be filled with strangers.

George Earlsfield is stabbed to death in a theater in the right town, but his name does not start with the right letter. He was sitting near Roger Downes at the time, which suggests that the killer stabbed the wrong man. A maid sees Cust washing his bloody hands and goes to the police. Cust is gone, but a box of stockings is found in his hotel room, along with a collection of the travel guides. The story of his coincidental trips to the murder sites triggers an attempt to interview Cust, but he takes alarm and bolts.

Cust, an epileptic, collapses and is arrested and charged. Poirot is the only one who seems to have reservations about his guilt. A problem arises because Cust has a solid alibi for the second murder. Poirot concludes that he was manipulated by the real murderer, who sent him letters purporting to be from his company, which sold stockings. Other items were planted in Cust's room, and his frequent blackouts made him believe that he had committed the crimes.

The real killer is Franklin Clarke, who feared that his brother would marry Grey after his wife died, depriving him of the ability to inherit the estate. The other murders were simply camouflage. Clarke tries, but fails, to kill himself and is taken into custody.

Murder in Mesopotamia (1936) takes place in Iraq and is mostly an account by Amy Leatheran, a professional nurse hired to help Louise Leidner, who is marred to Dr. Eric Leidner, head of an archaeological expedition. She is recommended by Dr. Reilly, a physician, whose daughter Sheila is a frequent visitor to the site and who dislikes Louise.

Leatheran meets all of the expedition members very quickly. Bill Coleman is a rather unserious young man who is infatuated with Sheila Reilly. Reilly, however, has her eyes set on David Emmott. Richard Carey is an architect, and Leatheran notices that he seems seriously worried about something. Anne Johnson is an older woman, who hero worships Eric Leidner. Father Lavigny is a French monk who translates tablets, but there is a hint that he might be a fake. Leatheran also sees him engaged in a clandestine meeting with an Iraqi man.

Joseph and Marie Mercado are a married couple. Marie is extremely jealous of Louise, but also accuses Leatheran of flirting with her husband. Carl Reiter is a young man who keeps mostly to himself and is responsible for the group's photography. They all live in a rectangular compound, a diagram of which is provided. There is a distinct feeling of tension at the site.

Louise has been spooked by a tapping at her window, a mysterious face, and other incidents that might be practical jokes or hallucinations. One night there are mysterious sounds from a store room which cause Louise to panic. She is not the only person to hear them but no intruder is found.

Louise then tells Leatheran that her first husband – Frederick Bosner - was reported killed during the war, and not honorably. He was a German spy who was captured, escaped, and then died in a train wreck. But the body was disfigured and she fears that he might have survived. She has periodically received letters warning her not to remarry, and now that she has, they have become death threats. She fears that either Frederick is still alive, or that his younger brother William might be tormenting her. Shortly after their marriage, someone entered their apartment and tried to kill them with gas. Leatheran sees one of the letters and notices that the handwriting strongly resembles Louise's own.

Louise is bludgeoned to death in her room and her husband finds the body. All of the members of the expedition were on their own at the time and each technically could have committed the murder except for Coleman, who had driven to the nearby town. Carey was at the dig site and her husband was on the roof during the entire period in question. Or so it seems. Servants were present at the outside gate and it seems impossible that an outsider could have entered or left.

Hercule Poirot happens to be in the country and he agrees to investigate. He conducts the usual preliminary interviews. The most likely theory is that one of the Bosner brothers is a member of the expedition, under another name. This would seem to leave out all of the women, plus Carey, who is the wrong age. There are rumors that Carey was having an affair with Louise, but he appears to genuinely hate her.

The mask that was used to scare her is found in its hiding place. Johnson has some kind of emotional crisis and tells Leatheran that she knows how the murder was done but that she has to think it over before she can say anything. That night she dies when someone puts poison in her drinking glass. The following morning they discover that Lavigny has disappeared. Poirot reveals that he was an impostor and that he has been stealing valuable artifacts and replacing them with fakes.

Leidner, who seems to be above suspicion, is actually the killer. He lured Louise to the window and dropped a heavy stone onto her head, killing her instantly. It was tied to a rope which he used to pull it up to the roof. Since he was the one who discovered the body, he moved it from the window to where it was found before raising the alarm. The gimmick is quite well done.

The motive, however, is terribly implausible. Leidner is actually the older Posner. He imitated Louise's handwriting and sent the threatening letters to keep her close to him. She was having an affair with Carey – which he hated but could not end – and this pushed Posner over the edge. The possibility that she could remarry the man she had not seen in fifteen years and never notice is too remote to be believable.

Cards on the Table (1936) features Poirot again. He is invited to attend a dinner by a rich, eccentric named Shaitana. Shaitana collects gossip and he claims to have identified several murderers who were never found guilty of their crimes. They are to be among the other guests at this ominous event.

The first guest whom he meets is Ariadne Oliver, who writes detective stories and who will reappear in several later novels. The second is Superintendent Battle, who has appeared previously in Christie's work and will also reappear in the future, the least known of her recurring detectives. The others include Colonel Race – another reprise, Dr. Geoffrey Roberts, Mrs. Lorrimer, Miss Meredith, and Major Despard.

The party is a success. The meal is followed by some bridge, two tables, with only Shaitana not playing. The bridge session lasts for quite a while and when it finally breaks up, it is discovered that Shaitana has been stabbed to death in his chair. All eight of the players have been away from their tables at least once during the evening, although Battle and Poirot are obviously not suspects.

Poirot and Battle believe that they plus Race and Oliver were meant to be the four detectives and that therefore the other four are Shaitana's murderers. The opening interviews provide no revelations. The only way forward is to look into the past of each of the four suspects.

Roberts seems to have had an uneventful career. One patient claimed that he was poisoning her, but she had said the same about previous doctors and had moved to another before she died. He had never received more than a token legacy from any of his patients. The only likely blackmailer had died while she was abroad.

Poirot interviews Lorrimer again. She remembers virtually every card that was played but unlike Roberts, she cannot remember the furniture very clearly. Oliver goes to see Meredith, who lives with Rhoda Dawes. She tells Meredith that she suspects Roberts. Shortly after she leaves, Despard shows up to tell her she needs to employ a lawyer. And after he leaves, Battle arrives. She tells him the truth, but leaves out one of the jobs she had held before moving in with Dawes.

Roberts did have words with a man who died soon thereafter, the husband of one of his patients, but it does not appear to have been serious. Despard tells Poirot that Shaitana indulged in emotional blackmail with his victims. Dawes tells Oliver that Meredith once worked for a woman who died after "accidentally" taking poison. Despard was at one time on an expedition where one man died, supposedly of fever, but a native had later claimed that he had been shot to death. Poirot interviews the widow, who admits that Despard shot her husband, but insists that it was self defense. Her husband had been feverish and mad with unjustified jealousy. Despard admits that he killed the man, but that he had meant only to wound and the husband had died only because his wife joggled his arm and then went into hysterics.

The woman who was poisoned probably died accidentally. Meredith had no motive and the facts supported the idea that she had chosen the wrong bottle. Poirot concludes that Meredith is both a liar and a petty thief. Poirot and Battle believe that for psychological reasons, Meredith, Roberts, and Despard could not have killed Shaitana.

Lorrimer admits to Poirot that she killed Shaitana on the spur of the moment because he knew she had poisoned her husband. She is now terminally ill and is unlikely to live long enough to stand trial. Poirot believes she is lying in order to protect Meredith, whom she sees as another version of her younger self. She actually saw Meredith kill Shaitan.

Poirot tries to convince her that Meredith will be emboldened if she gets away with this second murder. Lorrimer obviously is unconvinced because she writes a confession and some odd letters to the other three, and then dies of an overdose of sleeping pills, But there is evidence suggesting that she did not in fact write the letters, which turns out to be true. They were forged.

Battle and Poirot arrive as Dawes, Meredith, and Despard are sitting near the river. They see Meredith deliberately push Dawes into the water. Despard goes to the rescue, and saves Dawes, not Meredith, who drowns. But there is a final twist. It was Roberts who stabbed Shaitana, and then killed Lorrimer and forged the letters. A window cleaner happened to see enough to reveal the truth.

Poirot Loses a Client (1937, aka *Dumb Witness*) begins with the strange provisions in a will left by Emily Arundell, an elderly woman whose death is presumed to be by natural causes. Arundell's live-in companion was Wilhelmina Lawson.

The story jumps back to a dinner party a short time before

Arundell's death. There were four house guests, Bella Tanios and her husband Jacob, Theresa, and Charles Arundell. Bella is Arundell's niece. She married a Greek man despite her aunt's disapproval of the match. Theresa is engaged to Doctor Rex Donaldson. She is also a niece and Charles is her brother. Arundell disapproves of Theresa's flamboyant life style and considers Charles untrustworthy. The Arundell's friend, Caroline Peabody, was not invited. Lawson dislikes Charles, who is always broke. Theresa has money of her own but wants more. Tanios is on the brink of bankruptcy.

On the last evening of their visit, Donaldson comes to dinner as well. Late that evening, Arundell falls down a staircase, but survives. She is firmly convinced that someone attempted to murder her. She quietly writes a new will and sends a letter to Hercule Poirot, who is currently working with Hastings. Poirot is intrigued because the date on the letter is two months prior to his having received it.

When they arrive, they discover that Arundel has died and has left the house and a large fortune to Lawson. The letter to Poirot was found by a servant and belatedly mailed. Although Arundell may have died of natural causes, Poirot is certain that at least one attempt was made to murder her. He uses various ruses to question her doctor and others who knew her.

Lawson was interested in spiritualism and Arundell amused herself by attending an occasional séance with the Tripp sisters. Her final attack had come shortly after one of them. Charles hints that Lawson was aware of the new will despite her insistence that it came as a complete surprise. Arundell had shown him the document, but he expected that she would eventually revert to her original plan to leave everything to her family. There is a tension between the siblings.

A visit to Lawson reveals that she knew that a modfied will had been written, but claims not to have known its contents. She mentions that Arundell believed, correctly, that Charles had stolen some petty cash. Bella Tanios is concerned that Theresa might be spreading lies about her husband. He arrives and she is considerably less frank from that point on. It is clear that she is concealing something.

Despite her doctor's repeated assertion that Arundell died of natural causes, Poirot is convinced that it was murder. Poirot drops all pretense and tells Lawson about the letter. She is miffed that the maid mailed it without telling her. She also insists that she saw Theresa kneeling at the top of the stairs on the night of the accident, which suggests she arranged a tripwire in order to kill her aunt. But her story is not convincing.

Bella tries to see Poirot but misses him. Her husband shows up later and tells Poirot that his wife is suffering a mental breakdown. Theresa's violent objection to an exhumation convinces them that she knows that Arundell was murdered. She died of an apparent liver disease and Donaldson has been working with serums related to that kind of malady. He had told Theresa their effects. Bella takes their two children and leaves her husband. She secretly moves in with Lawson and then tells Poirot she is convinced her husband murdered Arundell.

Poirot fears another tragedy and convinces Bella to take the two children to a hotel without telling anyone. Nevertheless, she dies of an overdose of sleeping pills that night. It was suicide. She knew that Poirot had identified her as the killer. She fashioned the tripwire and she added phosphorous to her aunt's medication in order to mimic liver troubles. She had not known about the new will and she also wanted to leave her husband. She had probably been planning to kill him and ingratiate herself with Lawson.

Death on the Nile (1938) is the story of Linnet Ridgeway, a beautiful young woman who has recently inherited an immense fortune. She has just restored a mansion and is pleased to show it off to her friend, Joanna Southwood. She has also invited another friend, Jacqueline de Bellefort. She has been seeing Charles Windelsham, but is in no hurry to get married. Her maid, Marie, was planning to marry an Egyptian but Ridgeway investigated and discovered that he was already married.

Bellefort is engaged to Simon Doyle and prevails upon Linnet to give him a job. Linnet is used to having her own way and she quickly lures Doyle away from her friend and marries him. To add insult to injury, the newlyweds decide to take the honeymoon in Egypt that Bellefort had planned.

We are quickly introduced to the other characters who will be on that journey, including Poirot. Tim Allerton is friendly with Southwood, but is devoted to his mother, who will accompany him. George Wode detests Linnet because she bought his family home and transformed it until it is unrecognizable. Cornelia Robson is the companion of Mrs. Van Schuyler, and the two of them will be traveling together. Andrew Pennington is one of two men who manage Linnet's investments, and they are alarmed and surprised when they learn of her marriage. Their concerns are not disclosed but Pennington rushes off to "accidentally" meet and join the party. Jim Fanthorp's motives are not revealed, but when he learns that Pennington is with Linnet, he immediately flies to Egypt. Rosalie Otterbourne and her querulous mother have been in the Mideast for a while and they have become bored.

Poirot observes the newlyweds and makes two observations. Linnet is suppressing some severe tension. Doyle's voice is familiar, but Poirot cannot place it. Later he realizes he sat next to Doyle and Bellefort in a restaurant once when they were still engaged. Bellefort shows up. She is shadowing the couple to make them as uncomfortable as possible. Mrs. Otterbourne turns out to be the author of sexy romance novels. Linnet asks Poirot to stop Bellefort from following them. He refuses and points out that she is doing nothing illegal, but he talks to Bellefort to try to convince her that she is demeaning herself. She has a handgun and tells him she has considered using it.

The newlyweds decide to sneak away using a false name. Bellefort is not fooled. Tim Allerton dislikes Poirot for some reason. A man named Ferguson joins the group, and lectures constantly about the evils of capitalism. During an excursion on shore, a boulder rolls down a hill and nearly kills Linnet. Doyle was with her and Bellefort was still on their cruise boat, so neither of them could have been responsible, but Poirot does not believe that it was an accident.

Colonel Race, the government agent from *Thirteen for Dinner*, returns. He is pursuing a revolutionary believed to be on the cruise, but he does not even have a description. The fugitive has already committed several murders. That evening Bellefort gets drunk and pulls out her handgun. Doyle struggles with her and is shot in the leg. Only Fanthorp and Robson were present. Bellefort is hysterical and is taken to her cabin. She is never alone before a nurse arrives and the nurse stays with her all night, Doyle's wound is serious and he cannot walk. He spends the night in the cabin of Dr. Bessmer, and is given a narcotic strong enough to knock him out.

In the morning, Linnet is found shot to death in her bed, presumably with Bellefort's weapon. Fanthorp had tried to find it several minutes after the altercation the night before, but someone had taken it away. The letter "J" is scrawled in blood on the wall, but this is obviously fake because Linnet would have died instantly. So the two people with the strongest motives are both apparently innocent.

Poirot eliminates several others from the boulder incident, but not the shooting. These include both Allertons, Van Schuyler, the nurse, Doyle, and Bellefort. Two fresh suspects appear. A crew member named Fleetwood is the man who tried to marry Linnet's maid, bigamously. Doyle mentions that Linnet saw a name on the passenger list that bothered her because it was the son of a man whose father had been ruined in business by her father. Linnet's valuable pearl necklace is missing as well.

Van Schuyler saw Rosalie Otterbourne drop something into the water at about the time of the murder. The young woman flatly denies it. The murder weapon is brought up by divers. Poirot correctly guesses that the item Rosalie threw overboard was her mother's secret stash of alcohol. The nurse brings the pearls to Poirot and explains that Van Schuyler is a kleptomaniac. The pearls, however, are fakes.

Linnet's maid mysteriously disappears. A search of the boat turns up nothing except that several passengers are carrying handguns, including Rosalie, who denies it later. The maid is found stabbed to death and Poirot suspects she tried to blackmail the killer. He also thinks that Rosalie saw someone leaving Linnet's cabin, but she refuses to answer when he asks her directly.

Mrs. Otterbourne saw the maid with one of the other passengers and starts to tell Poirot and Race, but she is shot and killed in front of them. The murder weapon was Pennington's handgun, although he insists that someone must have taken it from his luggage. The person whose father had been ruined by the Ridgeway family is Cornelia Robson, but she does not resent the past. The professional killer turns out to be one of the minor characters, and he had no connection to any of the new murders.

Fanthorp explains that he works for Linnet's English attorney, who suspected Pennington of having embezzled some of Linnet's money. Pennington confesses to this when questioned, and also claims that the boulder that almost hit Linnet was dislodged when he "fell" against it. Tim Allerton confesses that he and Southwood have been stealing valuable jewelry by replacing it with substitutes. He had taken Linnet's pearls, unaware that she was lying dead in the darkness. Van Schuyler had made off with the fakes. Poirot uncharacteristically lets him go in return for the surrender of the real pearls.

The actual killers were Doyle and Bellefort, who have been working in collusion all along in order to acquire Linnet's fortune. The shot that supposedly hit Doyle actually missed. He used red nail polish to suggest that he was bleeding. While the others were taking Bellefort to her room and summoning help, he ran to Linnet's room and shot her, then returned and wounded himself, after replacing one spent round in the handgun. When the maid tried to blackmail him, he contrived an excuse to talk to Bellefort, who used one of the doctor's scalpels to stab her. She also pilfered Pennington's gun to kill Otterbourne when she realized that she had been seen. She has a second weapon – the one that was previously hidden in Rosalie's bag – and uses it to kill Doyle and herself before they can be turned over to the police.

Appointment with Death (1938) takes Poirot to Jerusalem. The story begins when Raymond and Carol Boynton, siblings, decide that their stepmother must die. The Boyntons are a party of American tourists who are completely dominated by the older woman. The other members of the group are Lennox and Nadine, a married couple, and a younger sibling named Jinny, who is the woman's only actual child. Nadine wants her husband to move out of the house, but he has no money, no friends, no job skills, and is thoroughly browbeaten.

Sarah King is also visiting the area and she decides that she dislikes Mrs. Boynton and wants to rescue Raymond. She mentions the family to Dr. Theodore Gerard, a famous psychologist, whose observations of the family disturb him. Jefferson Cope is also an American in Jerusalem. He is in love with Nadine and Mrs. Boynton tolerates him because she wants him to steal Nadine away. King and Gerard both believe the old woman is insane, but it is Jinny who begins to display symptoms of delusions.

An excursion is planned and the party is joined by the domineering Lady Westholme and a quieter woman, Amabel Pierce.

All of the main characters gather at a remote site, an abandoned city, and they are going about various tasks when one of the guides finds Mrs. Boynton dead, possibly of natural causes. The last person who admits to having spoken to her is Raymond, who claims it was just a brief greeting, although in context we know that he intended to assert his independence.

The group and the body return to Amman where Dr. Gerard expresses some concerns to the local police chief, whose guest is Poirot. He had been asleep during the crucial time period, recovering from an attack of malaria, and King had examined the body. She was quite certain that the woman had been dead for long enough that Raymond could not possibly have talked to her. Gerard also noticed that someone had "borrowed" and returned his hypodermic needle. This leads him to have some concerns that the death was not actually due to the hot weather and a weak heart.

Poirot begins to interview the potential suspects. Nadine tries to convince him to accept that it was a natural death. Pierce tells him that she saw one of the Boynton sisters throw away a box, which she later found. It contained a hypodermic, which King noticed and claimed that she had dropped.

Poirot sorts it all out. The Boynton's all suspected one another and they were lying to cover up the real time of death and other aspects of the case. The actual murder was committed by Westholme, who had been a prisoner when Mrs. Boynton had been the wardress at a prison. She had been recognized and threatened with exposure, so she stole the hypodermic, killed the woman, then invented a cover story which she convinced Pierce was true so that their stories were the same. Westholme commits suicide before she can be arrested.

A Holiday for Death (1938, aka *Hercule Poirot's Christmas*, aka *Murder for Christmas*) is relatively short. Stephen Farr has recently arrived in London from South Africa. He does not like being there, but he admires Pilar Estravados, a young woman he notices when they are on the same train. She has come to England to stay with relatives and to escape the Spanish Civil War.

Simeon Lee is the rich and rather domineering father of four sons. Harry ran off and has not been home in many years. Alfred lives with his father, along with his wife Lydia, who does not like her father-in-law. George is dependent upon his father financially and his wife Magdalene wants him to show more loyalty. David blames his father for his mother's death but his wife, Hilda, has been urging him to let the past go and reconcile. They are all invited to spend Christmas together, along with Stephen and Pilar. The staff at the Lee house includes Tressilian, the butler, and Sydney Horbury, valet, a devious man who is generally disliked.

There was also a sister, Jennifer, who died, but her daughter has never met the rest of the family. She is Pilar. Simeon tells the others that Harry will be there as well. Magdalene is concealing her copious bills from her husband, which cannot be paid even with the generous allowance from his father. Simeon has a bag of uncut diamonds in his safe, which he shows to Pilar. He also mentioned once ruining a business rival in South Africa. Harry arrives and it is clear that he and Alfred despise one another.

Farr arrives unexpectedly. His father was Simeon's partner in South Africa. Simeon pretends that he is about to write a new will. Horbury is very nervous when a policeman visits the house. The policeman – Superintendent Sugden – is just arriving on a supposed social visit - when there is an uproar from Simeon's room. The door is broken down and he is found dead, clearly murdered, but no one else is in the room. Pilar tries to conceal something from Sugden but he sees her do it. The item is an enigmatic bit of rubber which Sugden considers immaterial.

Poirot is visiting in the area and is naturally invited to help. Sugden reveals that his supposed innocent visit had secretly been at Simeon's request. Simeon had told Sugden that the diamonds had been taken from his safe and that he suspected two people, one a servant, the other a relative. But he did not identify them and asked Sugden to return a short time later. This resulted in the second visit just as the murder was discovered. Everyone was in the house at the time except for Horbury. Simeon's throat had been cut but there seems to be too much blood in the room, and the overturned furniture appears excessive as well.

The suspects were well scattered about at the time of the uproar. Alfred and Harry appear to have been together, and David was apparently playing the piano accompanied by his wife. George and Magdalene both claim to have been on the telephone at the time, but there is only one instrument so one of them has to be lying. Pilar claims to have been with Farr, but Farr says he was alone. Horbury is caught lying about his knowledge of the diamonds.

Simeon's existing will leaves half to Alfred, with the balance distributed equally among the other three of his children. A check with the telephone company indicates that no one was using the telephone at the time of the murder. Poirot finds the diamonds in a miniature garden designed and built by Lydia. Tressilian had seen her looking out one of the windows when the shouting started, so it does not seem possible that she is the killer. Horbury has a previous conviction for extortion.

A decorative cannonball disappears. A cable from South Africa proves that Farr is not the person he claims to be. A booby trap nearly kills Pilar. Farr admits that his name is actually Grant. He asserts that he was a friend of the Farr family and decided to impersonate the son because he was infatuated with Pilar. In fact, he is Simeon's illegitimate son and he had come to see what kind of person his father was. Pilar is also a fake. The real one died in the fighting in Spain.

Pilar saw someone standing outside Simeon's room just before the noises began. Hilda admits that she was that person, but insists that the door was locked and she could only hear the tumult through the door. The real killer was Sugden, another illegitimate son. Simeon died during his visit – which Sugden initiated. He quietly overturned some of the furniture and spread pig blood over the room. The rest of the furniture was piled up with a rope attached, the other end out the window, so that it could be pulled down when he "returned." He locked the door from the outside when he left. The cry was created by a pig bladder balloon, which is what Pilar had picked up.

There is one small error in the book. Poirot describes one of Simeon's physical mannerisms, but he never met the man and that gesture has not been mentioned in any of the conversations he had with the suspects.

Easy to Kill (1939, aka *Murder Is Easy*) briefly brings back Superintendent Battle. Luke Fitzwilliam, a retired police officer, has just returned to England after an extended period abroad. Due to a mix up with trains, he ends up sharing a carriage with an older woman, Lavina Fullerton, who is en route to Scotland Yard. She wants to reports a series of deaths which she believes were murders. Fitzwilliam is only mildly disturbed when he reads the paper the following day and learns that Fullerton was killed by a hit and run driver before she could tell her story.

Fullerton had mentioned the same of the next victim, a local doctor. Fitzwilliam does get disturbed a few days later when the doctor's obituary appears. He considers the matter worth further investigation and a friend puts him in touch with his cousin, Bridget Conway, who lives in the village where the murders are taking place. Conway is the fiancé of Lord Easterfield, a rather unpopular man who owns several small newspapers. His cover story is that he is writing a book about rural superstitions.

Fitzwilliam soon hears about some odd deaths. Amy Gibbs supposedly picked the wrong bottle in the dark and drank poison. Dr. Humbleby died of a presumed infection. Conway introduces him to the rector, Alfred Wake. He also learns about the village lawyer, Abbot, and the new doctor, Geoffrey Thomas, who is in love with Humbleby's daughter Rose.

More suspicious deaths. Tommy Pierce was cleaning windows when he fell to his death. He had gotten the job through the intercession of Miss Waynflete, an elderly spinster. Henry Carter, who worked in an inn, fell into a river and drowned while alone. It is clear that Conway suspects that his cover story is false, and that some of the villagers are refraining from expressing their suspicions about the high incidence of sudden deaths. Mr. Ellsworthy operates an antiques shop. Major Horton raises bulldogs. His wife recently died of gastritis.

Conway confronts Fitzwilliam, who tells her the truth. Fitzwilliam's prime suspect is Abbot, who had words with Carter, fired Pierce, and disliked Humbleby. Ellsworthy, who is interested in black magic, was also at odds with several of those who died. Fitzwilliam eliminates some minor suspects because their whereabouts were known at the time Fullerton was killed. Rose Humbleby tells him that Fullerton was worried about Conway.

There are a lot of interconnections. Gibbs was seeing Carter and Ellsworthy without the knowledge of her boyfriend. She had been working for the Hortons when the wife died, and had visited Abbot and Humbleby. She had also worked for Easterfield. Pierce once worked for Easterfield and had been a member of Ellsworthy's secretive occult group. Fitzwilliam is sure the killer is a man because Gibbs was probably killed by someone who climbed into her room from the roof. He decides the potential killer must be Thomas, Ellsworthy, Horton, or Abbot.

Fitzwilliam effectively drops the cover story and visits the scenes of some of the deaths. He realizes that he may now have become a target for the killer. He happens upon a violent altercation between Easterfield and his chauffeur. Waynflete was once engaged to Easterfield when he was using the name Gordon Ragg, a person of lower class before his financial success.

Fitzwilliam burglarizes Ellsworthy's house and find some suggestive but circumstantial evidence. Conway decides to marry Fitzwilliam instead of Eastwood. Ellsworthy may have had blood on his hands, literally, just after the chauffeur was killed by a fallen piece of concrete in an obviously contrived accident.

Dr. Thomas discounts Fitzwilliam's conviction that Ellsworthy is a madman, and he begins to have doubts himself when Easterfield goes on a quasi-religious rant and names the victims as people who had previously wronged him. When he learns that Easterfield's car was probably the one that killed Fullerton, and that his earlier engagement was broken off when he killed a canary in a jealous rage, Fitzwilliam is convinced, though Scotland Yard still has reservations.

He is wrong, of course, and it turns out that Conway is right. The real killer is Waynflete. Her story about the end of their engagement is false – he broke it off because he distrusted her mental stability. She has hated him for years and decided to kill several random people and frame him for the crimes. Conway tricks her into revealing the truth and Battle arrives in time to make the arrest.

And Then There Were None (1939, aka *Ten Little Indians*) is the acknowledged basis for at least three movies, and the concept has been stolen for a good many more. Soldier Island has been purchased by the mysterious Mr. Owen, who invites ten people to visit, but forges signatures and uses other pretexts so that they think they are being invited by old friends or potential employers. None of them actually know "Owen."

The first we meet is Lawrence Wargrave, a retired judge. Vera Claythorne thinks she is going to be interviewed for a new job. Philip Lombard is an adventurer who suspects that he is being hired for something shady. Emily Brent has been hired as a cook. General John Macarthur is under the impression that he is going to attend a reunion with old army friends. Dr. Edward Armstrong has been paid to provide a consultation. Tony Marston is a gigolo who never turns down an invitation for free food and drink. William Blore is a private detective, also believing he is going to be hired for an unspecified job. Thomas Rogers and his wife Ethel are to act as household servants.

They all arrive at approximately the same time and all are surprised that there is no host or hostess present. They are served a fine meal after which a recording is played which accuses each of them of a specific murder for which they escaped punishment. They compare notes and conclude that they have been lured to the island by a homicidal maniac. They also notice a set of ten figurines, and the reader has twice been exposed to the rhyme about the ten doomed little Indians.

Most declare their innocence. Marston admits having run over two people while driving under the influence. Lombard asserts that h did abandon some native bearers in South Africa and that they died as a consequence. There is no way off the island except by the local boat, which is supposed to visit every morning.

Marston dies of poisoning while they are all having a drink. Ethel Rogers passes away in her sleep of unknown causes. There are only eight figurines left. The boat that was supposed to call never shows up. Marston might have been a suicide, but most of the others believe he was murdered. They organize a search of the island, looking for Mr. Owen, but they find nothing. Obviously he is one of the supposed guests.

Macarthur is bludgeoned to death while sitting in a chair. Rogers is hit with an axe during the night and Brent is injected with poison the following morning. Lombard had brought a handgun but it has disappeared. Wargrave is found unconscious and Armstrong soon indicates that he is dead. Armstrong disappears. Lombard finds his weapon and refuses to relinquish it. Blore dies and Armstrong's body turns up, leaving only Lombard and Claythorne.

The trick ending is that neither of them is using the right name. Both came in place of someone else, so both are innocent. The real killer is Wargrave, who takes poison after assuming that Claythorne killed Lombard and will be arrested for all of the murders. He convinced Armstrong to help him fake his death in order to "find" the real killer, but the other two faked Lombard's death for the same reason.

Sad Cypress (1940) opens with a brief prologue in which we learn that Elinor Carlisle is on trial for the murder of Mary Gerrard. The story then jumps back to show what led up to this. Carlisle and Roderick Welman are cousins by marriage and are engaged to marry one another at some as yet undecided future date. Carlisle is completely supported by her rich Aunt Laura Welman, and Roderick Welman in part. Laura Welman has had a stroke and is bedridden, partially paralyzed. She is assisted by Nurses O'Brien and Hopkins, plus the volunteer help of a young local woman, Gerrard. Peter Lord is her doctor.

Gerrard is routinely abused by her father, Ephraim, but seems honestly devoted to the invalid, who provides money to ensure that she is properly educated. The nurses both like her but Mrs. Bishop, the longstanding housekeeper, thinks she is only after her employer's money. Carlisle receives an anonymous letter accusing Gerrard of dishonest motives. Ted Bigland has been courting Gerrard, but she is not really interested in him. During a visit, Roderick meets Gerrard and falls in love with her instantly, to the dismay of Carlisle who releases him from the engagement.

The aunt has a second stroke and belatedly asks to see her lawyer, but she dies during the night. It turns out that she had never made a will so her entire state goes to Carlisle. Although Carlisle clearly has reason to dislike Gerrard, she promises her a sum of money sufficient to allow her to train for a new profession and establish herself somewhere. Elinor promptly makes a will leaving everything to Roderick.

The house is sold and Carlisle and Gerrard meet for tea during the clearing out process. Gerrard collapses and dies, having been poisoned. Nurse Hopkins is missing some morphine, which disappeared the night the aunt died. Lord, who has fallen in love with Carlisle, asks Poirot to find out the truth. Ephraim dies and in his final moments he tells Hopkins that Mary was not his daughter, that she was the daughter of an unnamed gentleman. This could not be the aunt's husband because he died quite young, but there was a lover, Lewis Rycrift, who was killed during the war.

An exhumation proves that the aunt was also poisoned with morphine. Poirot's interviews ferret out the information that Mary Gerrard was actual Laura Welman's daughter, father by Sir Lewis

Rycroft. She was placed with the Gerrards to avoid a scandal. He also learns that Lord's car was parked near the house at the time when the poison was placed in a sandwich, although Lord denies it. He could not have known that the sandwiches were meant to be shared with Gerrard.

The solution cheats a bit. Hopkins is actually named Riley and she is the sister of Gerrard's adopted mother. Hopkins convinced her to write a will leaving everything to Mary Riley because she knew she was legal heir to Laura Welman's entire estate. She killed both of them with morphine and planted evidence implicating Carlisle. Lord also tried to introduce bogus evidence – his car – in order to cast doubt on the prosecution.

One, Two, Buckle My Shoe (1940, aka *An Overdose of Death*, aka *The Patriotic Murders*) features Poirot. Henry Morley is a rather grumpy dentist who lives with his sister Georgina in a flat above his office. His secretary is Gladys Nevill, whom he finds very competent, though he disapproves of her new boyfriend, Frank Carter. Among his patients are Sainsbury Seale, Alistair Blunt, a man named Amberiotis, Colonel Ambercrombie, and Hercule Poirot. A young man, Alfred Biggs, also works at the office doing odd jobs. Morley's partner is named Reilley.

A few hours after Poirot has his usual checkup, Poirot is told that Morley has killed himself. He never believes it for a moment and he remembers that Morley had mentioned a new patient who looked familiar to him. The last patient Morley had seen had been Amberiotis. Nevill had not been working that day – she was visiting a sick aunt. He was shot in the head and his sister insists that she has never seen the handgun before. Nevill returns, indignant because the telegram about her ailing aunt was not true.

One of Reilly's patients – Howard Raikes - walked out without seeing Reilly during the crucial time period, and Carter showed up briefly, unaware that Nevill had been called away. Reilly appears genuinely sad about Morley's death. Blunt, a prominent banker, tells Poirot and Inspector Japp that Morley seemed in good spirits. Blunt's niece, Jane Olivera, acts slightly odd when she hears about Morley's death.

Amberiotis dies before he can be interviewed. He was apparently poisoned by the painkiller administered during his dental visit. Japp believes this might be the motive if Morley did commit suicide.

Amberiotis has a history involving espionage and blackmail. Another of Reilly's patients is a retired government official and he tells Poirot that he suspects Morley was being pressured to help quietly assassinate Blunt, that he balked, and that he was killed to prevent him from talking.

Seale disappears from the hotel where she has been staying. Poirot questions Raikes, who is hostile and openly contemptuous of Blunt, whom he assumes has employed Poirot. Carter, who has a new lucrative job about which he will not speak, is truculent and uncooperative. The inquest results in a verdict of suicide, but Poirot disagrees. Olivera confesses that she is in love with Raikes despite his politics.

A month later, there is still no sign of Seale. She returned from India on the same ship that carried Amberiotis, but there is nothing indicating that they had ever met. Her body ostensibly shows up, stuffed in a trunk in the rooms rented by a Miss Chapman, who has abruptly disappeared. The body is badly damaged and identification is not absolutely certain. Chapman told one of her neighbors that her husband was a spy for the British government. Barnes confirms that Chapman was an agent, supposedly now dead. The woman's body is belatedly identified as being Mrs. Chapman and not Seale.

Blunt sends a note asking for Poirot to visit him, and a woman calls anonymously and threatens Poirot's life if he goes. Japp has been ordered to close the case because of concerns by the Foreign Office. Someone attempts to shoot Blunt but misses. The supposed gunman is apprehended – apparently by Raikes, although it turns out that he grabbed the wrong person. Blunt invites Poirot to spend a weekend with his family, and Poirot recognizes that Olivera's supposedly empty headed mother was the woman who threatened him.

Poirot is rather puzzled to discover that Carter is working as Blunt's gardener, and under an assumed name. Another shot is fired in Blunt's vicinity, and Raikes captures Carter this time. Carter insists he found the gun and did not fire it. He is in fact telling the truth and the means by which the gun was remotely discharged is never explained.

A maid finally confesses to Poirot that she saw Carter enter Morley's treatment room just before the body was found. Carter admits that this is true but insists that he found Morley dead and ran off in a panic. Seale approached Blunt shortly after she returned from India and insists that she was a good friend of his wife, but he insists he has no recollection of her, and given that his late, very wealthy wife was from the moneyed class, it seems like an unlikely friendship.

There is a clever double reversal, because the dead woman really was Seale after all. Mrs. Chapman took her place and has been impersonating her ever since. Their dental charts had been switched – this also is never really explained because they had two different dentists. Chapman is Blunt's real wife. They concealed the marriage so that he could marry the rich woman, and she remained as his mistress afterwards.

Blunt had sneaked back into the building and killed Morley, then rang the buzzer to summon Amberiotis. A chance remark by Seale had led Amberiotis to realize the truth about Blunt's marriage and he was blackmailing the man. Blunt's impersonation of a dentist and his ability to prepare a poisoned injection are not explained either. The Chapman identity is also false. She has been living as Blunt's poor cousin and has barely appeared in the story previously. In a final twist, Barnes tells Poirot that he knew something was wrong because he was Agent Chapman and he had never married.

Although there are some nice twists, this is not a very good mystery. Too many things are unexplained. There are multiple unlikely coincidences. Poirot learns the truth through a key piece of evidence that is withheld from the reader – the shoes on the dead body were similar to but not the same as those he had seen when he met the real Seale. They were too well worn and the wrong size to have been hers.

Evil Under the Sun (1941) features Poirot, who is vacationing at the Jolly Roger Hotel on a kind of island connected to the mainland by a causeway. The other guests include Odell Gardener and his wife Carrie, Emily Brewster, Rosamund Darnley, Reverend Stephen Lane, Patrick and Christine Redfern, Horace Blatt, and Major Barry. A family of three consists of Captain Kenneth Marhsall, his wife Arlena – a famous actress, and his daughter by a previous marriage, Linda.

Both Lane and Brewster say outright that they consider Arlena to be an evil person. Patrick Redfern is obviously attracted to her and his wife is quietly furious. Darnley and Kenneth Marshall knew each other in the past but met again at the hotel purely by chance. Linda Marshall hates her stepmother.

The following morning Arlena sets off on a supposed solitary walk, although Poirot suspects an assignation. Redfern shows up and sits on the beach, obviously hoping that Arlena will appear, so it is clearly not with him. He and Brewster take out a small rowboat and they find Arlena on a remote beach. She has been strangled. The context seems to eliminate both of them as suspects. Ken Marshall had gone off to work in his room and Odell Gardener was oddly long in retrieving some yarn, but both seem to have had no chance to commit the murder. Darnley had gone for a walk, while Linda Marshall was with Christine Redfern.

Christine Redfern tells the police that she overheard the dead woman talking to an unknown man and that he was clearly blackmailing her. Blatt, Lane, and Barry had all gone off individually during the critical time period. Linda Marshall secretly purchased some candles on the morning of the murder, but her purpose is unclear. A letter found in the dead woman's room is clearly from a former lover to whom she had paid some money. Darnley mentions that someone threw a bottle from a hotel window into the sea that same morning.

A container of heroin is found in a cave near the murder site. Darnley belatedly claims to have seen Marshall typing – providing him with an alibi – and he belatedly claims to have noticed her – returning the favor. Linda has a book about witchcraft in her room, which suggests the reason she purchased the candles. Lane retired because of mental problems – an obsession with evil women – and there are two unsolved cases of strangled women which happened near his church. Blatt's income has big jumps which lead Poirot and the police to believe he has been smuggling heroin.

Poirot proposes a picnic, to which everyone comes except for Kenneth and Linda Marshall. Linda takes an overdose of sleeping pills and leaves a note indicating that she murdered her stepmother. She had performed a ritual to that effect and may have physically acted – there is a flaw in her alibi. She may also have been convinced that her father was guilty and was trying to protect him. His mutual alibi with Darnley also falls apart, assuming that they were working together to kill Arlena.

The truth, however, is that the Redferns were working together to kill Arlena, just as they had previously killed at least one of the other cases – the victim was Patrick's wife at the time, under another name. The explanation is rather complex. The bottle thrown from the window contained a skin darkener so that Christine could pass for Arlena at a distance. Patrick had been defrauding rather than blackmailing Arlena. Christine pretended to be the dead body on the beach so that Brewster would confuse the time of death. Arlena had been hiding in the cave and Patrick strangled her and moved her body to the right place. Linda recovers.

N or M? (1941) is a Tommy and Tuppence story. Tommy is recruited for a counterespionage mission, replacing a man who was recently murdered. He is not supposed to tell Tuppence anything, but she sets out for the same destination under an assumed name. They pretend not to know one another.

They meet Carl von Deinim, a refugee from Germany at a large hotel where they are both staying. The hotel is believed to be unofficial headquarters for a group of German spies. The chief spies are known only as N or M and von Deinim has to be considered a prime suspect. His stated history seems quite convincing, but he may not be the real von Deinim.

Both of our heroes end up staying separately at the hotel where von Deinim is living, under the names Blenkensop and Meadowes. The hotel is managed by Mrs. Perenna, whose daughter Sheila is romantically involved with von Deinim. They are actually Irish and Sheila's father was executed as a saboteur when he was caught working for the Nazis. Other guests include the stuffy Major Bletchley, the apparently dimwitted Mrs. Strop and her three year old daughter, and Commander Haydock. A mysterious woman believed to be a refugee has also been seen in the area.

Although Tommy and Tuppence are both rather clumsy as spies, they begin to suspect von Deinim more seriously when he meets with the mystery woman clandestinely. He also admits that he is still loyal to Germany – just not the Nazis. The story takes a surprising turn when the mystery woman kidnaps the toddler. She is tracked down by a group of people and is threatening to kill the child when Strop shoots her in the head from a considerable distance. This is described as a very lucky shot, but the reader will likely suspect that there is more to Sprot than has been revealed.

Von Deinim is arrested under suspicion that he was an

accomplice to the abduction. Haydock tells Tommy that he is working for British intelligence and wants Tommy to help him with surveillance. This is a lie and instead Tommy is taken captive – at which point Haydock explains much of the mystery to him rather than shooting him out of hand. Tuppence offers herself as bait in a trap and Haydock and Sprot are both arrested, while Tommy is rescued.

The Body in the Library (1942) was the second full length novel featuring Jane Marple. Arthur and Dolly Bantry are a retired couple who are upset one morning when the servants report finding a woman strangled to death in their library. No one recognizes her but there is a report of a missing person who fits the description. Ruby Keene is a young professional dancer who was working at a hotel/resort a few miles away and she disappeared the previous evening between performances. Her body is identified by a cousin and co-worker, Josephine Turner.

Early suspicion focused on Basil Blake, an obnoxious young man who works in the film industry, though he is not an actor. Blake had been seen recently with a woman who looks very similar to Keene, but Deborah Lee is very much alive. Dolly Bantry enlists the help of an old friend, Jane Marple, whose presence is also mostly welcomed by the police.

Keene had been keeping company with Conway Jefferson and his family. Jefferson was an older man whose wife, son, and daughter were all killed in an airplane accident that also left him with both legs amputated. His health is declining and he is reasonably wealthy. The family living with him consists of his daughter-in-law, Adelaide Jefferson, and her nine year old son by a previous marriage, Peter Carmody, and occasionally Mark Gaskell, his son-in-law. Both of his dependents had already received large amounts of money, but they are secretly both in financial straits and are unhappy when Jefferson announced his plans to adopt Keene and leave her the bulk of his estate.

There are two more potential suspects, George Bartlett is a rather stupid young man who used to dance with Keene from time to time, and whose car disappeared on the night of the murder. Raymond Starr was Keene's professional dancing partner, but he had been paired with Turner until a small accident left her unable to dance temporarily. She does not appear to have liked Keene. Turner tells the police that Keene occasionally danced with Blake and that she personally disliked the man.

Another, slightly younger woman also disappeared that night. Pamela Reeves left her friends, supposedly to shop near the hotel, and never came home afterward. Bartlett's car is found burning a few miles away and there is a charred body inside which is presumed to be Reeves. The supposition is that she saw something incriminating and had been silenced. Everyone except Bartlett appears to have a solid alibi for the murder of Keene, but the time of death for the other body cannot be accurately determined.

A friend of Reeves eventually confesses that the dead girl had not gone shopping, that she had been offered a screen test, to be conducted in secret at the hotel. The police clearly believe that Blake is the murderer and that he broke into the library and left the body there. Although they arrest him, Marple – who has discovered that Blake and Lee are married – does not believe he is guilty. He admits finding her body in his own cottage and moving it to the Bantry home to avoid becoming involved.

Marple reveals the truth – some of which is just guesswork. Gaskell and Turner are secretly married. They drugged both of the victims. The body identified as Keene was actually Reeves, and vice versa. This was done to mislead police about the time of death and thereby establish their alibis. There is no proof, however, so Jefferson announces a new will giving everything to charity, but he is actually just acting as bait. Turner attempts to kill him and is caught in the act. Gaskell breaks down and tells the whole story.

Murder in Retrospect (1942, aka *Five Little Pigs*) features Poirot. His latest client is Carla Lemarchant, whose mother – Caroline Crale – was convicted of poisoning her father sixteen years earlier and who died in prison. Lemarchant is convinced that her mother was innocent.

Poirot interviews the defense lawyer, who admits that he thought his client was guilty, though perhaps with some justification. Her husband, an artist, had been consistently unfaithful and they had quarreled violently for a long time. His current mistress had been a young woman, Elsa Greer, the spoiled daughter of a wealthy businessman. The poison bottle had been found in Crale's bedroom and she admitted stealing it, ostensibly because she was considering suicide.

The poison had been in a glass of beer. Crale had brought the bottle, but there was no poison found in it. Her husband's fingerprints were the only ones on the bottle, but their position suggested that someone had pressed his hand against it. Potential suspects include Philip Blake, a friend of the family who had been staying with them, and Blake's older brother, Meredith who was a neighbor. Angela Warren was Crale's half-sister and there had been a governess named Cecilia Williams.

Poirot talks to various lawyers who were involved in the case. No one seems to have any doubt that Crale was guilty. She had just threatened to kill her husband, and had been overheard by several people. The police built an almost unassailable case although they admit that none of the other suspects had an adequate alibi.

Poirot interviews the various parties next. Philip Blake openly despised both Crale and Greer, although he appears to have liked Warren. His brother Meredith asserts that he had admired both women and had at one time considered proposing to Crale before her marriage. Both men agree to write down detailed accounts as far as they can remember and Meredith shows Poirot the murder scene – although the property has changed owners and is much changed.

Greer surprises him. She has been married for a third time and is wealthy, but she appears to have no interest in life. She clearly hates Crale and was in love with her husband, however, so she agrees to also provide an account. Williams favored Crale over her husband, but thought that both of them tended to ignore their daughter. She also insists that she has secret information that proves Crale poisoned her husband. Warren refuses to believe that her sister administered the poison and tells Poirot that she thinks Crale may have been involved with Philip Blake.

The accounts written by the Blake brothers add a few details but nothing startling or contradictory. Greer provides a good deal of additional information about her own personality but nothing factually new and relevant. Williams reveals that she saw Crale pressing her dead husband's fingers to the beer bottle and that this is why she is convinced of her guilt. But there was no poison in the bottle at any time, and if anything this actually supports the fact that she was ignorant and possibly covering up for another person. Warren's statement is vague – she does not remember much of what happened that day. Meredith Blake proposed marriage to Greer but was turned down.

The solution is fairly obvious from some of the details. The dead man was suffering symptoms before his wife brought him beer. She was covering up for Warren under the assumption that Warren had poisoned the beer, which was not true. A few other statements seem out of place. He had actually been about to send Greer away and she overheard him talking about it, so she administered the poison. But this had resulted in an oppressive sense of guilt that had bothered her ever since.

The Moving Finger (1942) features Miss Marple. The narrator is Jerry Burton, who is convalescing with his sister Joanna in a small village after an accident. The two of them have rented a house for a few months from Emily Barton, an elderly spinster. In short order they have met several of the local people including Dr. Owen Griffith, a lawyer named Richard Symmington, and a wealthy bachelor named Pye.

Then they receive an anonymous letter charging that they are not brother and sister but secret lovers. Griffith tells them that the letters have been troubling the local people for a long time. Their daily help quits after receiving a letter accusing her of sleeping with Jerry.

Megan Hunter is a young woman, stepdaughter of Symmington, and she appears to be quite naïve. She confides to Jerry that her family does not like her, nor does anyone else in the village. She is quite vehement on the subject, which suggests that she might have written the anonymous letters. Aimee Griffith, the doctor's sister, does not approve of Hunter and considers her lazy and disorganized. Elsie Holland is a governess working for the Symmingtons.

Caleb Calthrop is the local vicar. His wife Maud is quite upset about the letters – they have received three of them. The calm in the village is uneasy and it ends when Mrs. Symmington commits suicide after receiving a letter alleging that one of her sons was fathered by a lover. Her suicide suggests that it may have been a lucky guess.

The police get involved and are provided with a handful of the letters, including one to Symmington's secretary, Miss Ginch. A maid, Agnes Woddell, misses a social appointment and then fails to return to the Symmington house, where she works and lives. She is later found by Hunter, dead, and stuffed into a cabinet. The police assume that she knew something about the letters and was killed to keep her from talking. Holland appears to be the only named character who has yet to receive one of the letters.

The letters were all composed of words cut from a book that was obviously quite old. By chance, Jerry takes down one of the books from the library in the rented house and realizes that this is the source. Maud Calthrop decides that the police are getting nowhere so she calls on a friend, Jane Marple, who has not appeared in the first two thirds of the novel.

On impulse, Jerry arranges for Hunter to have her hair done and a new dress. The difference is quite striking. The following day he proposes to her but she turns him down. Joanna has been flirting with Dr. Griffith and has a traumatic day when by chance she is forced to help with a medical emergency.

Holland reports receiving her first letter. The police believe it was written by Aimee Griffith. They arrest her, but Marple insists it is a mistake. She talks to Hunter who pretends to have seen Symmington put poison in his wife's medicine and who demands blackmail money. The police are watching the house and arrest Symmington after he attempts to murder Hunter.

Aimee Griffith only wrote the last letter. She was in love with Symmington and wanted to scare off Holland. Hunter decides to accept Jerry's proposal after all. Joanna decides to marry Dr. Griffith.

Towards Zero (1944) has a brief prologue in which a lawyer ruminates about the fact that murders are often the culmination of years of small incidents. It switches to the hospital bed of Andrew MacWhirter, who recently tried to kill himself and resents the fact that he was saved. Superintendent Battle returns, in an unofficial capacity at first. His daughter Sylvia has confessed to a series of petty thefts at her boarding school. He quickly determines that she was not the thief but had been browbeaten into saying that she was.

Nevile Strange, a reasonably successful sportsman, lives with his second wife, Kay, but not entirely peacefully. She resents the fact that some of his friends and relations are unhappy that Nevile divorced his first wife, Audrey. They are expected to pay an extended visit every year to Lady Tressilian, widow of Nevile's one-time guardian. A substantial estate will come to her when Tressilian dies. Due to scheduling difficulties, the current year's visit will coincide with that of Audrey.

Tressilian and her companion, Mary Aldin, do not care for Kay and are fond of Audrey. They blame Nevile for poor judgment. Thomas Royde, recently back after years overseas, is courting Audrey. Ted Latimer, an admirer of Kay, has not entirely accepted that she is unavailable. Royde will be another guest and Latimer will be at a nearby hotel. Treves, the lawyer from the prologue, will also be at the hotel. And Battle is planning a short vacation with his nephew, Inspector James Leach.

The atmosphere at the house is tense. Kay is wildly jealous of Audrey. Nevile is embarrassed by her behavior and is feeling guilty about the way he treated Audrey. Treves is distressed when he finds out that the elevator at his hotel is out of order. He has to climb three flights of stairs and the strain causes a fatal heart attack. But the following day, the proprietress insists that the elevator was fine. The sign was a fake.

Nevile tells Kay that he wants a divorce so that he can try to get Audrey back. There is a loud scene. Someone drugs Tressilian's maid and then kills the older woman in her bed. The murder weapon was a golf club that has only Neville's prints on it. He and his wife inherit the bulk of the estate, but it is Audrey and not Kay who benefits. Bloodstained clothing is found concealed in his room. He is known to have had an argument with Tressilian shortly before she was murdered.

The police are skeptical because there is too much evidence and when the maid recovers consciousness, she tells them that she talked to Tressilian after Nevile left the house to take a ferry to the entertainment district. MacWhirter reappears briefly, no longer suicidal, and furious when he finds that the suit he brought to the cleaners has been swapped with another one. That night, he sees Audrey running toward the cliff and prevents her from killing herself.

Battle arrests Audrey, but is shaken somewhat when he learns that she was the one who was unfaithful to Nevile rather than the other way around, and she had no motive to hurt him in any way. He is reminded of the incident with his daughter earlier in the story and realizes that the point of the entire chain of events was to bring about Audrey's death. The mix-up with the suits at the cleaners was because Neville had swum back across the river in order to commit the murder and the suit had been stashed where it picked up stains from a dead fish. Neville is in fact quite insane. Audrey ends up marrying MacWhirter.

Death Comes As the End (1944) was an experiment. The novel is set in Egypt around 2000 BC. Renisenb is the daughter of a priest, Inhotep. She has three brothers, Yahmose, Ipy, and Sobek. Yahmose is married to Satipy and Sobek is married to Kait. Renisenb's husband died unexpected and she has returned to her home with her young son, Teti. The housekeeper is Henet, Hori is Imhotep's secretary, and Nofret is his mistress. Imhotep's mother Esa is still alive and living with him.

Satipy is an irritant. She spends a lot of effort trying to get Yahmose to assert himself. Sobek is also rebellious. The introduction of Nofret into the household causes additional tensions. Hori advises Imhotep to elevate one of his sons to a kind of priestly partnership in order to avoid misunderstandings when he is away. Henet appears to like Nofret, which puzzles the others. A young man named Kameni arrives in the area and Renisemb is attracted to him.

Kait and Nofret have a violent argument. Kameni assails Nofret for causing trouble and warns her that she is placing herself in danger. Satipy openly suggests that Nofret should be killed. Nofret is inevitably found dead, apparently having been killed by a fatal fall, although everyone suspects murder.

Imhotep questions everyone but there is no obvious culprit and it could have been an accident. There is increasing tension as time passes. Ultimately Yahmose is revealed to be the killer. He was seen by both Henet and Satify. Satify was clearly motivated to remain silent but Henet has a kind of blackmail in mind. The truth emerges at last.

Remembered Death (1945, aka *Sparkling Cyanide*) brings back Colonel Race. Irish Marle assumed that her sister Rosemary had committed suicide while depressed a year earlier, but Rosemary's husband – George Barton – thinks otherwise and is determined to prove it. Rosemary had become wealthy thanks to a bequest from a man who had loved, but failed to win, her mother. Barton is also reasonably well off.

Iris had been living with the Bartons and had chanced upon a distraught Rosemary who was in the process of writing a series of bequests. She died a few days later. Rosemary's money had gone to Iris rather than her husband. Following the death, Iris had remained at the house, now theoretically chaperoned by the docile Aunt Lucilla Drake.

Iris finds a letter written by her sister that clearly indicates that she was planning to leave her husband for another man, whom she calls Leopard. She suspects Leopard was one of two men. Stephen Farraday is an ambitious young politician and is unhappily married. The other was Anthony Browne, a mysterious young man who had not been seen since Rosemary's death.

Browne reappears, and now seems interested in Iris, who is flattered and increasingly infatuated. Barton clearly dislikes Browne and considers him a fortune hunter. At the same time, Aunt Lucilla is distracted by requests for money from her son, Victor, who is the black sheep of the family.

Ruth Lessing is Barton's secretary, competent and loyal, but she did not approve of Rosemary. Barton buys a country home, which is suspiciously close to that occupied by the Farradays. Barton finally confides to Iris that he has received anonymous letters claiming that Rosemary was murdered and, if that is true, it meant that one of the small group of people who had been at her birthday party was responsible. There are seven – Barton and Iris, the Farradays, Browne, Lessing, and Rosemary herself'

Lessing is in love with Barton. She acted as his agent in bribing Victor Drake to leave the country. Drake has also told Rosemary that Browne's real name was Morelli and that he had spent time in prison years earlier. She had taunted Browne about that and he had been very upset. Rosemary had also spent six months in an affair with Farraday. He is Leopard and he wants to break things off, unaware that his wife Sandra already knows about his infidelity. Barton was also aware of the affair, although he did not know the identity of the man involved.

So everyone present at the fatal birthday party had had a motive to want Rosemary dead. Barton decides to recreate the dinner party and everyone knows that he has an ulterior motive. The Farradays come to terms with the consequences of the affair. Browne asks Iris to run away and marry him but will not explain his reasons. Colonel Race, who had been invited to the fatal party but had been unable to attend, comes to visit Barton. He urges Barton to give up his plan to trap the killer.

The dinner party is held and, not surprisingly, Barton drinks poisoned wine and dies. The police are skeptical about a second suicide and now consider both deaths as murders. Race assists the police in interviewing the suspects. It appears that no one could have touched Barton's wine glass between the time he drank some of it and the time when they all returned from dancing. But somehow it was poisoned during that interim.

Browne reveals that he is actually a government agent and that he plans to marry Iris. He is the one who actually solves the case. Victor Drake was not in South America as everyone believed. He was in the restaurant when Barton was poisoned and he is the one who said no one approached the table. They had not met him and therefore would not have recognized him. Lessing had fallen in love with him. She was the one who poisoned Rosemary. The second victim was supposed to have been Iris, but a passing waiter placed her purse next to the wrong seat and when they returned from dancing, they all sat one position to the right of their former places without knowing it. If Iris died, her money would go to Lucilla, and effectively to Victor

The Hollow (1946) features Poirot. Lady Lucy Angkatell and her husband Henry are hosting a weekend party at their home. The guests include Midge Hardcastle, a cousin, John and Gerda Christow, Henrietta Savernake, a sculptor and also a cousin, David Angkatell, and Edward Angkatell, yet another cousin. Hercule Poirot is a neighbor and is coming to lunch one day. Edward had proposed to Henrietta but had been refused.

John Christow, a doctor, is romantically entangled with Savernake, who is clinical and often sarcastic. His wife Gerda is submissive and not very intelligent and he is often irritated by her for no discernible reason. Edward is still in love with Henrietta and knows about her relationship with Christow. Complicating matters further is a visit by a new neighbor, Veronic Cray. Cray had been engaged to Christow when they were both very young but he had broken it off because she was too assertive. Hardcastle is in love with Edward.

Christow goes off with Cray, but the experience makes him realize that he does not love her and does not have any interest in an affair. The following morning he goes to see her and tell her the truth. She is furious and vows vengeance, and a short time later someone shoots him.

Poirot arrives just as the other characters are all converging on the swimming pool. Christow says Henrietta's name and dies. Gerda is holding a revolver, which Savernake takes from her and "accidentally" drops it into the pool. The gun turns out to be a red herring. It is not the murder weapon. It is one of two guns which were stolen from Henry's collection, but it has not been fired. The real weapon is not found until much later when Poirot somehow concludes that it has been hidden in the hedge surrounding his own cottage.

One of the maids reveals that she saw Gudgeon, the butler, carrying a gun. Gudgeon tries to smooth things over but Lucy reveals that she had taken the gun out and was carrying it with her when the shooting occurred. It is not the murder weapon either. Edward proposes to Harcastle, who accepts, then breaks things off when she suspects Edward is still in love with Savernake. Edward tries to commit suicide and she saves him and decides he actually loves her after all. There is a good deal of Anthony Trollope in this novel.

The real killer is Gerda Christow, who believed incorrectly that her husband was still in love with Cray. She stole two guns and used one to shoot him, then concealed the other in a bush before the others arrived. There was no search at the time because she was seen to be holding what appeared to be the murder weapon. Savernake was initially taken in, but saw through the ruse and later moved the weapon to Poirot's hedge. She believes that the dying man's use of her name was to implore her to help Gerda.

Savernake realizes that the murder weapon had a holster, which must still be in Gerda's possession. She goes to warn her and Gerda tries to poison her protector. Poirot arrives in the nick of time and Gerda drinks the poison herself.

There Is a Tide (1946, aka *Taken at the Flood*) features Poirot. Gordon Cloade was killed in his home during an air raid. His wife Rosaleen was seriously injured but survived. Rosaleen had previously been married to Robert Underhay and remarried after receiving reports of his death. It appears, however, that he faked his demise and took up a new life under another name, Enoch Arden. The rumor reaches Jeremy Cloade, the dead man's brother, and that possibility affects the status of the family fortune.

Two years later Poirot is visited by Katharine, the wife of Lionel

Cloade, Gordon's younger brother. She wants him to find Underhay, supposedly to please Rosaleen, but Poirot is suspicious of her motives and turns her down. A few days later he sees a new story about the death of Enoch Arden. The story then reverts in time to Arden's arrival in England.

Lynn Marchmont has recently returned to civilian life and plans to marry Rowley Cloade. Rowley was running a farm with a partner, Johnnie Vavasour, who was killed in the war and who has never been replaced. Like all of the Cloades, he had expected financial support from Gordon, who had died intestate so that all of his money went to Rosaleen. Lionel is a doctor and Jeremy is a lawyer who had had a son, Antony, who died in the war. Jeremy's wife is Frances. Lynn's mother Adela was Gordon's sister and her father is dead. Rosaleen has a brother, David Hunter.

Jeremy has unwisely taken liberties with some of the funds entrusted to him and is facing financial ruin and even prison. Adela is so overwhelmed with expenses that she may lose her house. Rosaleen has access to all of the estate's earnings, but the principal is untouchable and will pass to Gordon's family upon her death. She is thoroughly under the thumb of her brother.

Hunter is attracted to Marchmont, but continues to be rude to everyone else in the family. Adela convinces Rosaleen to write her a check to cover her overdrawn bank account while Hunter is absent. Lionel and Katharine have independently requested substantial loans. Rosaleen, who is kindly but not very bright, makes a positive impression on Rowley.

A stranger comes to the village and registers at a local inn under the name Enoch Arden. Hunter visits him in his room and Arden blackmails him, threatening to reveal that Underhay is still alive, which would invalidate Rosaleen's marriage and take away her inheritance. Hunter agrees to pay him off. Unknown to either man, the manager of the inn, Beatrice Lippincott, has overheard their conversation from the adjacent room. Lippincott writes to Rowley and subsequently relates to him the entire conversation.

Lynn realizes that she does not want to marry Rowley and grows increasingly fascinated with Hunter. He calls her from London and indicates that he is planning to leave the country. The following morning, Arden is found murdered in his room. Rowley admits having visited Arden the night before. Roseleen is taken to see the body but insists that she does not recognize the man. But another man, Major Porter, who knew Underhay, confirms that he and Arden are the same man.

The inquest returns a charge of murder against Hunter. It appears that he is innocent, however, because Rowley spoke to Arden at nine o'clock and Lynn saw him running to catch a train ten minutes later. This latter point is not raised at the inquest and the alibi is in fact not very strong.

Lionel was the first doctor to examine the body, Ostensibly Arden was battered to death by a pair of fire tongs found next to the body, but he would have expected the weapon to have a different shape. Rowley is oddly distressed when he learns that Poirot plans to stay in the village for a few more days. By chance Poirot runs into an unpleasant woman who saw a younger one go in and out of the room where Arden died – at about ten o'clock.

Poirot goes to see Porter and finds that he has been shot to death, apparently a suicide. Frances asks to see Poirot and confesses that she arranged for Arden's appearance – he was actually her cousin Charles – and the blackmail scheme. But she insists that she had never met Porter and that his testimony had stunned her. Poirot believes that Porter killed himself because of shame about having put an innocent man in danger of execution.

Rowley realized that Arden was a fake and that his family was responsible. He is subject to sudden rages and when he confronted Arden, he struck him. Arden fell against the fireplace and was killed. He then used the tongs to make it appear that he was assaulted. It is not clear why he did this. He also bribed Porter into lying about the man's identity. Porter did in fact kill himself in remorse, but Rowley arrived and removed the suicide note.

Hunter had intended to pay the blackmail. He arrived to find the man dead. Knowing that he was likely to be the chief suspect, he went back to the house, dressed up as a woman, and made certain that he was seen after ten o'clock. But Hunter killed Rosaleen, who was not his sister. He was at Gordon's house when the bomb fell and he identified one of the servants as Rosaleen so that he could still enjoy the money she would inherit.

Lynn decides to marry Rowley after all, even though he would have killed her in a rage if Poirot had not intervened. The police are apparently uninterested in arresting him even though he committed manslaughter, fraud, bribery, mutilated a dead body, kept silent while another man was arrested for murder, lied to the police, etc. Both of these decisions are reprehensible and difficult to believe.

Crooked House (1949) is a standalone novel narrated by Charles Hayward, who has fallen in love with Sophia Leonides. They meet in Egypt and since Hayward will not be returning to England for two years, they postpone their engagement. Sophia's father is Philip and her mother is Magda, an actress. Her siblings are Eustace and Josephine. Her grandfather, Aristide, is very rich and has remarried a much younger woman, Brenda. Aristide's other son is Roger, whose wife is Clemency.

On the day Hayward returns to England he reads Aristide's obituary. When he meets Sophia, she tells him that she – and probably the police – suspect it was murder. Hayward's father works at Scotland Yard and he introduces him to Chief Inspector Taverner, who is in charge of the case. The entire family lives together – partly because of the recently concluded war – along with Edith de Haviland, sister of Aristide's first wife, who is now deceased.

Aristide was poisoned. The police suspect the wife, Brenda, who is reportedly quite friendly with Laurence Brown, who works as a tutor. The poison was probably substituted for the dead man's insulin. De Haviland did not like Aristide and the rest of the family disliked Brenda. Taverner, however, has some doubts about Brenda's guilt, because it looks like she might have been framed.

Because Hayward has previously worked with the police and because of his insider relationship, he is sent to help Taverner with the investigation. He tells Sophia everything up front and she is actually pleased that he is involved. All of the family members had been made financially independent years earlier, and although they would now inherit an even greater sum, there is no reason to believe that money was the motive.

Josephine is a difficult, secretive, and inquisitive child. She tells Haycraft that her parents lost most of their money producing a play that failed, and that Roger and Clemency were about to run off to Europe quietly because he had embezzled some money. She also claims to have read love letters between Brenda and Brown.

The will is discovered, but despite the fact that Aristide had read it to his assembled family and signed it, the document bears no signatures at all. There are multiple legal questions but it appears that Brenda would benefit most from reversion to an earlier will. The police investigate Roger's company and it is indeed on the verge of failure, although apparently through mismanagement rather than embezzlement. But Roger provides proof that Aristide had decided to provide the funds to keep the company afloat, which means that his death was not to their advantage.

Hayward is concerned that Josephine might be in danger given her fondness for spying out secrets. Magda suddenly decides that she should be sent away to school in Switzerland. Shortly after that she is struck on the head and falls into a coma. It was a booby trap specifically designed for her. Josephine kept a notebook which is not at the scene, and her bedroom has been violently searched. Fortunately she recovers.

A new will turns up, one that Aristide created secretly. Other than a settlement for Brenda, his entire fortune is left to Sophia. Hayward finds the love letters which Josephine had stolen from Brown. Sophia promptly fires Brown, who is then arrested, along with Brenda, for the murder. Sophia tells Hayward that she knew about the surprise will because Aristide had told her about it.

One of the servants drinks some cocoa that had been meant for Josephine and dies, poisoned. De Haviland announces that she is taking Josephine away from the house for a few hours for her safety, but instead she drives over the edge of a quarry, killing them both. She left behind a letter revealing that she was not likely to live much longer and confessing to the murder of Aristide and the servant. But she also left behind Josephine's notebook. It was Josephine who had poisoned her grandfather and the servant, and faked the booby track accident – almost killing herself in the process.

A Murder Is Announced (1950) is a Jane Marple novel. Mrs. Swettenham is one of the first to notice a formal announcement of a murder, posted in the personal column, and scheduled to happen that very day at the house presided over by Letitia Blacklock. She and her son Edmund believe that it is a variant of a murder game and decide to attend.

Archie and Laura Easterbrook come to the same conclusion, as do Amy Murgatroyd and Hinchcliffe, who share a cottage, as well as Reverend Julian and Diana Harmon. The Blacklock residence is also home to Patrick and Julia Simmons, who are younger cousins, Dora Bunner who is old friend with no money of her own, a laborer –

Philippa Haymes, and an emotional cook named Mitzi.

All of the various characters appear and at the precise moment predicted, the lights go out. A man opens the front door and someone fires a handgun several times. One shot grazes Blacklock slightly. The intruder then appears to have shot himself. When the lights are back on, some of those present recognize him as Rudi Scherz, who worked as a clerk at a hotel. There were suspicions that he might have been responsible for some petty theft, but no real evidence was ever found.

Blacklock tells the police that Scherz had approached her a few days earlier looking for money on a flimsy excuse and that she had refused. The interviews with the witnesses provide nothing of particular interest. Marple is staying at the hotel where Scherz had worked and she had just caught a check that he had altered. But she is convinced he would never have tried an armed robbery. It was too daring. She believes he was hired to participate in a joke, that he had never carried a gun and that someone else had fired the shots, then killed the accomplice. And she is reasonably sure that it was Blacklock who was supposed to die.

Mitzi claims that Haymes had been secretly meeting an unidentified man. Haymes denies the story but seems nervous. The police discover that a door in the house that has supposedly been locked for years has been freshly oiled and opens soundlessly. That means that anyone in the house at the time of the shooting could have quietly gotten behind Scherz.

Blacklock was once secretary to a very rich man. When he died, he left his estate in trust for his wife, but it passes to Blacklock when the wife dies. If she dies before the wife – who is reportedly in her deathbed – the money goes to a niece and nephew, Philip and Emma. They obviously have a great deal to gain if Blacklock dies soon.

Edmund Swettenham is unsuccessfully courting Haymes. Easterbrook notices that his handgun has disappeared from his study. Hinchcliffe realizes that the door where the intruder stood does not stay open and wonders how he managed the door, the flashlight, and the handgun. It disappeared after the shooting occurred. Marple learns that Blacklock had never met her two cousins before they came to live with her. Bunner reveals to Marple that she saw Patrick with an oil can shortly before the incident.

Blacklock tells Haymes that she is to be her main beneficiary under a new will, and she does so where Julia can hear her. Julia and Haymes have harsh words. Bunner takes some of Blacklock's aspirin and dies in her bed. The police suspect Sonia Goedler, sister of Blacklock's wealthy former employer, and discover that all of the photographs in which she appears have been removed from Blacklock's photo albums. She could be Hinchcliffe or Murgatroyd or Mrs. Swettenham.

Haymes' husband Harry was supposedly killed in the war, but he was actually a deserter. She denies having seen him since then. She is lying – she met with him secretly and gave him some money. But he was killed in an accident that occurred a few days before the shooting incident. Hinchcliffe has been investigating on his own and has figured out almost as much as have the police. Murgatroyd realizes that one of the women was not present in the room when the shooting took place, but before she can pass on the information, someone strangles her.

Blacklock receives a letter from the real Julia. Although Patrick is genuine, the woman posing as Julia admits that she is really Emma. Haymes then announces that she is Pip, Emma's sister. They had been separated while still toddlers and did not recognize each other.

Other revelations follow. Mitzi claims to have seen Blacklock do the shooting. Blacklock tries to murder her but is discovered in the act. She is actually Letitia's sister Charlotte, believed long dead. It was really Letitia who had died of influenza, but Charlotte adopted her identity. She had told the truth to Bunner, who happily agreed to go along with the impersonation.

They Came to Baghdad (1951) concerns espionage. Two British agents – Crosbie and Dakin – rather cryptically discuss the upcoming, clandestine visit of a major head of state to Baghdad. They also allude to an agent named Carmichael, who has discovered something extraordinary, and is supposedly en route with the proof. Unknown parties are determined to ensure that he does not arrive alive. The agents also mention Anna Scheele, who is the trusted secretary of Otto Morgenthal, an international banker.

The protagonist is Victoria Jones, a young woman whose penchant for silliness and imaginative stories has just cost her a job as a typist. She meets a young man in the park named Edward who tells her he is leaving for Baghdad with his employer, who owns a chain of bookshops, but that he thinks there is something odd going on. She feels an immediate connection to Edward and decides to go after him.

Scheele is followed during her visit to London. She is aware of it but gives no sign that she notices. Jones is delighted to hear that a Mrs. Clipp has broken her arm and needs someone to accompany her to Baghdad. Her forged letters of recommendation gain her the job. Carmichael escapes an assassination attempt and realizes that there has to be an informer within his own organization.

Richard Baker is in Baghdad to join an archaeological expedition which is coincidentally led by a man named Jones. He is an old friend of Carmichael, who tries to enter the British consulate disguised as an Arab. The two recognize each other just before an Englishman tries to shoot Carmichael. Carmichael passes to Baker an apparently innocuous note – probably a code. Baker recognizes its significance and conceals it, then creates an alternate version, which is stolen from him within hours.

Victoria flies to Cairo on the same plane as Sir Rupert Crofton Lee, a renowned world traveler. Sir Rupert is involved in the preparations for the mysterious meeting. He decides to stay at the Tio Hotel, which is where Victoria has just checked in. Victoria's money is running very low. The hotel is managed by Marcus Tio. Victoria has to find Edward, and all that she knows is that he is working for a Dr. Rathbone. She tracks down Rathbone but Edward is away and will not return for several days. Victoria suspects that Rathbone is a fraud. She meets Dakin at the hotel.

Carmichael asks Victoria to hide him in her room. She successfully bluffs the police but Carmichael dies of a stab wound, speaking only three words: Lucifer, Basrah, and LeFarge. Dakin enters the room and she tells him what she little she knows. He helps dispose of the body and offers to hire Dakin, warning her that it is dangerous. He also provides a rather murky overview of international politics. Then, absurdly, he tells Victoria that he is sending her to Basrah to find the information Carmichael was carrying – but without any guidance about whom to see, what to look for, or how to get by. He – and the author – claim that beginner's luck is important.

Victoria finally finds Edward, whose last name is Goring. Dakin has mentioned Scheele in passing and Edward has heard her name.

The usual adventures follow. She is briefly kidnapped, works for a while under the façade of being the niece of an archaeologist, and she stumbles toward the solution. Edward is actually the chief villain, which makes his encounter in the park a retrospectively glaring anomaly. Victoria acquires the information to safeguard the conference, in conjunction with Baker, who will presumably be her romantic interest going forward. A thoroughly implausible novel.

Mrs. McGinty's Dead (1952) brings back Poirot. An old acquaintance asks him to look into a murder case. The elderly Mrs. McGinty was bludgeoned to death and robbed. She lived alone except for a lodger, James Bentley, who was broke. The money was found hidden nearby, there was blood on some of Bentley's clothing, and other evidence suggested his guilt and he was convicted. But the acquaintance, a police officer, has doubts and does not want to see an innocent man hanged.

Poirot rents a room at the decidedly inferior lodgings run by John and Maureen Summerhouse. McGinty had done cleaning for them, among others. Bessie Burch, McGinty's niece, was not close to her aunt. Her husband Joe seems slightly uneasy around Poirot, who is pretending to know more than he actually does in order to provoke some kind of response.

The money was so poorly hidden that it was clearly meant to be found. The murder weapon has never been identified. The only possible clue he discovers initially is that McGinty bought a bottle of ink two days before the murder, presumably in order to write a letter. Among the dead woman's belongings is a news clipping of a story about four women who probably changed their names and vanished. Each was connected to a violent death.

An inquiry suggests that McGinty wrote to the newspaper, referring to a photograph related to the story and asking for a reward. The paper had not been interested. Poirot decides to talk to McGinty's various customers. Dr. Rendell seems affable, but his wife Shelagh is clearly apprehensive. Mrs. Weatherby is a hypochondriac. Her adult daughter is Deirdre Henderson. The older woman is quite upset when Poirot suggests that Bentley is innocent. Roger Wetherby is curt and it is obvious that he and his stepdaughter dislike one another.

Laura Upward and her son Robin are to be his next interview, but before he arrives he encounters Ariadne Oliver, who has appeared once before, a mystery writer with an abrasive personality. Robin is supposed to be dramatizing one of her books. Robin seems mildly nervous when Poirot is introduced. Guy and Eve Carpenter pretend not to have known McGinty, which is clearly a lie.

Someone attempts to push Poirot in front of a train. He shows pictures of the four mystery women to the others at a get together, and Laura Upward remarks that one of them looks vaguely familiar. Poirot privately cautions her to be careful. Shelagh Rendell approaches Poirot and insists that he is really investigating something else entirely, alludes to anonymous letters, and then rushes off. Poirot spots a tool in the Summerhouse lodge which he believes was the murder weapon. Maureen tells him that they got it from the Wetherbys.

The Weatherbys have just lost their maid and Poirot has met Maude Williams, who wants to help Bentley. She agrees to accept a job as cook and housekeeper. That night, Laura Upward is murdered in her home. It appears that Upward invited several women to her house on the night and one of them killed her. A photograph is planted to implicate the Summerhouses, but Poirot is not fooled.

Robin Upward was adopted. His real mother was one of the mystery women, who was almost certainly a murderer. McGinty saw the picture he kept of her and he killed her to protect his secret. This revelation is somewhat telegraphed because we are twice told that when he left Laura Upward alone to go to the theater on the night when she was killed, he briefly returned to speak to her. The incident with the train may have been an accident after all.

The other secrets are unconnected. Henderson actually has all the money in her family and her stepfather and mother are dependent upon her. Eve Carpenter was a dance hall girl in her youth and does not want that revealed publicly. Dr. Rendell's first wife died under mysterious circumstances and his present wife is worried that the investigation will be reopened.

Murder with Mirrors (1952, aka *They Do It With Mirrors*) is a Jane Marple novel. As a young woman, Marple had been close to a pair of sisters whom she now sees only at great intervals. It has been more than twenty years since she had last seen Carrie Louise Serrocold. The sister has lunch with Marple and tells her that she visited Carrie – who with her husband runs a large educational and psychological center for juvenile delinquents – and indicates that she is worried that something is seriously wrong.

Marple goes to visit by means of a subterfuge and quickly meets all of the significant characters. Mildred Strete is Carrie's only daughter, by her first husband, and is widowed. Gina Hudd is the daughter of Pippa, who was adopted before Mildred was born, but who died when Gina was an infant. She was raised by Carrie Louise and is married to a sullen young man named Wally. Her second husband has also died and his two sons, Stephen and Alex Restarick, were also raised in part by Carrie Louise. Christian Gulbrandsen was the son of her first husband, who is also dead.

Juliet Bellever is the housekeeper. Lewis Serrocold is the current husband and an avowed fanatic about reforming young men who have committed petty crimes. Edgar Lawson is one of his subjects, a particularly irritating person who is both arrogant and whiny. Dr. Maverick is head of the psychiatric staff.

Almost immediately, Marple observes that Stephen Restarick is in love with Gina Hudd and that Wally Hudd does not enjoy living at the sprawling mansion/educational center. Carrie Louise has reservations about their marriage. Gina is not enthralled with Lewis' obsession and Lawson dislikes her.

Gulbrandsen has a brief conference with Lewis, parts of which Marple overhears. He has reason to believe that someone has been slowly poisoning Carrie Louise. Her husband suggests that she discontinue her medicine and a subsequent analysis proves that it contains arsenic.

Someone has convinced Lawson that Lewis is his father and leads an imaginary plot against him. He uses Wally's gun to threaten Lewis in his locked office while the others try to decide what to do. Lawson fires two shots but fails to hit Lewis, who then turns him over to Dr. Maverick. In the meanwhile, however, someone has fatally shot Gulbrandsen in his room. Lewis tells the police about Gulbrandsen's suspicions.

Carrie Louise's will is complex. The larger of two fortunes would be split between Gina and Mildred. There is a second but still substantial fortune that would largely benefit the Restarick brothers, and Bellever. She has already signed over a substantial amount to Lewis and Marple is convinced that he is devoted to his wife. Carrie Louise tells Marple that Gina's grandmother was hanged for poisoning her husband with arsenic.

The murder weapon is found hidden in the piano stool where Stephen had been sitting. A box of chocolates arrives, ostensibly from Alex, but he did not send them. He suggests to Gina that she leave Wally and marry him. One of the delinquents, Ernie Gregg, lets slip that he sneaks out of the confined area at night and knows something about the murder. Subsequent events prove that this is not possible. The Hudds quarrel and both claim to want a divorce.

Gregg disappears. Evidence suggests that he was lying about being able to get around the locked gates. Then he is found dead, along with Alex. Marple contemplates magic tricks and then realizes what really happened. Carrie Louise was not being poisoned after all. That was not what Gulbrandsen was concerned about. There had been embezzlement from the trust fund, which certainly had to have been done by Lewis. He had enlisted Lawson's help in creating the illusion that he was locked in his office while he committed the murder.

The conclusion actually occurs off stage. Lawson panics and drowns in the lake. Lewis dies as well, while trying to save Lawson. The Hudds become reconciled and go back to America. Lawson was in fact Lewis' illegitimate son.

Funerals Are Fatal (1953, aka *After the Funeral*) features Poirot. Richard Abernethie was the strongest character of six siblings, but the opening scene is the reception following his funeral. The family is introduced through the eyes of Richard's lawyer, Entwhistle. Helen is the widow of his brother Leo, and Richard was very fond of her. Timothy Abernethie was Richard's brother. He is an invalid and his wife is named Maude.

George Crossfield is the son of Richard's sister Laura. She and her husband are both dead. George has no money and works for a disreputable firm. Rosamund is a niece whose parents have both died. She is married to Michael Shane. The other niece is Susan, who is married to Gregory Banks. Cora Lansquenet was Richard's youngest sibling and is also a widow. Richard had intensely disliked her husband.

Richard had planned to leave everything to his son Mortimer, but the son had died of natural causes a few months earlier. A new will divides the bulk evenly into six parts – Timothy, Susan, Cora, George, Helen, and Rosamund. Helen and Cora's bequests are in the form of a trust. Upon their deaths, the balance goes to the four full recipients. Richard died rather suddenly and Cora rather blatantly assumes that they all know that it was murder.

The trouble is smoothed over, but shortly after returning to her home, Cora is murdered by what appears to have been a burglar, although the police think otherwise. Entwhistle is troubled and interviews the woman who lived with Cora, an older woman named Gilchrist. She tells him that Richard had visited a few weeks earlier, unannounced, and had told Cora that someone was poisoning him. Not surprisingly, none of the others has an alibi for the time of the murder.

Entwhistle visits each member of the family – and his observation is that Timothy is not an invalid despite his claims – and he is sufficiently troubled to consult his friend, Hercule Poirot. Susan goes to settle up Cora's estate and is approached by Alexander Guthrie, who claims to be an old friend of Cora. A fancy cake is delivered to Cora's companion, but she does not recognize the name of the sender. Gilchrist eats the cake and is hospitalized with arsenic poisoning.

Poirot uses a detective agency to check the alibis. George lied about being at the racetrack. Michael lied about meeting a theater producer. Instead he rented a car and put just enough mileage on it for a trip to Cora's cottage and back. Susan and her husband were not together for most of the day despite claiming otherwise. Helen had gone shopping alone. Timothy had been home alone. Maude had been marooned because of car trouble, but could have taken a train and committed the murder. Susan arranges to have Gilchrist work temporarily for Timothy and Maude.

Christie telegraphs a clue. There have been three separate references about nuns going door to door, including the homes of both Richard and Cora. A Pocketbook paperback edition makes this even more obvious by putting a nun on the cover. Banks at one point prior to his marriage had a nervous breakdown. Poirot uses a subterfuge to gather all of the concerned parties for a few days stay at Richard's mansion, which is about to be sold. Gilchrist mentions that a nun came to Timothy's house and suspects she was the same woman. She professes to be too frightened to remain alone and accompanies them.

Rosamund has known all along who Poirot is and she announces that he is a detective to the group as a whole. Poirot arranges to have something taken from Gilchrist's room, which we later discover is an original Vermeer painting which Cora had purchased for almost nothing. Helen is assaulted when she tries to call Entwhistle, having realized what struck her as wrong at the funeral. She is concussed but recovers.

Poirot reveals the truth. Richard was not murdered. He died of natural causes. Gilchrist eavesdropped on his conversation with Cora, which had nothing to do with poisoning. She then drugged Cora and impersonated her at the funeral so that she could drop her bombshell. Her real intent was to murder Cora and steal the painting. Helen realized that Gilchrist had disguised herself in a mirror, which was a reversed image of the real Cora. Gilchrist is arrested but is clearly insane.

A Pocket Full of Rye (1953) begins with Rex Fortescue drinking tea in his office and suddenly falling violently ill, dying a short time later. The doctors determine that it was a slow acting poison which he probably ingested at breakfast, not in the tea. Fortescue was married to Adele, his second wife, who was much younger. He had three children by his first wife. Lancelot and his wife Pat live out of the country and are estranged from the family. Percival is a partner in the firm. His wife is Jennifer. Elaine is the daughter, who has not married.

The immediate oddity is that Fortescue had a handful of rye grains in his coat pocket. The police had been interested in him in the past because some of his business transactions came close to breaking the law. The family is all away from home when the police arrive, so they talk to the housekeeper, Mary Dove, who is very competent, very forthright, and provides devastatingly critical portraits of all the family members except Elaine. The household also includes Miss Ramsbottom, sister of Rex's first wife. Adele appears to be having an affair with Vivian Dubois.

Lance arrives at the house but Pat stays temporarily in London. One of the maids, Gladys, appears to know more than she is saying. Gladys has a boyfriend whom no one has met. She disappears shortly before his arrival. Adele drinks tea with cyanide in it and Gladys is found strangled in the yard, where she was working on the clothesline. Someone placed a clothes pin on her nose. Marple realizes that the rye, the clothesline, the damaged nose, and the poisoned mistress of the house are all elements of the rhyme from which the title is derived. She immediately asks about blackbirds and discovers that someone had introduced them to a pie in the kitchen some months earlier.

One of Rex's business projects had been a supposed gold mine in Africa, the Blackbird. He and another man had been partners and the partner had reportedly died in the jungle. His widow, who had two children, was named MacKenzie and was reportedly in a mental institution. She had vowed vengeance against Rex, whom she believed had murdered her husband.

Gerald Wright arrives. He is informally engaged to Elaine, is clearly a fortune hunter, and he admits having gone for a walk from his hotel about the time of the two recent murders. Dubois also admits having approached the house in search of love letters he had written to Adele. Although he insists that he did not enter, there is evidence to the contrary.

Adele's will leaves everything to Dubois, but her large legacy from Rex will not be included because the will states that she must survive her husband by at least a month. The police interview MacKenzie, who admits she demanded that her children avenge their father. But her son died in the war and she has apparently disowned her daughter for not remaining loyal.

Marple provides the solution, although some of it was inspiration rather than logic. Gladys' boyfriend was Lance – he had been in the country to see his father but had been rebuffed. The reconciliation is completely fabricated. Lance convinced Gladys to substitute some poisoned marmalade which he claimed contained a truth serum. He then had to kill her before he could turn up as Lance. It was not difficult for him to slip some cyanide into Adele's tea cup because she was sitting alone at the time. Adele's legacy would have forced the company into bankruptcy, and he did not want that to happen.

Lance wanted to take the Blackbird mine as part of his share of the company, apparently because it was found to contain uranium rather than gold. Pat knew nothing about any of this. Jennifer is MacKenzie's daughter and she put the blackbirds in the pie as a mean spirited prank, but she had no interest in avenging her father. Dove, however, is both a blackmailer and the scout for a team of burglars. Nothing can be proven but she will be watched closely in the future.

So Many Steps to Death (1955, aka *Destination Unknown*) is another attempt at an espionage thriller. It is not a success. The premise is that brilliant scientists are being abducted by a foreign power, identity unknown, which has distressed the governments of various Western nations. When Tom Betterton disappears, the alarms are particularly strident. His wife has no explanation when the authorities interrogate her.

Hilary Craven has come to France in an effort to put her unhappy past behind her, but discovers that she is just as bored and morose as ever. She is contemplating suicide when she runs into an agent named Jessop, who has a better use for her. Betterton's wife has died by accident and he wants Craven to impersonate her. They hope that she will be snatched by whoever has her husband and they plan to watch her closely.

Her adventures are low key and eventually take her to Morocco. There is a secret, multi-national gang run by a very rich man who wants power to match his money. He is behind the plot, which involves both volunteers and involuntary recruits. He is thwarted by the end of the novel, but is still free to pursue his efforts in other areas. Jessop would return in a later novel.

Hickory Dickory Dock (1955, aka *Hickory Dickory Death*) is a Poirot novel. His secretary, Miss Lemon, is preoccupied because of problems related to her sister, a widow named Hubbard. Hubbard took a job as matron at a student Hostel run by Mrs. Nicoletis. Although she mostly enjoys her job, she has been lately disturbed by a series of petty crimes. The thefts are odd in that most of the items are worth very little and some of them have subsequently turned up, usually having been destroyed.

The only valuable item is a diamond ring, stolen from Patricia Lane and returned by being placed in a bowl of soup served to Valerie Hobhouse. Both of them are students. Poirot observes that it was the only object whose loss might result in a call to the police, and that might be why it was promptly returned. Len Bateson, a medical student, lost a stethoscope. The other items have included a book, a lipstick, a box of chocolates, light bulbs, etc. Colin McNabb lost a pair of pants and Sally Finch lost one shoe.

The incidents continue. Someone pours ink over the notebooks of Elizabeth Johnston. The ink apparently belonged to another student, Nigel Chapman. Following Poirot's hunch, Hubbard finds the missing shoe at a nearby lost and found. Celia Austin is a nonstudent, a hospital worker who stays at the hostel and who is in love with McNabb.

Poirot arranges to give a small talk at the hostel so that he can meet the students. His ruse is exposed almost immediately. McNabb corners him later with a detailed psychological profile that points to Austin, and she in fact confesses almost immediately afterward. But she denies taking the stethoscope or pouring ink on the notebooks. Then she denies responsibility for a few more of the minor items.

Poirot tells Hubbard that Celia undoubtedly did some minor pilfering, but primarily to attract McNabb's attention. This is not entirely convincing but does not affect the main plot. Some of the incidents seem to him to be more disturbing. Lane appears to be in love with Chapman.

McNabb and Austin announce that they are going to be married, but the following morning she is found dead in bed, a drug overdose, and there is an ambiguous suicide note. The note is almost immediately revealed to be bogus, which means it was murder. Most of the students, including Jean Tomlinson, could have visited Austin at her hospital job and taken the poison from the unlocked cabinet.

Chapman admits to having stolen some morphia from the hospital, in order to win a bet, by stealing the stethoscope and pretending to be a doctor. Finch tells the police that she thinks there is something peculiar about Nicoletis. She also saw Austin leave the house after she had supposedly gone to bed on the night she died. Johnston believes that Austin had figured out who destroyed her notebooks and that it had something to do with a forged passport. Poirot also learns of a student who had been sought by the police but whom Nicoletis had already evicted.

Nicoletis is clearly very frightened. She meets someone she knows in a bar and something is placed in her drink. Poirot has purchased a rucksack like the one that was slashed to pieces at the hostel and he cuts his up as an experiment. Hobhouse admits to Poirot that she talked Austin into the supposed kleptomania in order to attract McNabb's attention. The ring that was returned had been modified – the valuable diamond replaced by a cheaper gem. Poirot accuses her of having made the substitution.

Poirot believes that the rucksacks are used to trick unsuspecting students into smuggling drugs or gems from the continent into England. The coincidental presence of a police officer on an unrelated matter panicked someone into destroying the one in the hostel – and that was prior to the other incidents. Poirot also suspects that Nicoletis is involved – she manages several similar establishments – but she cannot be questioned because she dies, poisoned.

There are some brief, sometimes confusing scenes in which we discover that Chapman changed his name and thus has a contradictory passport, that the stolen morphine was removed by Pat Lane because she thought it was dangerous, only to have it stolen from her room, and that Lane thinks she has something out. Naturally before she can reveal what she knows, she is murdered.

Poirot reveals the truth. Hobhouse and Chapman are behind the smuggling operation and Chapman committed all three murders. Years earlier, he had poisoned his mother. Nikoletis was Hobhouse's mother. She did not condone the murders but was unable to find a way out of the trap she had built for herself.

Dead Man's Folly (1956) was a reworking of an earlier manuscript that was later published in its original form as *Hercule Poirot and the Greenshore Folly* in 2014. Ariadne Oliver calls Poirot and practically demands that he come to see her in a remote village on the next train. It is clear to him that she is not specific because she fears being overheard, so he does as he has been asked.

Oliver has been hired to arrange a murder party at the sprawling mansion owned by Sir George Stubbs and his wife Hattie. It is to be part of a large charitable lawn party open to the public. Hattie is rather dull witted. Although she had worked out all of the details, she has subtly been influenced to alter some of them and she suspects that she is being manipulated for a purpose. But she cannot see what the purpose is, or who is responsible.

The other participants include Michael Weyman, an architect hired to design a tennis pavilion. There is already a folly, a kind of stone temple. The housekeeper is Amanda Brewis. Alec and Peggy Legge are neighbors. Jim Warburton works as agent for another neighbor, the Mastertons, Wilfred and Connie. The elderly Amy Folliat lives in a cottage on the property. Her late husband once owned the mansion. A young girl, Marlene Tucker, has been recruited to play the victim, whose body will be inside the boat house.

Poirot's early observations are not obviously significant. Alec

Legge is a rather rabid idealist who recently had a nervous breakdown. Brewis despises Hattie Stubbs but Folliat considers her a harmless child. Weyman may be flirting with Hattie. A letter arrives announcing that Etienne de Sousa, Hattie's cousin, is about to arrive on his yacht. She tells Poirot that her cousin is a bad person and she would prefer that he not come.

The cousin arrives. Hattie has disappeared and no one knows where she is. Oliver and Poirot go to the boat house to check on Tucker and find her strangled. The police begin to search for Hattie. Brewis, who is in love with Sir George, tells Poirot that Weyman is interested in Peggy Legge, whom he knew before she married Alec.

Poirot knows that Peggy is lying about her whereabouts at the time of the murder. She was actually in the folly. He also discovers that Alec has been secretly meeting a young man from the nearby youth hostel and that he is unhappy about it. Hattie's hat is found in the river. If she was thrown into the water, she might have been swept out to sea.

Two weeks pass with no progress. Poirot has returned to London. Then an elderly man who spends his time on the river bank is found drowned. It looks like an accidental death but clearly he saw something he should not have. Peggy Legge leaves her husband to be with Weyman. Poirot has figured out the truth.

Folliat's two sons were both supposedly killed in the war, but one actually deserted. He changed his name and became George Stubbs, and obviously his mother helped him with the masquerade. He was not actually rich. Hattie was the one with the money, although he had convinced her to sign everything over to him. The elderly man had known as well, but had kept his mouth shut. Nevertheless, he had to be killed. Stubbs also killed Hattie and the young girl. George had earlier married an Italian woman, and she had impersonated Hattie on their first night in their new home, and ever since. The real Hattie is buried under the folly.

What Mrs. McGillicuddy Saw (1957, aka *4:50 from Paddington*) features Jane Marple. Elspeth McGillicuddy is on her way by train to visit Marple when she glances into the windows of another train and sees a man strangling a woman. She tells the porter, who is skeptical but agrees to pass on the information. Marple insists that she repeat her story to the police, but no body turns up, either on the train or alongside the tracks.

McGillicuddy is off to Ceylon for a visit. Marple tells herself to drop the issue but cannot do so. Instead she determines which train must have been the scene of the crime and examines maps of the area. Marple is not agile enough to search on her own so she enlists the assistance of Lucy Eyelesbarrow to do the legwork. Her theory is that the body was thrown off the train near a steep slope and then later retrieved and removed. The house at the foot of the slope belongs to the Crackenthorpe family and Marple wants her friend to apply for a housekeeping position there. Marple will be staying with another friend who lives nearby.

Luther Crackenthorpe owns the house. He is an irritating miser, but his daughter Emma is quite pleasant. Luther has three living sons – Cedric, Harold, and Alfred. His daughter has died but her husband, Bryan Eastley, and his son Alexander are still considered part of the family. Alexander comes to visit during a school vacation. Luther had collected art objects in his youth which are stored in a run down outbuilding. One of these is a sarcophagus and inside is the missing body. Lucy calls the police.

The family all comes home but no one admits to recognizing the dead woman. The clothing she was wearing suggests that she is French. Emma wonders if it might be Martine, who was engaged to the fourth brother who died during the war. No one in the family has ever met her. Emma had recently had a letter from her proposing to visit, then a telegram saying that she had to return to France. The telegram was sent around the time of the murder. She has a son, who would inherit his father's share of the estate, which would include the very valuable real estate. Emma is interested in the family doctor, Quimper.

A ballet dancer who was using an assumed name disappeared at the right time, but it is not clear if she is the dead woman, or Martine, or neither. Harold and Alfred are both in poor shape financially. Cedric claims not to be interested in money. Harold and Alfred both suggest partnerships with Lucy, and Alfred even proposes marriage. So does Luther a short time later.

Alexander and a friend have been looking for clues and they find a letter thrown in with some old trash addressed to Martine Crackenthorpe. They believe it proves she came to the house and give it to the police. Unfortunately, the inspector thinks that it is a fake Lucy concocted to entertain the boys. This scene is very implausible given that he recognizes that it has a real postmark and looks very authentic. Fortunately he later checks with Lucy. It is the letter that Emma sent to Martine in France.

No one has a good alibi. The missing ballet dancer sends a postcard indicating that she is alive. Everyone in the house except Lucy is mildly poisoned – arsenic in the curry she cooked but did not eat. The doctor suspects that a second dose will be administered to one person, a fatal dose, and goes to the police. It is too late. Someone poisons Alfred's tea and he dies.

The story takes a sudden radical turn. The real Martine shows up. She is living in England, but she never married Emma's brother and never wrote her a letter. Someone sends medicine to Harold, supposedly from his doctor, but the tablets are poisoned and he dies. McGillicuddy returns and Marple arranges for her to meet the various suspects. She positively identifies Quimper as the strangler, as Marple had expected.

Quimper was married to the ballerina, although they had been separated for years. He needed to kill her because he hoped to marry Emma, who would eventually be rich. He faked the letter from Martine, murdered his wife, and poisoned the family – it was not in the curry after all. He added it after the fact to provide himself with an alibi for the time of the supposed poisoning.

Ordeal by Innocence (1958) is a standalone novel. Arthur Calgary returns from two years in Antarctica to discover that his absence has caused a tragedy. Jack Argyle was convicted of murdering his mother and sentenced to life in prison, where he died of pneumonia a few months later. Jack had always been a troubled young man, had quarreled with his mother over money, and had been found with cash on his person that was traceable to his mother. His alibi was that he had been in a car with a stranger who had never been found. Calgary was that stranger and he knows that Jack was innocent. A concussion followed by his hasty departure for Antarctica prevented him from hearing of the case until he had returned.

Leo Argyle is the head of the family. His daughter Hester lives with him. She is romantically involved with Dr. Donald Craig. His secretary is Gwenda Vaughan. Kirsten Lindstrom is the housekeeper. Leo's daughter Mary is married to Philip Durrant, who had polio and was an invalid. His son Michael is unmarried, as is a daughter,

Christina All of the children were adopted. The family is understandably unhappy to have the issue reopened because it obviously suggests that someone else in the family was responsible for the crime.

The family lawyer brings Calgary up to date. On the night of the murder, Michael and Christina were absent but all of the others were in the house. Michael had not had an alibi and was close enough that he could have come to the house. Although the dead woman, Rachel, was very wealthy, most of her estate is tied up in charitable trusts and her money does seem likely to have been the motive. Jack had left a widow behind, Maureen, who is now married to Joe Clegg.

Rachel Argyle had been generous and charitable but also smug and controlling. It is entirely possible that one of her adopted children might have struck her down in a moment of rebellion, and her husband was by then already in love with Vaughan. Michael resented having been taken from his mother – an alcoholic who had effectively sold him to the Argyles. Philip wants to play detective. Dr. Craig recognizes that Hester might have struck her mother down on impulse. Only Tina appears to have loved Rachel.

Hester appeals to Calgary for help. Tina admits that she drove to the house at the time of the murder but insists that she did not go inside. She overheard two unidentified people, whose words she retroactively interprets as apparently planning Rachel's murder. Philip gets too close and he is stabbed to death. Tina is stabbed in the back and rushed to the hospital. Calgary reveals the truth. The killer is Lindstrom, who was working in consort with Jack. He expected to be exonerated by Calgary. She had let him go to prison rather than helping when she found out he had been secretly married.

Cat Among the Pigeons (1960) is a Poirot novel with a rather large cast of characters. The setting is a respected school for girls operated by Miss Bulstrode, who is on the verge of retiring. Her second in command is Miss Vansittart and her secretary is Ann Shapland. Miss Johnson is the school matron.

Several staff members are introduced briefly including Miss Springer, who is in charge of athletics, and Mademoiselle Blanche, who is new to the school. The only student of note at this point is Julia Upjohn, whose mother used to work for British Intelligence and who notices someone she recognizes while she is dropping off her daughter. The reader, of course, has no idea who it is.

MASTERS OF DETECTION

Princess Shasta is from Ramat, a small middle eastern nation whose ruler, Ali Yusuf, has been attempting to modernize the country. He is a close friend of Bill Rawlinson, whom he has known since college. Ramat is in the midst of a revolution and the two men are trying to flee the country. Yusuf asks Rawlinson to smuggle a fortune in gems to safety in England. Rawlinson conceals them inside an unidentified object carried by his sister Joan Sutcliffe and her daughter, Jennifer, who are vacationing in the country. Unbeknownst to him, a woman is watching him from another room and knows where it was concealed.

The plane that was carrying Rawlinson and Yusuf out of the country reportedly crashed, killing everyone aboard. The Sutcliffes successfully returned to England along with their luggage. Ronnie Goodman is a young government agent who is posing as a gardener in order to keep an eye on the princess. Another agent, Robinson, is set to watch over the Sutcliffes because he is certain they are unknowingly carrying the gems. A third agent, O'Connor, contacts the Sutcliffes directly, suggests that something might have been hidden among their belongings, and goes through them with the mother, finding nothing. Her room is subsequently burglarized, but nothing is taken.

Jennifer is sent to Bulstrode's school. Various predictable events follow, friendships formed, the unpopularity of Miss Springer is noted, letters are sent to parents by reasonably contented daughters, and the Princess has some difficulty acculturating. Bulstrode is trying to settle on her successor. She is impressed by Eileen Rich, who is new to the school but intelligent and organized.

Everything seems normal until Springer is shot to death in the gymnasium. The working theory is that she was investigating an intruder, although it is also possible that she was meeting someone clandestinely. The students have some of their clothing and equipment stored there, but nothing of obvious value. Interviews with the staff are unproductive. The Princess insists that someone is plotting to kidnap her. Goodman reveals his true identity and the nature of his assignment to the officer in charge.

Blanche has been seen poking around in places where she had no business. Bulstrode remembers Mrs. Upjohn's comments about seeing someone familiar. An unidentified woman trades a new tennis racquet to Jennifer for her old one and runs off. But Jennifer had already traded with Julia Upjohn, so Julia has the one which presumably contains the gems.

A few nights later, Vansittart is bludgeoned to death in the gymnasium. The Princess, meanwhile, has ostensibly been kidnapped by men impersonating embassy officials. Julia discovers the gems concealed in the handle of her tennis racquet. She decides to leave the school to consult Hercule Poirot and writes a note to Bulstrode. Poirot takes custody of the gems and then drives Julia back to the school.

The police welcome Poirot's assistance. Bulstrode invites Rich to become a partner and her eventual successor. Goodman reveals himself to Poirot. Blanche knows who murdered Springer and tries blackmail, only to be murdered herself almost immediately. The Princess turns out to be an imposter, enrolled at the school because it is believed that the gems would be conveyed to her at some point. She was not kidnapped. Rich was in Ramat at the time of the revolution, but this is a red herring. Mrs. Upjohn returns and identifies Shapland as a foreign agent. Shapland is the killer, although her motive is not clear.

The Pale Horse (1961) is another standalone. Mark Easterbrook, an historian, is a friend of Ariadne Oliver, the mystery writer who has appeared in some of the Poirot stories. She has been invited to sign copies of her books at another country fair.

Father Gorman is called to the bedside of a Mrs. Davis, who is dying of pneumonia. He listens to her final confession – which is not revealed to the reader – and is troubled after she has died. On his way back to his church, he is bludgeoned to death by an unknown attacker. He had written down a list of names told to him by Davis, but the paper had been tucked into his shoe and his attacker had not found it. It falls into the hands of the police.

One of the names on the list is Mrs. Hesketh-Dubois, who recently died of natural causes. Easterbrook is her godson. Easterbrook runs into the police surgeon, Dr. Jim Corrigan, who is curious about his godmother and whose name also appears to be on Gorman's list. He and Corrigan were at college together. Another name on the list is Tuckerton, and Eastbrook happened to see her in a bar fight shortly before she died in a nursing home.

Eastbrook had already met Pamela Stirling briefly in a nightclub and she had mentioned the Pale Horse. He has grown curious about it and looks her up, but she later denies ever having mentioned it and is clearly very frightened. The Pale Horse was once an inn and is now a private home owned by Thyrza Grey, who claims to have occult powers. Sybil Stamfordis currently lives with Grey, as does a cook named Bella. All three women are considered to be witches by local tradition.

Venables is a wealthy local man who helps sponsor the charity festival, which is a great success. He is confined to a wheelchair. He is reticent about his past. Easterbrook manages an invitation to have tea with the ladies, and feels rather foolish about it. Grey and her companions spout a good deal of arcane nonsense to their guests. Grey tells Easterbrook that she can kill people from a distance by remote control.

The man seen following Gorman just before he was killed is identified by a witness as Venables. Easterbrook decides that the Pale Horse is an organization that kills people for fees and that the supposed natural deaths are all actually murders. There is a good deal of not very convincing plot development. Easterbrook wants to trap the bad guys into revealing themselves. Venables is an imposter, not paralyzed at all, and sends a genuine polio victim to his doctor whenever he is due for a checkup. Certain drugs have been developed that bring on apparently natural deaths from various causes. The fake Venables is the head of the gang.

The Mirror Crack'd (1962, aka *The Mirror Crack'd from Side to Side*) is a Jane Marple novel. Marple is feeling her age and is largely confined to her home village. She also has a companion living with her, Miss Knight, who is more than slightly cloying. Marple slips out for a solitary walk and meets Arthur and Heather Badcock.

Heather tells her that the actress, Marina Gregg, has taken a house in the village with her latest husband, Jason Rudd. He is her fifth, although no one knows who the first one was. They bought the house from Mrs. Bantry, a friend of Marple from *The Body in the Library*. Rudd's secretary is Ella Zielinsky and Hailey Preston works for both of them as a kind of administrative assistant.

There is a large party at Gregg's house and very briefly she reacts in obvious shock to someone she sees, although she recovers quickly. A few minutes later, Heather Badcock feels sick and promptly dies of an overdose of a drug commonly used to reduce tension. Gregg quite logically believes that the doctored drink was meant for her.

The people at whom Gregg may have been looking when she grimaced include the mayor and his wife, a pair of photographers, and Ardwyck Fenn, a movie executive who was once quite close to Gregg. Lola Brewster is an actress whose husband divorced her to marry Gregg, many years earlier. Gregg adopted three children, who no longer live with her, and had one child of her own, born mentally deficient and institutionalized.

The police are sure that Gregg is withholding information, even after she reveals that she has received some threatening notes. The photographer who was present is Margot Bence, who turns out to have been one of the children Gregg had adopted. Another attempt to poison Gregg fails. Zielinsky is considering blackmailing someone, presumably having seen them tampering with Gregg's cocktail. She is poisoned soon after making a telephone call, but survives.

Fenn tells the police that Zielinsky called him and threatened to expose him as the poisoner, but he denies that she was right. That evening, Gregg's butler is also killed, shot to death. A servant believes that Badcock spilled her own drink deliberately. Marple convinces the servant to leave the village for a few days. Arthur Badcock is revealed to have been Gregg's first husband.

The killer is Gregg herself. Badcock had just told her that they had met years earlier while she was suffering from German measles, which is the reason her son was born impaired. She doctored her own drink, forced her victim to spill her own, and then killed the butler and Zielinsky because they were blackmailing her. She takes an overdose of sleeping pills and dies.

The Clocks (1963) opens at a secretarial school run by Katherine Martindale. The staff includes Sheila Webb and Edna Brent. Webb is sent to the house of Millicent Pebmarsh, who is blind, with instructions to wait inside if no one is home when she arrives. She enters the house and finds the dead body of a man on the floor, just minutes before Pebmarsh returns from shopping.

The narrator, Colin Lamb, is looking for an address when he encounters the hysterical Webb and examines the body and calls the police. There are some immediate oddities. The supposed call from Pebmarsh asked for Webb specifically, but they had never met. All but one of the clocks in the house is an hour fast, and stopped, and several of these were in the house when Pebmarsh left to go shopping. Pebmarsh did not call for Webb or anyone else.

A business card suggests that the dead man is R. Curry, an insurance agent. Pebmarsh does not know the name. Lamb is a friend of Inspector Hardcastle and accompanies him during his initial inquiries. The woman who cleans for Pebmarsh left at noon and the mysterious clocks were not there at that time.

Lamb is actually a counter intelligence agent. Another agent had recently been killed and a scrap of paper suggested a possible address, which is what Lamb had been looking for. The address is the home of Josaiah and Valerie Bland. Bland is a somewhat shady building contractor who recently inherited a large sum of money.

One of the clocks is missing. It appears that either Pebmarsh or Webb took it away before the police removed the others and its absence was overlooked until the following day. The insurance company mentioned on Curry's card does not exist and it is uncertain what his real name is.

The next door neighbors are James Waterhouse and his rather domineering sister Edith. James was at work all day, but Edith is able to confirm portions of Pebmarsh's account of her movements, and Pebmarsh seems to have taken an unusual route to do her shopping. Another neighbor is Mrs. Hemming, who seems oblivious to the outside world and who is obsessed with cats. The Bland house is behind Pebmarsh's and they also insist that they saw nothing unusual. Finally the Ramsay house. Mrs Ramsay is overwhelmed by the energy of her two sons, both home from school. Her husband is frequently out of the country. The boys give Hardcastle a collection of odds and ends they retrieved from Pebmarsh's garden, which includes a foreign coin. The last neighbor is a retired professor named Angus McNaughton, who lives with his wife.

Web's real first name is Rosemary and the missing clock had that name inscribed on it. She was raised by an aunt and believes her parents died when she was an infant, but in fact she was illegitimate, her mother disappeared but is probably still alive, and she never identified the father.

The inquest is predictable except that it reveals that the dead man was drugged before he was stabbed. Brent wants to speak to Hardcastle because something said during the proceedings was wrong, but the reader is not told what it was or who said it. Lamb tells the whole story to his friend, Hercule Poirot. The murder weapon is found in the shrubbery.

Webb shows Lamb a postcard she received from someone named R.S. Webb that refers to a time – the same time the four clocks were showing when they stopped. She does not know what it means. Brent is found strangled in a telephone booth. No one admits having seen her since the inquest.

Ramsay's husband has a suspicious list of engineering assignments and has lied to his wife, Merlina Rival, about where he is being sent. The dead man is tentatively identified as Harry Castleton, who apparently supported himself by seducing women, getting engaged or even married, and then appropriating their money. He apparently went into hiding after one of his victims became pregnant.

Lamb talks Webb into admitting that she stole the clock. She recognized it as her own, which she had lost a week before the murder. Ramsay admits that her husband has defected to Russia. Lamb notices a young girl in a house directly across the street from Pebmarsh – whom the police unbelievably have not spoken to. She saw an unfamiliar laundry truck deliver a very large basket of laundry to Pebmarsh shortly before the body was discovered.

Hardcastle, meanwhile, has discovered that Rival lied in her identification of her husband. She promptly calls someone and tells them she wants out of their agreement, and she is stabbed to death within hours.

Poirot reveals the truth. Martindale lied about the telephone call and later killed Brent to avoid being exposed. The inheritance that the Blands received should have gone to his first wife, not his present one. The dead man had come from Canada and would have recognized that she was the wrong woman and that they had committed fraud. Mrs. Bland's sister is Martindale. Martindale had been secretary to a writer of thrillers and the clocks were inspired by an uncompleted manuscript. Bland drugged, moved, and killed the man and presumably Rival. Pebmarsh turns out to be Webb's mother, but also a dedicated communist spy, who is also arrested. The clocks are an elaborate and totally unnecessary element.

A Caribbean Mystery (1964) features Jane Marple, who is on vacation in the West Indies, staying at a hotel run by Tim and Molly Kendal. One of the other guests, Major Palgrave, is garrulous and tells her that he once heard of a case where two wives committed suicide under odd circumstances that were very much alike, and a photograph – of which he has a copy – proves that they both had the same husband.

Palgrave seemingly becomes very flustered by the arrival of two married couples, Greg and Lucky Dyson, and Edward and Evelyn Hillingdon. Presumably one of the men is the person in his snapshot – although that turns out not to be the case. The other guests include Mr. Rafiel, who is elderly and rich and requires a wheelchair. He is accompanied by his valet, Arthur Jackson, and his secretary, Esther Walters. Canon Jeremy Prescott is there with his sister Joan.

Palgrave is found dead in his bed. Marple pretends that she loaned him a picture of her nephew in order to retrieve the one he started to show her, but it has disappeared. There is disagreement about whether or not Palgrave suffered from high blood pressure. The medication for it found in his room had never been there before, according to the housekeeper, Victoria, who cleaned for him. Molly begins to have nightmares about persecution and has blackouts. Marple discovers that Palgrave told a different murder story to some of the other guests, with the wife as the killer. She finally tells the whole story to a local doctor, who consults with the police.

Victoria is considering blackmailing someone. Edward Hillingdon is having an affair with Lucky Dyson. Greg Dyson makes an unsuccessful pass at Molly and apparently has done the same with other women. Edward tells his wife that he helped Lucky poison Greg's first wife and that he has come to hate her.

Predictably, Victoria is found stabbed to death. Palgrave apparently told stories about both male and female murderers, so everyone is a suspect. Marple and Rafiel compare notes. Jackson is spotted sneaking a look at Rafiel's papers. Molly takes an overdose of sleeping pills but survives. There is some suspicion that she did not actually try to commit suicide.

Lucky Dyson is found drowned. She was wearing Molly's shawl and looked much like her in the dark. With the assistance of Jackson, Marple prevents Tim Kendal from poisoning his wife. His guilt had been obvious because events followed the pattern developed in Palgrave's story. Tim was also having an affair with Walters, who would probably have been his next victim. It was Palgrave's realization that he recognized the resort manager that shocked him and led to his death.

At Bertram's Hotel (1965) also features Miss Marple. As the title suggests, the focus is a revered hotel that mixes modern and Edwardian elements. Lady Selina Hazy is having tea there when she runs into an old acquaintance, Colonel Derek Luscombe. The manager is Humfries and Miss Gorringe is the receptionist. Other current guests include Bess Sedgwick, Canon Pennyfather, and, of course, Jane Marple. Sedgwick has led an adventurous and somewhat notorious life.

Marple notices that Sedgwick reacts sharply to the arrival of two women in the lobby. One of the women is Elvira Blake, Sedgwick's daughter. The other is an older woman named Carpenter, apparently a chaperone. Luscombe is Blake's godfather. Blake will gain control of a substantial trust fund when she turns twenty-one. They are having a somewhat awkward conversation when Ladislaus Malinowski rather ostentatiously leaves a note for Sedgwick at the front desk. Malinowski is a racing car driver and adventurer.

At Scotland Yard, the higher ups are concerned about the apparent existence of an organized criminal gang with very large ambitions. They also notice that in some of the cases attributed to them, there have been misidentifications of prominent people with impeccable alibis, all of whom had at the time been staying at Bertram's Hotel.

The hotel doorman is Michael Gorman, who was at one time Sedgwick's lover. He hints mildly at the possibility of blackmail. Blake spots her mother and then consults with a friend, Bridget, over a plan to secretly flying to Ireland for a brief time. Blake steals a bracelet from a jeweler and pawns it to get some cash. Pennyfather mixes up dates and returns to his room on a night when he had expected to be elsewhere. Someone is inside and he is knocked on the head. Blake returns from Ireland, redeems the bracelet, and returns it to the jeweler.

When Pennyfather does not return to his home, the police are notified. Marple sees Blake meeting Malinowski. Humfries and Gorringe are clearly discomforted by the police presence in the hotel, and not just because of the potentially bad publicity. Pennyfather wakes up in a strange room. A married couple tell him that they found him lying unconscious in the road and brought him to their home. Since he was a clergyman and might have been drunk, they decided not to call the police. When he recovers, he speaks to the police but has no memory of what has happened to him.

The owners of the hotel turn out to be the Hoffman brothers, both very rich, both suspected to have been involved in questionable financial affairs from time to time. An unknown person tries to shoot Blake in front of the hotel. Gorman comes to her assistance and is killed. Blake tells the police that someone tried to poison her when she was at school in Italy. Bridget denies the poison story but confirms that Blake has been seeing Malinowski for some time.

The murder weapon is found discarded and it belongs to Malinowski. Sedgwick admits that Gorman was the first man she married, although she believes that the ceremony was fake. Blake overheard part of a conversation and the trip to Ireland confirmed that the marriage was valid. Sedgwick is head of the crime syndicate, which includes most of the hotel staff. She confesses to having murdered Gorman and is then killed trying to escape. But Gorman was actually killed by Blake, who incorrectly thought that her illegitimacy, if revealed, would invalidate the will leaving her a large fortune.

The Third Girl (1966) begins with Poirot feeling his age. A prospective client, a young woman, has aborted her visit because he is "too old." It appears that she was indirectly sent to him by Ariadne Oliver, who met her at a party. The girl, Norma Restarick, suggests that she "might have" committed a murder.

Restarick is a "third girl," that is, a third tenant of a flat whose presence is required to keep the rental fees low for the other two, who are friends. Andrew Restarick is married to his second wife, Mary, who has been suffering from a suspicious ailment that might be poison. They live with their aging uncle, Sir Roderick Horsefield, who was privy to confidential information during the war. Poirot prevails upon Oliver to arrange an introduction to the family.

Intrigued herself, Oliver contrives a meeting with Norma's roommates, Claudia Reece-Holland and Frances Cary. They tell her that Norma is away but the truth is that they have no idea where she has gone. Poirot visits the Restaricks, where he briefly meets David Baker, an obnoxious young man who has dated Norma but who has been banned from the house. He also meets Sonia, Sir Roderick's secretary.

There is a story that Norma fired a handgun outside her apartment a few days earlier, and there were drops of blood suggesting she might have hit someone. Reece-Holland works for Andrew Restarick. Oliver happens to be in a restaurant and sees Norma talking to a young man whom she assumes is Baker. Norma thinks that she may have poisoned her stepmother during a blackout and is very upset.

Oliver follows Baker to his loft and shortly after he leaves, she is knocked unconscious. Poirot confronts Norma, who is as vague and silly as ever. Norma then tries to throw herself in front of a bus, but is rescued by a doctor named Stillfleet, and agrees to stay at a kind of nursing home temporarily. Stillfleet appears to have an unusual amount of interest in her.

Oliver is hospitalized. She is convinced that Baker attacked her, but did not see him at the time. Sir Roderick wants to hire Poirot because some confidential papers and letters may have disappeared from his house. By luck, Poirot discovers that Sonia has secret contacts with a foreign embassy. Poirot belatedly learns that a woman fell or jumped to her death from a window and that she was a neighbor of the three young women. Sonia visits Poirot and insists that she did not steal the missing papers. She also expresses the opinion that Mary is having an affair.

The dead woman was named Louise Charpentier. Andrew Restarick had left his wife for a woman named Louise, but their affair had lasted less than a year. Charpentier was once the mistress of Reece-Holland's father, who is a Member of Parliament. The art gallery where Cary works was recently involved in the sale of forged paintings.

Stillingfleet is working for Poirot and calls to tell him that Norma has disappeared again. Cary returns to the apartment and finds Baker stabbed to death. Norma confesses to having killed him during another blackout. Andrew confirms that Charpentier was the woman he had run off with. Norma has been drugged to bring about the memory lapses and disorientation and has done nothing wrong.

Cary is actually Mary Restarick without a wig, which is rather improbable given that some people knew them both quite well. Andrew is an imposter as well and Charpentier was killed to prevent her from discovering the truth. Baker was blackmailing him. The missing documents turn up – Sonia had not taken them. They had simply been misplaced and are a red herring. Norma inherits the family fortune and becomes engaged to Stillfleet.

MASTERS OF DETECTION

Endless Night (1967) is narrated by Michael Rogers, a young man who feels out of place in the modern world. By chance he notices that a piece of property called Gypsy's Acre is for sale. The area is believed by the local people to be under a curse. He is friends with an architect named Santonix whom he met while working as a chauffeur. He also discovers that he shares interest in the property with a young woman, Fenella Goodman.

They are both warned about the curse by Miss Lee, who is granted use of a cottage by Major Phillpot. Goodman comes from a wealthy family, but her life is strictly controlled and her only friend is Greta Andersen, who worked for the family briefly. They arrange to meet again and during the interim Rogers has a testy visit with his mother. Their romance continues but neither has met the other's family, and Rogers has not yet met Greta.

Goodman purchases Gypsy's Acre. The two of them marry and hire Santonix to design their new home. They honeymoon in Europe. Goodman's real name is Guteman. Rogers does not want her to meet his mother, and she tries to avoid any meeting between him and her family and associates. She has just come of age and there is some resentment about her deceptions.

This one was more psychological suspense than mystery, although in the second half the undercurrent of danger becomes more explicit. It also contains a good deal of ambivalent supernatural content – apparently Miss Lee really does have psychic powers. Guteman eventually becomes ill and dies. Only then is it revealed that Andersen and Rogers had contrived the entire sequence of events in order to marry her, quietly murder her, and then live on her money.

By the Pricking of My Thumbs (1968) is a Tommy and Tuppence story. They are on the brink of being elderly at this point. Tommy is feeling guilty about not having recently visited his Aunt Ada, who is in a kind of nursing home. They meet some of the staff and the other residents. Three weeks later, Ada dies in her sleep. They are settling up her affairs when her close friends, Mrs. Lancaster, disappears from the nursing home.

They also hear disturbing rumors of possibly poisoned stew and some other strange events. They begin to investigate both the nursing home and the neighboring community, and promptly place themselves in danger as they begin to unmask a criminal conspiracy.

Fortunately, they survive and reveal the truth.

Hallowe'en Party (1969) is a Poirot story and a further adventure of Ariadne Oliver. Oliver is visiting an old friend, Judith Butler. A community party for children is being planned in conjunction with Rowena Drake, a schoolmistress. One of the students, Joyce Reynolds, claims to have once witnessed a murder, but no one believes her. Sometime during the party, she is deliberately drowned in a bucket where the party goers had been bobbing for apples.

Oliver immediately goes to see Poirot, who agrees to help. He asks for a list of people who had died within the past few years whose deaths may not been classed as murders or whose killer had never been found. The first considered is the death by presumed natural causes of an elderly woman named Smythe who left all of her money to a much younger, foreign woman – Olga Seminoff – whom she had engaged as a companion. Smythe was Drake's aunt and there was some concern that her recently altered will leaving them nothing might be a forgery. Legal action was being prepared when the companion suddenly disappeared, leaving many of her belongings behind.

The second possibility is Charlotte Benfield, a young woman who was beaten to death in a wooded area. Lesley Ferrier was a law clerk who had been stabbed to death and who was rumored to be having an affair with a married woman whose husband was known to be violent. Janet White was a school teacher who had been strangled.

One of the attendees, Elisabeth Whittaker, tells Poirot that she saw Drake drop a vase during the party when she happened to glance at the door of the library, which is where Reynolds was drowned. Poirot briefly reviews the four cases, then meets Michael Garfield, the gardener who designed an elaborate garden near where White was killed.

Harriet Leaman says that she is one of the people who witnessed Smythe signing the codicil that left her money to Seminoff and reveals that she read it herself and that it was authentic and not a forgery. But there was another version of it, which was forged, and with a different witness. It is also possible that someone convinced Leaman to lie about it. Seminoff never returned to her home country and no one knows where she went.

Joyce's younger brother is murdered, drowned in a brook. Drake tells Poirot she thought Leopold had killed his sister. Seminoff's body is found in an abandoned well. Butler's daughter Miranda runs off with an unidentified man, but is rescued before he can kill her.

The killers are Drake and Garfield. They suppressed the authentic will and produced the forgery to discredit Seminoff, then killed her. Drake murdered Joyce – who had lied and had repeated a story told to her by Miranda. Miranda is Garfield's daughter, but she does not know that. Garfield killed Leopold, who was blackmailing him. He also killed Ferrier, because he knew too much. The movie, *A Haunting in Venice*, is supposedly based on the novel but has no similarities to the plot whatsoever.

Passenger to Frankfurt (1970) is a standalone novel. Sir Stafford Nye is a not particularly notable diplomat who is traveling in Europe when he is approached by a woman in the Frankfurt Airport. She tells him that her life is in danger and that since she looks very much like him, she wants his passport and coat so that she can get to Geneva. He agrees. Her name is Daphne Theodofanous. Nye takes a knockout drug and later claims that his passport was stolen.

Back in England, security is not convinced that he is telling the truth. Someone searches his apartment. An advertisement in the personals column leads him to a rendezvous point where a woman passes him a note. This is to set up another meeting at another location.

Unfortunately the plot becomes unfocused after that, blended with long stretches of uninteresting dialogue, musings about the difficulties of old age, fear of fascist leaders returning to power, disillusionment with youth, etc. The core of the story is a worldwide plot to add some drug to the environment that will make everyone much nicer. New characters – some of them world leaders – are introduced in large numbers and often vanish suddenly. The locale moves from England to the United States and elsewhere before coming to a climax in Scotland. Christie never learned how to write potboilers.

Nemesis (1971) is a Jane Marple story. It opens with her reading the obituary of Jason Rafiel, who appeared in *A Caribbean Mystery*. Rafiel left her a substantial legacy on the condition that she solve a crime that has been bothering him, but his letter of explanation includes no references to any event, persons, or problems.

She contrives to encounter Esther Waltons – now Anderson –

who had served as Rafiel's secretary. Nothing promising arises. Then she receives communications for Rafiel's lawyers suggesting that she take part in an organized tour of houses and gardens. The tour, which consists of a bit more than a dozen people, gets underway and Marple sets about identifying and studying her fellow travelers. This is horribly contrived because Rafiel could easily have provided the information to start with, saving her wasted time.

There is nothing immediately suggestive, although Marple thinks that she might have seen a Miss Cooke sometime in the past. Later she remembers a chance encounter at her home when a passerby had discussed gardening with her. One house they visit was the scene of a murder, but during the 17th Century. Marple discovers that another tourist, Elizabeth Temple, was a teacher, one of whose students had at one time been engaged to Rafiel's estranged son. The son had reportedly died.

Cooke and her companion, Miss Barrow, are acting a bit oddly. Marple thinks that her chance encounter with Cooke was designed to let Cooke know what she looked like. At one of the stops, Marple is approached by Lavinia Glynne, who tells her that Rafiel had suggested that they meet at this particular time and place. Glynne invites her to stay with her and her two sisters, Anthea and Clotilde, for a night or two because the tour involves considerable physical effort for that period. Although things are ostensibly quite peaceful, Marple detects tension among the sisters.

Marple learns that Michael Rafiel, the son, was convicted of murder and sentenced to prison. Temple is badly injured in an "accidental" rock fall. Another tour member, Professor Wanstead, approaches Marple and tells her quietly that Rafiel had arranged for him to take the tour in order to protect her. He and Rafiel had both believed that Michael was a confirmed delinquent, but not a killer and had been convicted in error. Several other young women were murdered about the same time.

Temple dies of her injuries but mentions the name Verity Hunt, another of the murdered women. This leads Marple to the correct conclusion. Clotilde murdered Hunt because she loved the girl and did not want her to marry Michael. She then killed another in order to frame him for murder. When Marple confronts her, she decides to murder Marple as well, but Cooke is actually a private detective hired to keep Marple safe and Clotilde is apprehended.

Elephants Can Remember (1972) brings back both Poirot and Oliver. Oliver is at a social event when Mrs. Burton-Cox raises the subject of Celia Ravenscroft, Oliver's goddaughter, who is engaged to marry her son Desmond. Celia's parents had been found shot to death years earlier and it was never clear whether it was murder and suicide or two murders. Oliver is offended, but also curious, and she consults her friend, Hercule Poirot.

Oliver also talks to Ravenscroft, who has no idea about her parents' death and is in fact rather curious herself. Poirot interviews the police officers who handled the investigation. Oliver talks to some old, mutual friends and learns that Lady Ravenscroft's sister was confined to a mental institution. Celia's brother Edward had not been on good terms with his parents, but he had not been home at the time. The boy's tutor had been named Edmunds and his father had not cared for the man.

There are various stories – a love affair discovered, a fatal illness, etc. Poirot interviews Desmond Burton-Cox, who reveals that he is adopted. The dead woman and her sister were twins. Poirot eventually sorts everything out. The mentally unstable twin had taken the place of her sister. Celia's father realized this, wanted to avoid the scandal if the insanity and murder were known, so he then killed the imposter and himself. It is not clear why he thought a murder and suicide would be less scandalous than a mentally ill relative.

Postern of Fate (1973) brings back Tommy and Tuppence. It was the last novel Christie wrote, although two others were published posthumously, by design. It is not one of her better efforts, however. The twosome have just bought a new house, which contains a number of items from the previous owners, including some books. Tuppence happens to notice some odd underlinings in one of the books, copies the words out, and the first letters of each indicate that a decades old death was a murder.

The death involves some secrets involving international politics, but the mystery and its investigation are almost after thoughts. Most of the novel consists of long conversations and then regurgitations of those conversations in order to try to put together the solution. They do, of course, and receive the quiet gratitude of the government.

Curtain (1975) was Poirot's last case. Hastings, now a widower, has returned to England. Poirot is staying at Styles, now a small resort, and is gathering some of his old acquaintances. The owners are Colonel George Luttrell and his wife Daisy. Hastings' daughter Judith has also come. Poirot is confined to a wheelchair because of arthritis.

Stephen Norton, an amateur ornithologist, is also a guest, as is William Carrington, formerly a government official in India. The others are Dr. Franklin in his wife Barbara, a man named Allerton, and a woman named Cole. There is also a nurse named Craven. Poirot tells Hastings that one of the people in the house is a murderer. He summarizes five murder cases in which there was always a single suspect, although they were not always convicted. But another person whom he calls X, who had no motive in any of the cases, is connected to all five.

Poirot will not identify the killer. Hastings discovers that the Franklins knew the family in one of the five cases of interest. Allerton and Craven both have connections to at least one of the crimes. Craven is contemptuous of Barbara Franklin, whom she considers silly and useless. Luttrell is obviously frightened of his domineering wife.

Hastings stumbles around but does discover that each of the inmates of the house has a connection to at least one of the critical murder cases. Luttrell shoots his wife, apparently by accident, but the wound is superficial. There is a subplot in which Judith seems to be falling in love with Allerton, whom Hastings despises.

Barbara Franklin is poisoned and dies. Poirot's testimony convinces the jury at the inquest that she committed suicide, but he tells Hastings confidentially that it was murder, but that he wanted the investigation terminated so that the killer would be off guard. Then Norton is found shot to death, apparently by his own hand. Poirot insists this too is a murder.

Poirot dies during the night. The cause of death was a heart attack but Hastings does not believe it. The solution comes in a letter several months later. Norton had a unique ability to convince people to do things out of character, and he talked people into committing the various crimes in the past. Poirot – rather implausibly – contrives a way to shoot Norton fatally and make it appear to be suicide, after which he did die of natural causes.

Sleeping Murder (1976) was Christie's final published novel and features Jane Marple. Gwenda Reed is from New Zealand and is in

England looking for a house for herself and her husband Giles, who will join her in a few months. She buys a largish property from a widow named Hengrave and modernizes and furnishes it. She does note an odd placement of forsythia and makes a note to change that when she has time. There also appears to be a wall where one would expect to find a door to the next room. Gwenda is convinced that she is having psychic flashes because she knows things about the house that she had never been told.

Gwenda goes to visit Raymond West and his wife. West's aunt is Jane Marple. Gwenda is an orphan so it is fairly obvious to the reader that she is remembering things from a childhood that she has suppressed. A chance scene in a play reminds her of having seen a woman named Helen, who had been strangled. She decides to consult with Marple.

Gwenda talks with the aunt who raised her and learns that she did briefly live in England during her father's short and unhappy second marriage. Giles arrives. Marple, rather uncharacteristically, advises them to forget about the past. Contradicting herself somewhat, Marple decides to investigate on her own.

The Reeds are able to confirm that her father briefly rented the house, but after twenty years and a war, there are few records that are reliable. But her father married someone named Helen Kennedy, who supposedly ran off with another man. They find Helen's half-brother, a doctor, who says that he has not heard from his sister in many years. Gwen's father was in poor health and died two years later, after sending Gwen to New Zealand to live with her aunt.

Her father died in a mental institution, insisting that he had strangled his wife. Dr. Kennedy believes this was a delusion because he received letters from Helen several times after she had disappeared. Gwen's father, Major Halliday, killed himself because of his feelings of guilt, although it is not completely clear that he actually killed his wife.

Helen had once been involved with Walter Fane, who might have held a grudge. Gwen makes an excuse to meet Fane, who strikes her as a quiet and good natured person. One of the women who worked as a maid at the time had noticed that although Helen had taken a full suitcase when she disappeared, the clothes she had selected had seemed random and unlikely. Marple, however, knows that Fane once assaulted and tried to kill his brother. Marple finds two more of Helen's admirers, Major Erskine, who also accepts that she ran away, and Jackie Afflick, who believes that he was framed and lost his job because he was too attentive.

Lily Kimble also worked for the Hallidays. She sees a newspaper notice asking for information and arranges a visit, but she is murdered before she arrives. The police find Helen's body, buried under the forsythia. Someone poisons the brandy in the Reeds' house and the housekeeper almost dies. The killer reveals himself, trying to kill Gwenda. It is Dr. Kennedy, who is insane and was very possessive of his sister.

MASTERS OF DETECTION

SHORT STORIES

Christie's short stories have been collected and cross collected many times. They usually but do not always involve her more famous protagonists, but some also involve Parker Pyne, Harley Quin, Tommy and Tuppence, and others. Although most are quite readable and a few very good, she was never as successful in the short form as she was at novel length, presumably lacking the room for a truly complex plot.

"Accident" is a very short tale in which a man suspects that a woman poisoned her husband. His suspicion is borne out, but not soon enough to prevent a second death.

"The Actress" is very short. A blackmailer threatens a successful actress with revelations about her past, so she tricks him into thinking that she has committed a murder and framed him. He decides to leave the country rather risk being arrested.

"The Adventure of Johnny Waverly" concerns a kidnapped child. The boy is never in any danger because he was kidnapped by his father to extort money from his mother, and Poirot solves the case.

"The Adventure of the Cheap Flat" starts when Poirot hears about a couple who have rented an expensive apartment at an astonishingly low rate. He soon uncovers a pair of spies who are hiding out from the Mafia while trying to sell the secret plans they have recently stolen. They wanted to use the couple as bait.

"The Adventure of the Clapham Cook" begins when Poirot surprises Hastings by accepting a job to find a cook who disappeared suddenly from her job. The answer is that, rather implausibly, it was an elaborate ruse to secure her large trunk in which a killer wanted to conceal a body.

"The Adventure of the Egyptian Tomb" takes Poirot to Egypt where he pretends to believe that a curse is real in order to trick a serial killer, the expedition's doctor, into revealing himself.

"The Adventure of the Italian Nobleman" begins with the murder of a man at a small dinner party. He was a blackmailer, and Poirot correctly deduces that he was murdered by his own valet, who then made it look as though he had had guests, one of whom had killed him.

"The Adventure of the Sinister Stranger" is a Tommy and Tuppence story. Someone has been searching the papers of a doctor who is researching untraceable poisons. Some bogus police officers turn out to be responsible.

"The Adventure of the Western Star" involves two fabulous jewels owned by two different women. Each claims to have received letters threatening theft by Chinese fanatics. Poirot sees through the ruse. There is only one real diamond. The other is paste. The threats are fabricated to cover up blackmail.

"The Affair at the Victory Ball" is a rather routine account of Poirot solving a murder performed in the middle of a public festival.

"The Affair of the Pink Pearl" involves the theft of a valuable gem. Tommy and Tuppence take the case and the former notices soap on the hands of a maid and concludes – correctly – that she has concealed the jewel inside a bar of soap.

"The Ambassador's Boots" is a story of espionage. Some baggage is missing from an ocean liner and Tommy and Tuppence track it down.

"The Apples of the Hesperides" features Poirot. A valuable goblet was stolen just as it was about to be sold. The case is complicated because the man supposed to have stolen it died a short time later. No trace of it has turned up subsequently. Poirot tries to talk to the dead man's daughter, but she has recently passed away as well while living in a convent. The missing cup had been given to the convent in atonement for her father's sins.

"The Arcadian Deer" is the story of a young man who falls in love with the maid working for a famous dancer. The maid disappears and he convinces Poirot to find her. He discovers that it was actually the dancer herself, pretending to be her maid so that she would not overawe him.

"At the Bells and Motley" briefly strands Mr. Satterthwaite at a remote inn where he seeks a meal while his car is being repaired. Harley Quin happens to be staying there for the night and the two of them hear the story of Captain Harwell, who brought home his new bride a few months earlier, only to promptly disappear. If it was murder, the suspects include an arthritic gardener and a recently fired employee, but how did either of them dispose of a body? In a rather large leap of intuition, Quin connects these events to a family of acrobats who committed several burglaries in France. Harwell was the supposed gardener and the whole plot was to sell the stolen goods as part of his wife's legacy.

"The Augean Stables" is somewhat problematic because Poirot is induced to suppress the truth about a political figure's corruption because he favors the political policies of that particular party. A disreputable newspaper is about to print the truth, so Poirot tricks them into accepting and publishing false information about the Prime Minister's wife. The subsequent lawsuit puts them out of business. The acceptance of this dishonesty is appalling.

"The Bird with the Broken Wing" is clearly supernatural. Harley Quin communicates with Satterthwaite through a Ouija board and sends him to a house in the countryside. One of the guests is murdered – it is made to look like suicide – and Satterthwaite solves the crime with no help from Quin, who appears only very briefly at the end.

"Blindman's Bluff" has Tommy pretending to be blind in order that he and Tuppence can apprehend a fake duke.

"The Bloodstained Pavement" involves a romantic triangle. A man and his mistress contrive to murder his wife, but Miss Marple catches them.

"The Blue Geranium" is a Miss Marple story in which a nurse impersonates a fortune teller in order to manipulate a woman into leaving her a substantial amount of money. It is discovered that the nurse has murdered at least one previous patient.

"The Call of Wings" is fantasy. After seeing a man die in an accident, a rich but selfish man hears things inaudible to everyone else and eventually gives his entire fortune to a church.

"The Capture of Cerberus" takes Poirot to a nightclub whose theme is Hell itself. An old friend is part owner but Poirot suspects that it is a criminal front for a drug dealer. He manages to extricate his friend from the consequences when the club is raided.

"The Case of the Caretaker" involves a man who bribes a woman to harass his wife and then arranges for the latter to have a fatal accident. Miss Marple sees through the ruse.

"The Case of the Missing Lady" has Tommy and Tuppence searching for an explorer's fiancé, who disappeared just as he returned from a year out of the country. In fact, she had gained a great deal of weight and was attempting to shed it before he saw her again.

"The Case of the Missing Will" is a simple story about Poirot locating a will hidden somewhere in a farmhouse.

"The Case of the Perfect Maid" describes Miss Marple's discovery that a maid is actually burglarizing the neighbors.

"The Chocolate Box" takes place when Poirot still worked for the Belgian police. He is asked to look into the supposedly natural death of a prominent politician and, he admits to Hastings, it was the first and only time he ever failed to find the correct solution.

"The Clergyman's Daughter" is an incomplete Tommy and Tuppence story involving a small inn which appears to have a poltergeist. The second half is "The Red House."

"The Coming of Mr. Quin" introduces Harley Quin. Mr. Satterthwaite is hosting a house party and is puzzled by the Portals, English husband Australian wife. The wife dyes her blonde hair black and her husband is clearly afraid of her. Eleanor Portal is visibly shaken when she learns that the previous owner of the house shot himself at a similar gathering. Quin shows up late that night, explaining that his car broke down, and the old suicide becomes the topic of conversation. Satterthwaite is convinced that Quin somehow managed the entire scene. Quin eventually convinces them that the suicide had poisoned the husband of a woman he loved, and committed suicide when he learned that the body was being exhumed. The woman changed her name and appearance and is now Eleanor Portal.

"The Companion" is the story of a woman who drowns her companion during a trip abroad and impersonates her in order to gain some of her wealth. She then fakes a suicide but Miss Marple is too smart for her.

"The Cornish Mystery" is a Poirot story. Poirot knows that a man is guilty of having poisoned another, but there is no evidence of consequence so he makes use of a ruse to trick the man into confessing.

"The Crackler" pits Tommy and Tuppence up against a counterfeiter, who is quite easily discovered and foiled.

"The Cretan Bull" is a rather transparent story about a man who believes that he is going insane. He breaks off his engagement and ends his naval career. Poirot easily discovers that a supposed friend of the family has a long standing grudge and is arranging incidents to deceive the man about his mental health.

"The Dead Harlequin" is an odd story about Satterthwaite's purchase of a painting of a dead harlequin in an actual room where a man is believed to have committed suicide. Shortly afterward, a famous entertainer and the owner of the house where it is set both offer extraordinary amounts of money to buy it from him. Quin shows up, almost magically, as all the parties come together. The suicide turns out to have been murder and the widow realizes that her husband was not having an affair after all.

"Dead Man's Mirror" is a novella featuring Poirot. He receives a letter from Gervase Cheminix-Gore asking for help. He crosses over to the Harley Quin universe by consulting with Satterthwaite about his potential new client. The man's wife is Vanda and they have an adopted daughter, Ruth, and a nephew, Hugo Trent. Cheminix-Gore is elderly, eccentric, and very rich. The story follows the same plot as "The Second Gong" but is longer.

"Death by Drowning" is a Marple story. A young barmaid becomes pregnant and is found drowned. Marple does not believe it was suicide and reveals that she was murdered by a woman with whose husband the girl had been having an affair.

"The Disappearance of Mr. Davenheim" is a rather obvious Poirot story in which a banker disappears along with a large amount of cash and bonds. It is quite evident that he embezzled from the bank and has changed his identity.

"The Dream" is a Poirot story. An eccentric millionaire is troubled by a recurring dream in which he kills himself. Poirot clearly cannot help him and a few days later he takes his own life just as he had dreamed. Or did he? Poirot figures out that his interview with the man was actually with his secretary, in disguise, and that the murder was committed by shooting from one window to another and then being the person who finds the body – but only after rearranging things.

"The Dressmaker's Doll" psychically commands a woman to purchase her from a shop. Her servant and visitors find the doll disturbing without being to articulate what they are concerned about. The doll seems to move about by itself when people are not looking, but its owner thinks that the servant is responsible. Eventually even she is affected and she shuts it up in a room that she no longer enters. Finally, she attempts to destroy the doll but it is taken away by a child and is beyond her reach.

"The Edge" is a study in psychology. The protagonist lost the man she loved to a vindictive rival. By accident, she discovers that the wife is having an affair. Rather than expose her, she uses that knowledge to humble and terrify her enemy. The wife is, however, thoroughly in love with the other man, but frightened that a divorce would ruin both their lives. She finally commits suicide in order to save her lover from disgrace. The protagonist then becomes insane, crippled by guilt.

"The Erymanthian Boar" takes Poirot to an isolated mountain lodge where one of those present is actually a fugitive murderer and others are presumed to be members of his gang. The story involves impersonation and the unlikely rescue of Poirot by a gun-toting American tourist.

"The Face of Helen" begins with Satterthwaite and Quin noticing an unusually beautiful young woman at the opera. She has two admirers and when she accepts one's proposal, the other provides a wedding present – an unusual radio. But Quin knows that it is a device designed to release a deadly poison gas under certain conditions. He intervenes and the would-be killed commits suicide.

"A Fairy in the Flat" simply sets up Tommy and Tuppence as professional detectives.

"Finessing the King" is a partial Tommy and Tuppence story in which they decode a message, attend a costume ball, but fail to prevent the murder of a young woman. The story continues in "The Gentleman Dressed in Newspaper."

"The Flock of Geryon" is a direct sequel to "The Nemean Lion." The woman who kidnapped dogs now wants Poirot to help with a wealthy friend who has joined what would now be called a cult. It specializes in recruiting elderly people with money, several of whom have died suddenly, leaving everything to the cult. With her help, Poirot proves that the head of the cult is killing his followers for their money.

"Four and Twenty Blackbirds" is another story of impersonation. This time a killer impersonates his victim to confuse the estimated time of death, but Poirot spots anomalies in his behavior.

"The Four Suspects" mixes Miss Marple and espionage. A retired spy is killed and there are only four people who could have been the killer. She solves the case.

"The Fourth Man" takes place on a train when four men find

themselves in the same car. One is a clergyman, one a lawyer, and one a psychologist. The fourth man does not speak and looks foreign. They begin discussing split personalities, specifically a French woman who had four different personas and who eventually took her own life. The fourth man then speaks up, insisting that he knew the woman and that she had been tormented by another. After her death, her enemy became convinced that the dead woman was now inside her own mind.

"A Fruitful Sunday" describes what happens when a not very bright couple find what they think is a stolen necklace in a basket of cherries. It is actually a fake. Too coincidental to be plausible.

"The Gentleman Dressed in Newspaper" is a continuation of the Tommy and Tuppence story, "Finessing the King." A dying woman's final words suggest who murdered her, but it turns out to be someone else entirely.

"The Gipsy" is a fantasy about two men who encounter a woman who may have the power of seeing the future.

"The Girdle of Hyppolyta" draws two cases together. A valuable painting has been stolen and is believed to have been smuggled into France. At the same time, a school girl has disappeared mysteriously from a moving train and although she is found safe a day later, she is dazed and was perhaps drugged. Poirot figures out that the girl was kidnapped before she boarded the train and an imposter traveled in her place. The imposter changed her appearance and left the train unobserved at its destination. The trick was to include a disguised version of the stolen painting in her luggage.

"The Girl in the Train" is a spoof of stories of intrigue. A conceited young man meets a woman on a train, agrees to follow another man without explanation, indulges in various spying activities, and eventually gets to marry the girl. It is one of Christie's few genuinely funny stories.

"The Golden Ball" is a not very serious tale of a recently unemployed man who gets involved with a woman who has hired actors to pretend to menace them, in order to judge the characters of the men she meets.

"Greenshaw's Folly" is a convoluted story in which a housekeeper impersonates her employer in order to write a new will in her own favor. Miss Marple figures it out.

"Harlequin's Lane" was the last appearance of Quin, who makes enigmatic comments while Satterthwaite unravels a quasi-tragic love affair.

"The Harlequin Tea Set" is a Harley Quin story in which he nudges Satterthwaite into preventing murder by poison.

"The Herb of Death" features Miss Marple. A supposed accidental case of food poisoning is actually a very clever murder.

"The Horses of Diomedes" begins with a drug party that ends with a minor shooting. A doctor asks Poirot to help him shield a young woman who attended but whom he thinks has learned her lesson. The others will, of course, be turned over to the police.

"The Hound of Death" is a fantasy in which a nun once called upon some primordial power to destroy a body of enemy soldiers. The nun was left in a peculiar mental state and years later attempts to probe into her visions result in tragic deaths.

"The House of Dreams" is not a mystery. An unambitious young man discovers that the woman he loves has vowed never to marry because of a strong strain of insanity in her family. He decides to run off to Africa where he eventually dies. The title refers to his recurring dream of a house he cannot quite enter.

"The House of Lurking Death" begins with a box of poisoned chocolates from an anonymous sender. One of the victims hires Tommy and Tuppence but eats a poisoned sandwich soon afterward and dies. Tuppence figures out who is responsible, but the poisoner dies herself before she can be arrested.

"How Does Your Garden Grow?" takes Poirot to the countryside after the woman who sent him a letter requesting help dies suddenly. She left the bulk of her estate to her companion rather than her niece, and the fact that she was poisoned – apparently by the companion – immediately tells the reader that the niece was responsible. The method is a bit of a cheat – in the closing paragraphs Poirot reveals that the dead woman had secretly been given some poisoned oysters, the shells of which are now lining part of the garden.

"The Idol House of Astarte" is a grove of trees rumored to have once hosted a sacred temple. When a group of people visit the area, one woman seems to be briefly possessed and then one of the men is stabbed to death in open view – except that there is no weapon. Jane Marple hears the story and correctly deduces that the first person to reach him after he had fallen without injuring himself committed murder and concealed the weapon upon his person.

MASTERS OF DETECTION

"In a Glass Darkly" is a non-series story with some fantastic content. A man has a vision of another man murdering a woman in the future. He himself falls in love with the prospective victim, prevents her from marrying the killer, and marries her himself. But years later, he has a moment of insane jealousy and is about to kill his wife, and is stopped only because the vision recurs.

"Jane in Search of a Job" is an unemployed woman who agrees to impersonate an aristocrat who is in danger of being kidnapped. The abduction takes place, but it is all actually an elaborate cover story so that the aristocrat – who is an imposter – can steal some jewels and have a suitable alibi.

"The Jewel Robbery at the Grand Metropolitan" is a Poirot story. He is present in a hotel when a string of pearls is stolen, apparently by their owner's maid. It was actually two other people, using a complicated and perfectly timed trick that depended on a situation they could not possibly have foreseen. A very weak story.

"The Kidnapped Prime Minister" involves the substitution of a double to fool police into believing that the minister was abducted at a particular time. Poirot clears the matter up and the minister is rescued.

"The King of Clubs" shows Poirot reasoning from the fact that a card is missing from a deck used for a supposed bridge party to expose blackmail and reveal that a possible murder was actually an accident.

"The Lamp" is a rather conventional ghost story. A boy died in an old house. The new tenants have a son who can see the boy and wants to help, but he falls ill and dies. There are then two ghosts in the house.

"The Last Séance" is one of the author's occasional ventures into horror. A genuine medium has become so frightened that she vows that her next scheduled séance will be her last. The manifestations literally make use of a part of her body as material to form something solid. But the final customer breaks the rules when her dead infant appears and takes it away with her. The medium is found dead, with portions of her body missing.

"The Lemesurier Inheritance" is a slightly uncharacteristic Poirot story involving a family curse. The first born son in a wealthy family has not inherited for generations thanks to accidents and deaths from disease. Poirot is asked to investigate when the latest heir apparent survives a series of potentially deadly accidents. He determines that the boy's father is insane and is determined to validate the family curse.

"The Lernean Hydra" involves a doctor whose career is being ruined by rumors that he poisoned his wife in order to marry his assistant. There is enough circumstantial evidence for Poirot to instigate an exhumation, which reveals that she was indeed poisoned. But the murderer was her nurse, who was secretly in love with the husband.

"The Listerdale Mystery" takes an impoverished woman and her two adult children to a house offered at an amazingly low rent. It belongs to Lord Listerdale, who disappeared to Africa under mysterious circumstances more than a year earlier. Her son believes the man was murdered. There is something odd about the butler, who turns out to be Listerdale himself. He had undergone a midlife crisis and was trying to expunge his early sins. He ends up marrying the mother.

"The Lonely God" is a romance rather than a crime story. Two lonely people are both drawn to an obscure artifact in a museum and find each other.

"The Lost Mine" is owned by a Chinese businessman who disappears after traveling to London. Poirot figures out that the disappearance was faked and that the man who arrived in England was an imposter.

"The Love Detectives" is a Harley Quin story. He figures out the solution to a murder mystery by realizing that two clocks were altered in different ways.

"Magnolia Blossom" involves a lover's triangle. A woman in the process of leaving her husband decides to remain because he is facing bankruptcy. Then she discovers that his business dealings were crooked and that he was lying to her in order to cover his own sins.

"The Man from the Sea" is Harley Quin, who only appears on the last two pages. He is seen by a vacationer and his description convinces Satterthwaite that his mysterious friend has some to the island where he is taking a break from England. Sure enough, he has to solve a murder involving a man who is terminally ill.

"The Manhood of Edward Robinson" is a mildly humorous story about an insecure man who accidentally drives off in the wrong car, finds a stolen necklace in it, has a rendezvous with the thieves, carries off an impersonation, and returns to his normal life with a new sense of confidence.

"The Man in the Mist" involves a supposed ghost. Tommy and Tuppence run into an old friend who is posing as a clergyman. They discover a woman bludgeoned to death in her bed, presumably by the husband she has never identified to any of her family, who have never met him. They determine that the police constable who promptly answered their call for help was unrealistically quick and therefore was the murderer, still lingering at the scene.

"The Man Who Was No. 16" mixes Tommy and Tuppence with espionage as they are asked to identify a Russian agent surreptitiously operating in England.

"Manx Gold" was written as part of a tourism stunt for the Isle of Man, setting up a mystery whose clues would lead someone to a "treasure" concealed on the island. Two grandchildren of a notorious scoundrel find a letter from him following his death which suggests that he concealed a very large treasure somewhere on the Isle of Man.

"The Market Basing Mystery" is another case where Poirot sees through a clever subterfuge. A housekeeper murders her employer but arranges things so that it appears the guilty party is a house guest.

"The Million Dollar Bond Robbery" involves the theft of a bundle of negotiable securities from a locked case aboard a cruise ship. Poirot correctly determines the documents were never there in the first place, but the story makes this quite obvious much earlier.

"Miss Marple Tells a Story" is a routine tale of a murder committed by a woman disguised as a chambermaid, since hotel help is rarely noticed.

"Motive v. Opportunity" is a minor Miss Marple in which disappearing ink is used to write a will in order to mislead the potential heirs.

"Murder in the Mews" is a long Poirot story. A young woman is found in a locked room, the victim of an obviously staged suicide. Her flatmate had been away for a few days and called the police when she could not open the door to the victim's room. The dead woman was engaged to be married and had no financial or other known troubles. She was also paying blackmail to someone, perhaps a man who knew her when she was living in India. They arrest the blackmailer, but Poirot confronts the roommate. It was suicide after all, but she altered the physical evidence before calling the police in order to cast suspicion on the blackmailer, in revenge for her friend's death.

"The Mystery of Hunter's Lodge" is a standard puzzle story. A woman murders her husband but then disguises herself as a housemaid who establishes an alibi for her mistress, actually herself.

"The Mystery of the Bagdad Chest" revolves around a small party at a man's apartment, after which the husband of one of the guests is found stabbed to death in a large chest. Poirot notes that air holes have recently been punched in the chest and concludes that the dead man suspected his wife of infidelity, was spying on her, and was murdered by a third party who hoped to frame their host. A slightly different version appeared as "The Mystery of the Spanish Chest."

"The Mystery of the Blue Jar" describes a young man who keeps hearing calls for help that are inaudible to everyone else. He thinks he is losing his mind, but a professorial type tells him that he may have tapped into some kind of psychic link. In actuality, it is all a hoax designed to facilitate a theft.

"The Nemean Lion" is an unusual Poirot adventure. He is hired to discover who kidnapped a pampered Pekingese and returned the animal after being paid a ransom. He discovers a plot by an organized group of companions to wealthy but silly women. He is sympathetic and protects the perpetrators by revealing that the indignant husband pressuring the police to arrest the plotters poisoned his first wife.

"Next to a Dog" is a non-mystery about a woman who contemplates marriage solely so that she will be able to support a pet dog, and who backs out when the dog is accidentally killed.

"Philomel Cottage" is a suspenseful story in which a woman realizes that the man she married is a crook and plans to kill her. She is able to get a message to a former lover, but before he arrives she convinces the man she has poisoned him – which is not true – and he dies of fright.

"The Plymouth Express" is a train upon which a woman is murdered by her maid in order to steal her jewels. There is a bit of impersonation involved to confuse the issue but Poirot is not fooled.

"A Pot of Tea" has Tommy and Tuppence tracking down a missing young woman, but it is a major cheat because the woman and Tuppence are friends and arranged things to worry her boyfriend.

"Problem at Pollensa Bay" is a Parker Pyne story set in Spain. A doting mother disapproves of her son's fiancé because of her life style so Pyne finds another woman to act even worse, convinces the son to pretend to have switched affections, and the mother suddenly finds the fiancé more acceptable.

"Problem at Sea" involves a rich woman who is murdered in her cabin on a cruise ship. Poirot happens to be aboard and he correctly concludes that she was killed earlier than it appears and that her husband used ventriloquism to imitate her voice and confuse witnesses. Christie appears to have believed that voices can actually be thrown because the sounds came "through the door."

"The Rajah's Emerald" is another story of a man who stumbles into a crime. The protagonist steals the use of a private dressing room at a beach and ends up with the wrong pants and a stolen emerald. The real thief pretends to be a detective, but is tricked into betraying himself to the police.

"The Red House" is the second half of a Tommy and Tuppence story. They help a young woman marry the man of her choice by locating a treasure buried on her property.

"The Red Signal" begins with several people arguing about whether or not premonitions are real. The protagonist fails to heed a premonition of his own and gets trapped in a murder case.

"The Regatta Mystery" is meant to be a prank. A young girl claims that she can steal a valuable gem, but it disappears for real. Parker Pyne solves the crime – the girl and two other people are in collusion – but the number of people who had to be involved make it impossible for the reader to guess the solution.

"Sanctuary" begins when a woman finds a dead man in her church. Two people posing as relations are determined to have all of his possessions including a tattered coat. He is in fact an escaped convict who checked a bag filled with stolen gems and the baggage check is in his coat, but a suspicious woman takes the ticket and Miss Marple finds the truth.

"The Second Gong" is a Poirot story. He is invited to the home of a man who is pathological about promptness and a tightly scheduled dinner. When he fails to appear, the door to his study is forced to reveal him slumped dead in a chair, apparently having shot himself. Poirot figures out that the secretary killed the man to avoid being exposed as an embezzler.

"The Shadow on the Glass" includes an apparently genuine supernatural element, a window that shows a man's face even when the glass is replaced. The plot involves a complicated pair of interlocking romantic triangles and a double murder – two people fatally shot in the garden. Satterthwaite is on hand again and Harley Quin shows up on different business just as the police are about to make an arrest. A minor wound and other clues point instead to the dead woman's husband, who discovered she was in love with another.

"The Sign in the Sky" is a twisted smoke column from a train. When an innocent man is convicted of murder, Satterthwaite discovers that one of the maids was hurried out of the country with a cover story. Quin's questions lead him to realize that this meant the clocks in the house were displaying an incorrect time, so the alibi for the dead woman's husband is eliminated and he confesses.

"SOS" has a very familiar opening. A motorist has automobile trouble in the midst of a violent storm and takes refuge in a remote house tenanted by a somewhat peculiar family. The house is supposedly haunted. The houseguest notices something suspicious and uncovers a plot by the man of the house to poison one of his two daughters.

"The Soul of the Croupier" takes Satterthwaite and Quin to Monaco where a predatory woman has targeted a gullible young American tourist. There is no crime this time. The woman was once married to a croupier in the casino, who fakes things so that she wins some money, only to have her reject his pity.

"The Strange Case of Sir Andrew Carmichael" involves the supernatural. A young man has complete amnesia and eventually displays the personality of his deceased father. The cause of death was deemed natural but he was murdered. Once he has communicated this fact, the possession ends and the young man's original personality is restored.

"Strange Jest" has no crime involved. A man with an odd sense of humor dies and his substantial legacy is concealed. Miss Marple realizes that the stamps on his old letters are very valuable.

MASTERS OF DETECTION

"The Stymphalean Birds" are a pair of Polish women who are inadvertently drawn into a scheme to defraud a tourist by convincing him that he saw an accidental death which would ruin his reputation – it would be supposed that he was cheating with the dead man's wife – and agrees to bribe the authorities. Poirot proves that the death never took place and that he is being swindled.

"The Submarine Plans" is another Poirot espionage story. A man has been murdered and the specifications for a new submarine have disappeared under sinister circumstances, but they have actually been altered in ways that will make any attempt to use them unsuccessful. One of the women involved is found holding the murder weapon, which she claims she instinctively picked up.

"The Sunningdale Mystery" involves the murder of a man stabbed by a hatpin while he was walking on a golf course. Tommy and Tuppence are right and the police turn out to be wrong about the identity of the killer.

"Swan Song" is a tale of revenge. A famous opera singer arranges a situation in which a retired performer agrees to come out of retirement for one performance, during which she murders him because of an old affront.

"Tape-Measure Murder" involves the strangulation of a married woman. Suspicion points to the husband but Miss Marple determines that the killer is actually the dress maker who was at the door when the body was discovered, avenging an old grudge.

"The Third Floor Flat" is a variation of the locked room mystery. When their friend loses the key to her flat, two men decide to enter by means of the coal lift. They get off at the wrong floor and find a woman's dead body. Poirot figures out that the choice of the mistaken floor was managed and that one of the two men is the killer.

"Three Blind Mice" is a very suspenseful novella with none of Christie's recurring characters. A newly opened lodge has only four guests, one of whom is probably an insane serial killer motivated by a childhood grudge. A lone policeman arrives just before they are snowed in and the telephone line promptly stops working. One of the guests is murdered and one of the innkeepers almost follows before they discover that the police officer is a fake.

"The Thumbmark of St. Peter" involves the murder of a man whose final words are misunderstood, making the wrong person a suspect. Miss Marple figures out what he was really saying.

"The Tragedy at Marsdon Manor" has multiple layers of revelation. Poirot is hired by an insurance company after a highly insured man dies of supposedly natural causes. His initial investigation suggests that the dead man committed suicide and disguised it so that his widow could collect the insurance, but further study proves that the wife actually murdered her husband.

"Triangle at Rhodes" is a Poirot story. A romantic triangle at a resort leads to an attempt at murder by poisoning, but the wrong person drinks the tainted glass.

"The Unbreakable Alibi" does not involve a crime. Tommy and Tuppence are challenged to break an apparently perfect alibi. They figure out that there is a twin involved, which is cheating.

"The Under Dog" is a novella. Sir Reuben Astwell has been murdered and his nephew, Charles Leverson, has been arrested. The evidence against him appears to be overwhelming. Other potential suspects include Victor Astwell, his brother, Owen Trefusis, his secretary, and Lily Margrave, companion to Lady Astwell. Lady Astwell believes that Trefusis is the killer and calls in Hercule Poirot. The investigation turns up evidence that the dead man stole the rights to a gold mine years earlier, but it is in fact Trefusis who killed his employer, reacting to many years of abuse in a moment of rage.

"The Veiled Lady" is a supposed aristocrat who is being blackmailed by an odious man. Poirot burgles the man's house and recovers a compromising letter, along with some stolen jewels. The lady is an imposter who had a falling out with other thieves and wanted to make off with the jewels that they had already stolen.

"The Voice in the Dark" hints at the supernatural. A young woman is troubled by accusing voices in her bedroom and there is some evidence that other people have had weird experiences near her. She, however, does not believe in ghosts. Satterthwaite and Quin arrive. There is a séance at which the ghost of a dead aunt mentions things that only she could have known. Satterthwaite, quite on his own this time as Quin does not even fill his usual role as a catalyst, figures out that the aunt is suffering from amnesia, has fits of clarity, and is bitter about having been thwarted of her legacy by her sister.

"While the Light Lasts" is not really a mystery. A woman

marries after the man she loves is reported to have killed. Several months later she discovers that he is alive and is trying to figure out how to resolve her conflicting opinions when he commits suicide, convinced they can never be together.

"The Wife of the Kenite" is a widow who lost her son during the German invasion in World War I. The man responsible is a German agent in South Africa and by chance he ends up staying at her house, where she kills him.

"Wireless" (aka "Where There's a Will") is a cute if predictable story in which an elderly and wealthy woman whose heart is failing is given a radio by her doting but impoverished nephew. He is the chief beneficiary in her new will. He uses faked broadcasts to suggest that her long dead husband is coming for her and succeeds in scaring the woman to death. Only at that point does he learn that she burned her will, intending to write a new one, and her fortune reverts to an earlier legatee. And on top of everything else, she would only have lived a few more weeks in any case, so his efforts actually cost him the fortune.

"Within a Wall" is another character study. An obsessed artist becomes aware of his wife's sinister means of financing his career, and what he must pay in return.

"Witness for the Prosecution" presents an interesting problem. A man is accused of murdering an elderly woman he befriended after she made a will in his favor. He insists that he did not know about the will. His alibi is based on his "wife," but in fact they are not married because her husband is in an asylum. And she hates him and would like to see him hang. But this is all a ruse. She arranges to have herself exposed during testimony and he is acquitted. Only then does she tell his lawyer that he was actually guilty.

"The World's End" is a remote town in the mountains of Corsica where Satterthwaite runs into Quin once again. The plot involves a stolen jewel that was not really stolen, a man falsely sent to jail, and a murder plan that is canceled when Quin convinces the jailed man's fiancé that he was not framed.

"Yellow Iris" involves the re-creation of a party at a club where the host's wife died, apparently having taken poison. Poirot answers a summons from one of the guests, who senses something is wrong, and he averts a murder by the same method.

MASTERS OF DETECTION

A great many of Christie's novels have been adapted for the screen, perhaps most notably the PBS series of Poirot films (1989-2013) starring David Suchet. The summary that follows is not all-inclusive of even English language titles, let alone those made elsewhere.

The first of these was *The Passing of Mr. Quin* (1928, based on the story "The Coming of Mr. Quin." *Adventures, Inc.* (1929) was an adaptation of *The Secret Adversary* and *Alibi* (1931) was a version of *The Murder of Roger Ackroyd*. *Lord Edgware Dies* appeared in 1934. "Philomel Cottage" was made for television as *Love from a Stranger* in 1938. It was remade in 1947 and 1958.

The first major film was *And Then There Were None* (1945) which was
 remade in 1949 and 1959. *Witness for the Prosecution* was released in 1948 and remade in 1957. During the early 1950s, her work appeared in many television anthology series including Lux Video Theater, Danger, Suspense, and Studio One.

Murder She Said (1961) was based on *4:50 from Paddington*. *Murder at the Gallop* (1963) is from *After the Funeral* and *Murder Most Foul* (1964) is from *Mrs. McGinty's Dead*. *The ABC Murders* became *The Alphabet Murders* (1965), *Endless Night* (1972), *Murder on the Orient Express* (1974), *Death on the Nile* (1978), and *Why Didn't They Ask Evans?* (1980) were interspersed with uncredited versions of *Ten Little Indians*.

More adaptations followed including *The Mirror Crack'd* (1980), *The Seven Dials Mystery* (1981), *Murder Is Easy* (1982), and *Evil Under the Sun* (1982). The Agatha Christie Hour in 1982) provided versions of several of her stories and was followed by a remake of *Witness for the Prosecution* (1982), *A Caribbean Mystery* (1983), *Sparkling Cyanide* (1983), and *Ordeal by Innocence* (1984). 1984 also brought a television miniseries, *Partners in Crime*, and several other brief series including *The Body in the Library, The Moving Finger, A Murder Is Announced*, and *A Pocketful of Rye* all during 1984-1985. *Murder with Mirrors* and *Thirteen at Dinner* also appeared in 1985.

Dead Man's Folly appeared in 1986, as did *The Murder at the Vicarage*. *The Mousetrap* was another miniseries. 1987 saw the release of *Sleeping Murder, At Bertram's Hotel, Nemesis*, another version of *Ten Little Indians*, and a remake of *4:50 from Paddington*.

Appointment with Death reached the screen in 1988 and *The Man in the Brown Suit* in 1989, along with yet another *Ten Little Indians* and a remake of *A Caribbean Mystery*.

They Do It with Mirrors (1991) was followed by a remake of *The Mirror Crack'd* (1992). *Innocent Lies* (1995) was based on *Towards Zero* and *The Pale Horse* was remade in 1997. 2001 saw another version of *Murder on the Orient Express*. The pace slowed down after that. A new version of *Sparkling Cyanide* arrived in 2003, *By the Pricking of My Thumbs* screened in 2005, and another television series based on stories about Poirot and Marple ran from 2004-2005.

There were two audio versions in 2007 – *Evil Under the Sun* and *Towards Zero*. *Peril at End House* also appeared that year. *Crime Is Our Business* (2008) was adapted from *Partners in Crime*. A new version of *Witness for the Prosecution* arrived in 2016 as a miniseries. *Crooked House* (2017), *Ordeal by Innocence* (2018), another version of *The ABC Murders* that same year, a redo of *The Pale Horse* (2020), *The Hollow* (2020), a remake of *Death on the Nile*, and *A Haunting in Venice* (2023), allegedly based on *Hallowe'en Party*, are the most recent as of this writing. The last title has nothing to do with the book.

BY OTHER HANDS

There are also several continuations of her series by other authors. Charles Osborne has novelized three stage plays which Christie wrote early in her career, and Sophie Hannah is the author of several new Poirot novels. There is also an anthology of short stories featuring Miss Marple.

Osborne's first novelization was *Black Coffee* (1997). It features Hercule Poirot. Sir Claud Emory is a brilliant scientist whose newest discovery is an atomic bomb variant. The formula is stolen from his safe during a family gathering and just before Poirot arrives at his request, he dies after drinking some poisoned coffee.

The people present during this incident are his niece Barbara, his son Richard and wife Lucia, the latter of whom is Italian, his spinster sister Caroline, and his secretary, Edward Raynor. There is also a supposed friend of Lucia calling himself Dr. Carelli, also Italian, although it is obvious from the outset that he is blackmailing Lucia somehow. All of his relatives dislike Sir Claud, who is rather stingy, and no one likes Carelli either.

Just prior to the fatal event, a container of various poisons was examined by several of the suspects. It had been left over from the war when the house was used as a hospital. Lucia put some of these pills into a cup of coffee, but it is not clear if that was the one from which Sir Claud subsequently drank. She did in fact intervene when Raynor picked up a cup for his employer. We also learn that Lucia's valuable necklace disappeared a few months earlier, reinforcing the idea that she is being blackmailed.

An anonymous letter mentions Selma Goetz, a notorious spy who has recently died. Goetz had an adult daughter, who is clearly Lucia. These details emerge during Poirot's investigation and Lucia insists that she stole the poison, intending to kill herself. She believes that her husband killed his father and makes a transparently false confession.

Poirot is convinced, correctly, that the formula is hidden somewhere in the room where Sir Claud died. Carelli tries to flee and is arrested on unrelated charges – he has long been suspected to espionage as well as mundane crimes. The real killer is Raynor, who wanted to sell the formula to a foreign power. The formula is recovered.

Osborne's second novelization was *The Unexpected Guest* (1999). Michael Starkwedder has just returned to England and gets lost in the fog. He enters a remote house and finds Richard Warwick shot to death in his wheel chair. Warwick's wife, Laura, immediately confesses to having shot him and expects him to call the police, but Starkwedder hears her story and decides to help her out.

Warwick was a big game hunter who was mauled by a lion and could no longer walk. He was sadistic and vindictive and had made a hobby of shooting passing cats, dogs, squirrels, etc. The other residents of the house are unaware of the fatal shooting. They consist of Richard's mother, his mentally challenged younger half brother, a housekeeper named Bennett, and a nurse named Henry Angell.

They cannot contrive a plausible accident or suicide scenario, so they consider vaguely blaming the dead man's enemies from the past. The most likely is the father of a child Richard ran down with his car while speeding, MacGregor. Starkwedder arranges things to support the story that he was approaching the house, heard a gunshot, recovered the gun, and entered to find the body. The police tentatively accept the story and try to find out more about the old enemy, who lives in Canada.

A neighbor, Julian Farrar, tells the police that Richard was widely disliked because of his shooting of small animals and his arrogant personality. Farrar had left his cigarette lighter in the house and retrieves it. Laura and Farrar are clearly more than just friends. Starkwedder realizes that she does not even know how to take the safety off the murder weapon. It was Farrar who shot her husband.

Angell knows about the affair and tries to blackmail Farrar. He also saw Farrar leave the house just after the shot was fired. Farrar accuses Laura of being the killer and vice versa, which puts a strain on their relationship. The police are told that the old enemy has been dead for some time so he obviously is not the killer if that is the truth.

The older Mrs. Warwick then tells Starkwedder that she skilled her son because he had turned into a monster. He thinks she is lying and he is right. Jan is the real killer. He was afraid that Richard was going to have him put in an institution. Or is he? Startkwedder tells Laura that he is MacGregor, that he faked his death and changed his name and that he might have shot Richard. The identity of the killer is never confirmed.

The third of Osborne's adaptations was *The Spider's Web* (2000). Clarissa, wife of a diplomat, Henry Hailsham-Brown, is fond of games. As the story opens, Sir Rowland Delahaye and Hugo Birch are participating in a blindfolded wine tasting to determine how good a pallet each of them has. They and Jeremy Warrender are guests of the Hailsham-Browns. Clarissa has fooled them – all of the samples are from the same bottle.

Henry has a daughter, Pippa, by his first marriage. She is still in school and lives with them. Warrender is openly in love with Clarissa. Mildred Peake is the gardener. Elgin is the butler and his wife is the cook. Henry's ex-wife, Miranda, was a drug user, presumably cured, and has remarried since the divorce. Peake does not get along with the Elgins.

An unsolicited visitor tried to purchase a desk from the house and ignored Clarissa when she told him that they were renting the house furnished and that the desk did not belong to her. Pippa shows Warrender a secret passage. She also reveals a hidden drawer in the desk, from which she has taken autographs by Queen Victoria and others. There was a stamped envelope which she sold to a dealer for a small sum.

Oliver Costello arrives unannounced. He is believed to be the man who provided drugs to Miranda and is now her husband. The terms of the divorce left her with custody of Pippa, but there was a private understanding that she would stay with her father. Pippa is nearly hysterical when she finds him there. Clarissa is certain they are trying to extort money from her husband.

Henry arrives and tells her that there will be a secret conference between the Russian premier and the Prime Minister at their house that evening. It is very much secret and she is not to make an appearance. While they are elsewhere in the house, Costello sneaks in. He has just opened the secret drawer when someone emerges from the secret passage and strikes him on the head.

Clarissa finds Costello's body. Pippa arrives and insists that she did not mean to kill him. She calls her three guests back from their club and enlists their aid in moving Costello's body and his car to a nearby wooded area. Before they can do so, the doorbell rings, so they stash the body in the secret passage. There is a hint that while Pippa might have knocked Costello out, she did not deliver the fatal blow.

The police are at the door. They are responding to an anonymous telephone call about a murder, presumably made by the real killer. Clarissa is startled to discover that the Elgins, who had left for the cinema, are home after all. Mrs. Elgin is reportedly ill and they aborted their trip. An antiques dealer named Sellon previously lived in the house and had died of a fall down the stairs which the police were not entirely convinced was accidental.

The police find Costello's car. Clarissa admits that he was there earlier, but claims it was just to drop off some items that Miranda wanted to return to her ex-husband. Peake confirms that she showed Costello out, but she reveals the existence of the passageway and the police find the body. The story the others cobble together falls apart, so Clarissa is prevailed upon to tell the truth. The police do not believe that either, so she tells a lie about having struck the man because she thought he was a burglar. This time they believe her.

Meanwhile, the body has disappeared. Peake tells Clarissa that she hid it in one of the bedrooms. Pippa thinks she killed Costello by black magic, which means she is not the one who struck him down.

Sellon had a partner named Brown and Clarissa realizes that this was the person whom Costello had come to see. And it is also obvious that Mrs Brown is Peake.

The autographs from the secret drawer are a ruse. Heat brings out secret writing – the names of drug dealers who worked with Sellon, one of whom was Costello. But Clarissa has realized the truth. Warrenden was playing golf alone and could have sneaked back into the house. He admits that she is right, tells her the stamp on the envelope is worth a fortune, and then tries to kill her. The police are listening in and come to the rescue.

Marple (2020) is a collection of twelve original Jane Marple stories by different writers. No editor is credited. "Evil in Small Places" by Lucy Foley has Marple visiting an old school friend. A retired opera singer has moved into the town and has become quite unpopular, although her maid indicates that she was a lovely woman. The singer is found stabbed to death, clutching a note that suggests blackmail. The dead woman was rumored to have flirted with a local man and the murder weapon is found in his wife's purse. Marple concludes that her friend was the real killer, with her adult daughter as her accomplice. The motive was that the woman was a relative of the friend's first husband, whom she had secretly poisoned.

"The Second Murder at the Vicarage" by Val McDermid begins with the discovery of a woman's body, a few days after her lover ate poisoned mushrooms and died. Marple concludes that the two of them were planning to blackmail a local politician who had been having an affair. This story cheats a great deal, withholding some information until the end, using two people to commit the crimes, and having neither of them appear on stage at any time in the story.

"Miss Marple Takes Manhattan: by Alyssa Cole takes place in New York, where she has accompanied her nephew and his wife to see a play based on his novel. There is a feud among the cast and what appears at first to be a murder but turns out not to be.

"The Unravelling" by Natalie Haynes describes a petty fight between two men in a village street. The next morning one of them is found dead, killed by an arrow. The other party confesses, but witnesses prove he could not have done it. Then his wife confesses, but she did not do it either. The dead man was her real husband, father of her son. She was living with an impostor because she needed his help and believed her real husband was dead. Their son thought the dead man was going to upset his family and killed him.

"Miss Marple's Christmas" by Ruth Ware is a holiday gathering to which an odd couple is inadvertently invited. The situation becomes even more awkward when the alarm is raised about some missing pearls.

"The Open Mind" by Naomi Alderman is set in academia. A very unpopular, pompous professor is descended from a family that had connections with Oliver Cromwell. When he is poisoned at a formal dinner, a young woman almost dies with him. She recovers and Marple arranges for her to be caught stealing historical documents from the dead man's family vault, which was only unlocked because of the funeral.

"The Jade Empress" by Jean Kwok takes Marple on a cruise to Hong Kong, where she meets the wealthy Mr. Pang. Pang left his family to find a job in England, but when he had enough money to bring them over, the wife had already died and the son preferred to stay. Now he is going to meet his son, bringing his daughter by a second wife, who has also died. Pang is stabbed to death in his bed and his daughter is the chief suspect. Marple reveals the real killer to be Pang's son, who impersonated a steward.

"A Deadly Wedding Day" by Dreda Say Mitchell goes badly from the start. The groom's mother is indignant that her son is marrying for love rather than money. The bride has almost no personal guests at the ceremony. And then a woman whom no one appears to recognize dies at the beginning of the reception. Marple proves that the dead woman was accidentally responsible for her own death, which she had meant for another.

"Murder at the Villa Rosa" by Ely Griffiths appears to be narrated by a woman contemplating the murder of a long time friend. She has emotional and physical problems which Marple recognizes, but she is not actually a criminal. She is a writer who has decided to kill off the recurring character in her books.

"The Murdering Sort" by Karen M. McManus has Marple solving a murder by poison within a family she knows.

"The Mystery of the Acid Soil" by Kate Mosse starts when Marple, en route to visit an old friend, encounters an apparently troubled clergyman on a train. He was in love with a woman who has vanished. Her family claims she joined a theater group but he has already determined that this is false. The girl's mother had recently died of tetanus and some of the circumstances are suspicious. She was survived by her husband, stepfather to the missing woman, who was notoriously tight with his money. The doctor who attended the case also died mysteriously. Marple concludes that they were both murdered and that the missing woman is being secretly held in the house. A direct investigation proves her to be correct.

"The Disappearance" by Leigh Bardugo also deals with a missing person. Marple notices a friend's strange aversion to the garden she had previously doted upon and concludes that a body is buried there. Naturally she is right.

As of this writing, Sophie Hannah has brought Poirot back in five novels, starting with *The Monogram Murder* (2014), set in 1929. Poirot is living quietly in London, temporarily rooming with a Scotland Yard detective, Edward Catchpool – who is the narrator. He is in a small coffee shop one night when a regular patron, Jennie, arrives in a state of evident terror. She insists that she is in danger and that her death will be justified but does not explain why. When she runs off, the waitress tells Poirot that she works as a kind of housekeeper for an unknown woman.

Catchpool has that day been at the scene of three murders, in three different rooms at the same hotel. Each of the bodies had then been arranged in the same position, so obviously the deaths were related. Each victim has a cufflink in his or her mouth, all labeled PIJ. Jennie had blurted out that she did not want anyone to "open their mouths," which implicates her as well.

Poirot invites himself into the investigation. The three victims are Harriet Sipple, Ida Gransbury, and Richard Negus. The manager is named Lazzari, and the chief receptionist is John Goode. The victims had all checked in the previous day, but they were not traveling together. Their room keys are all missing. Each had separately ordered room service at precisely 7:15.

Gransbury apparently had company – two teacups. Negus is the only one whose window was open. Otherwise they appear to have been quietly poisoned and then formally arranged on the floor. The women have the cufflink between their lips, but Negus' is in his throat. The killer also left a note at the desk listing the three rooms involved.

Poirot finds Negus' key concealed in his room, but the other two are still missing. Negus booked all three of the rooms and the two women lived in the same village, although he did not. Rather belatedly Lazzari tells the police that he erred. The three had their suppers together in Gransbury's room. But no one knows how the sherry appeared in Negus' room.

Samuel Kidd was walking past the hotel on the night of the murders and tells police that he saw a woman run out, drop two keys, pick them up, and then disappear into the darkness. He was able to read the room numbers – which is very unlikely. Negus' brother Henry arrives. He does not know Sipple but his brother had at one time been engaged to Gransbury. Richard had given up his law practice and turned to drinking a few years earlier. His distress may have been connected to the death of the local vicar and his wife sixteen years earlier. The design of the monogram now appears to be PJI rather than PIJ.

Catchpool goes to their village for background. Victor Meakin, who runs the local hotel, seems vaguely hostile. A local man, Walter Stoakley, tells Catchpool that Sipple's husband died of a blood clot when they were quite young, and that she never recovered. Her personality took a sharp turn for the worse. Stoakley, however, is quite drunk and makes little sense thereafter.

A visit to the churchyard reveals that the dead vicar was Patrick James Ive, whose wife was Frances. Their graves are tended by Margaret Ernst, an older woman, who tells Catchpool that the local people would desecrate the graves if she did not watch over them. This portion of the novel is rather awkward. Catchpool does not speak to the local police – an obvious move – and the people he attempts to interview act unnaturally. Margaret's husband Charles was Patrick's replacement, until his recent death.

Kidd identifies the woman he saw as Nancy Ducane, a noted artist. Stoakely was Frances Ive's father. Ernst hints that Ducane has a motive to kill the three victims. She urges him not to talk to the village doctor, Ambrose Flowerday, and will only talk about the double death if her promises not to discuss it with any other villager. This is a very awkward and not credible scene.

The story is that a servant of the Ives told Sipple that Patrick was bilking villagers of their money by conducting bogus seances in the church. Ducane was the only one named as a victim. The villagers decided to believe Sipple's gossip. Negus and Gransbury, who were engaged at the time, promoted the rumor. Ducane confessed that she and Patrick were in love but insisted that nothing improper had taken place. Negus changed his mind, which brought an end to their engagement. Frances committed suicide and Patrick did the same a short time later. The servant who started the rumor is clearly Jennie.

Ducane denies being at the hotel when Kidd claims to have seen her there and a neighbor appears to confirm that they were together. But the two missing keys are found in her coat pocket, and the neighbor is missing a distinctive bowl which, in a convoluted fashion, might call her alibi into question. Catchpool returns to London and is immediately told that another murder has taken place at the hotel.

The body is missing but there is a pool of blood in one of the rooms. Jennie's hat is lying in the corner and a fourth cufflink has been placed inside. One of the hotel workers, Thomas Brignell, was seen with a woman on the ground who might have been Jennie. But she is not. Poirot now knows that Kidd has told several lies and he takes Catchpool to Kidd's house, where they find Jennie alive.

Jennie had put on an act to impress Poirot and with Kidd's help, tried to frame Ducane for the murders. She had prior knowledge of details which she could not have known otherwise. She insists that all three of those who died had come to see the error of their ways and that the four of them had drawn up a suicide pact to punish themselves for their past bad behavior. It appears then that the three who took poison had all arranged their own deaths.

The story has just been told when Catchpool learns that Ernst has been attacked and is dying. Poirot is convinced that Jennie is still lying. The solution is in fact very complex, involving tricks with timing, multiple impersonations, and other elements including red herrings. The three victims were killed much earlier than was believed. Ducane and Kidd impersonated two of them to mislead hotel staff members. Ducane's impeccable alibi is a lie. During the great reveal, Jennie fatally stabs Ducane. Negus did kill Grandbury, but Jennie killed him and Sipple.

Closed Casket (2016) begins with a meeting between Athelinda Playford, an author of children's books, and Michael Gathercole, her lawyer. She wants to write a new will, disinheriting her son Harry and daughter Claudia, and leave everything to Joseph Scotcher, her secretary. Claudia is engaged to Randall Kimpton, who is very wealthy, and Harry is married – his wife is Dorothy -and doing well in his profession. Scotcher is seriously ill and has only weeks to live.

Catchpool and Poirot are independently invited to Playford's mansion for a week. The other guests include the children and their partners, Gathercole, and another lawyer named Orville Rolfe. Scotcher is also present as is Sophie Bourlet, a nurse. The butler is Hatton, the maid is Phyllis, and the cook is Brigid. Claudia and Kimpton are exaggerated caricatures whose dialogue is artificial and awkward. The announcement of the new will has the predictable effect on all concerned. Scotcher asks Bourlet to marry him. Phyllis is dismayed because she is in love with him.

Rolfe seems to have been poisoned but it is only indigestion. He claims to have heard someone talking about open versus closed caskets. There is no explanation of why he took no steps after hearing his life threatened. Bourlet begins screaming and is found standing over the body of Scotcher, whose head had been battered until it is unrecognizable. She insists that she heard him talking to Claudia and then saw her kill him, but has no explanation of why she did not intervene in what would have been a lengthy process.

Claudia denies her story and seems to have a witness providing an alibi. Bourlet says that Claudia referred to someone named Iris, whom no one admits knowing about, or acts mysterious about, although there is no reason for them to do so. A great deal of the plot involves people doing things for no discernible reason. There are also contradictions. Playford insists that she already explained why she changed her will, but in fact she did not do so. She also claims that no one in the house is unkind, and we are told that she never lies, but almost every line of dialogue at this point has been deliberately unkind to the point of cruelty.

Kimpton, who is a doctor, recognizes that Scotcher had already been dead – poisoned – for a considerable time before his body was mutilated. Poirot somehow misses this fact despite ample evidence. The story is set in Ireland so the garda arrive, and the two detectives are so imbecilic that they are almost a parody. Iris is eventually identified as Iris Gillow, who was engaged to Kimpton years earlier, who broke off their engagement to marry Scotcher, and was then jilted by him in turn.

Playford expected that someone would try to murder her during the night, but does not say who. She asks Gathercole to hide in her room and surprise the killer. Kimpton reveals that Scotcher was not seriously ill at all, that he had been pretending for two years to gain sympathy. He also asserts that almost everyone knew this, including Playford and Bourlet. The autopsy supports his claim. He had somehow faked his visits to the doctor who was supposedly treating him.

Kimpton had also met Scotcher's brother, Blake, who bears a strong resemblance to his sibling. Kimpton is convinced in fact that it was Joseph in disguise. The police – absurdly – arrest Claudia because they think this will cause someone else to reveal the truth. Poirot tries to dissuade them because Claudia has an alibi. Poirot travels to England to interview the widower husband of Iris Gillow. He tells Poirot that Iris was pushed in front of a train by a woman disguised as a man, but he was not present so could not have known this, and it is also untrue.

Playford admits that she knew Scotcher was not dying – which makes her motive for changing her will nonsensical. She also admits being in love with him despite the difference in their ages. Bourlet also knew the truth, which makes her behavior equally illogical. Playford now asserts that her plan was to drive Scotcher into a position where he would either confess his play acting or try to murder her during the night. And she planned to forgive him and keep him on regardless of what choice he made.

The real Blake Scotcher died many years earlier. Kimpton tried to convince police that Gillow's husband killed her, although he believed it was Scotcher. The nonsensical explanation of this is that if he had accused Scotcher, it would have been attributed to personal animosity. He could simply have remained silent – he was not otherwise involved in the case. The author does not appear to have thought through this and several other elements of her plot.

Poirot contends that Scotcher killed Iris because she suspected he was not really ill, but he has no evidence to support his claim. Bourlet's account of things turns out to be have been largely delusional. Claudia admits having mutilated the corpse. Kimpton is the killer. For some arcane reason, Kimpton always carried a small vial of strychnine on his person. Claudia mutilated the body so that an autopsy would be performed and prove that he had never been ill. There would have been an autopsy in any case, and there was no reason why she should want to prove this after he was dead.

MASTERS OF DETECTION

The Mystery of Three Quarters (2018) begins when Poirot is confronted by Sylvia Rule, an irate woman who has received a letter accusing her of murder and signed by Poirot, although he knows nothing about it. The supposed victim, Barnabas Pandy, is unknown to him as well. Shortly thereafter, John McCrodden arrives, having received a similar letter accusing him. A third is sent to Annabel Treadway. Pandy was her grandfather and he died three months earlier, drowned in his bath, a presumed accident.

The fourth is sent to Hugh Dockerill, who appears to be much less upset than the first three. Dockerill is house master at the school where Pandy's great-grandson, Timothy Lavington, is a student. Pandy was in his late nineties when he died. Dockerill once proposed to Treadway. Lavington is spoiled by his mother, Lenore. Catchpool reappears. The other residents at the house include Treadway's niece, Ivy, and Pandy's manservant, Kingsbury.

An unidentified woman begins calling the recipients of the letters pretending to be working for Catchpool and asking questions about alibis. The superiors at Scotland Yard are so inane about insisting Catchpool and Poirot were responsible that the plot and momentum are fatally undercut and it is difficult to take the rest of the novel seriously. Right after Catchpool's superior blames Poirot for interfering with an official investigation, he places Poirot in charge of it and makes Catchpool his assistant.

Peter Vout, the family's lawyer, insists that the death was an accident, even though he was not present when it happened and can offer no evidence to that effect. Poirot investigates and eventually discovers that Treadway is in danger because she once placed the life of her dog ahead of the life of her niece. She confesses falsely to murdering her grandfather because he had planned to disinherit her and somehow concluded that she could only expiate her guilt by being hanged.

Pandy was going to cut off Lenore without a cent because she had refused to forgive Treadway. Pandy did die accidentally, although Kingsbury is murdered by Lenore, who then tried to frame her sister for the murder – and remarkably ineptly. She also tried to murder Treadway. Poirot figures it all out.

The Killings at Kingfisher Hill (2020) takes Poirot to the Devonport house. Richard Devonport's fiancé, Helen Acton, has been convicted of killing Richard's brother Frank and will be hanged if she cannot be exonerated within a few days. For some reason Scotland Yard has once again assigned Catchpool to serve as Poirot's assistant, even though the trial is over and the police have no further official role in the case.

They encounter a young woman, Joan Blythe, on the bus who loudly proclaims that she will be murdered if she does not change her seat. She was warned of her danger by a man who looks so much like Catchpool that she initially believes him to be the same person. Her seat is changed but she continues to act erratically until she disembarks. A third mystery is hinted at. Poirot interacts with an unnamed woman who is reading a book titled, *Midnight Gatherings*. All of this is later explained as an elaborate – and totally pointless – ruse.

The murder for some reason is not discussed at the Devonport house. Poirot's excuse for visiting is to meet Richard's father Sidney, and his friend Godfrey Laviolete. Laviolete's wife is Verna. Poirot is discussing this with Catchpool when several passengers, including the woman with the book and Blythe, exit the bus. Bloodstains are found on one seat, but this is a red herring. Poirot believes, however, that the unknown woman has committed murder. She is soon identified as Daisy Devonport.

More plot elements appear, including a possibly stolen design for a game similar to Monopoly. Daisy admits, sort of, to having murdered Frank. Sidney blows his stack and orders Poirot and Stackpoole to leave. The investigation continues at a distance. Daisy's confession leads to a stay in the execution order for Acton. Daisy is engaged to Oliver Prowd. Laviolete owned the house before the Devonports and is reluctant to talk about their having changed its name.

A woman is found bludgeoned to death in the Devonport home. Although her face is unrecognizable, Poirot believes it is Blythe. Acton recants and now insists that she saw Daisy kill Frank, whose shady activities were casting shame on the family. Blythe was actually Winnie Lord, who once worked for the Devonports. Daisy admits mutilating the body in a rather confusing series of contradictory statements. She also withdraws her claim to have murdered Frank. Blythe/Lord's story on the bus was complete imaginary – and totally unnecessary.

The truth is that Acton did murder Frank by pushing him out the window. He was on the verge of discovering that she and Prowd had engaged in the mercy killing of Prowd's father. Prowd then killed Lord because she knew too much.

Hercule Poirot's Silent Night (2023) is the most recent in the series as of this writing. It is 1931 and Christmas is about a week away when a fresh case arises. A very popular postal employee, Stanley Niven, is murdered while hospitalized, and no one can figure out how he committed the crime in the midst of the hospital workers.

Catchpoole is visiting Poirot – and he is as inept as usual. His mother, Cynthia, is introduced as well. She lives in a large rambling house near the hospital and insists that Poirot stay there while he investigates, and through the holiday season. Cynthia has a close friend who is scheduled to be admitted to the same hospital. The friend's wife is convinced, rationally or otherwise, that he will be murdered in turn if he goes there.

Poirot wants to solve the crime and leave before Christmas because he does not want to spend that day with Cynthia, who is unpleasantly overbearing. His investigation proceeds as quickly as possible and he eventually reveals that the wife is in fact the killer, though her friends are shocked at the revelation. The plot is coherent for the first two thirds – the best controlled book in this series – but founders a bit in the final third. Catchpoole would never have been able to sustain a career at Scotland Yard given his obtusity. He makes Hastings look like Sherlock Holmes.

INDEX OF TITLES

4:50 from Paddington (151)
The A.B.C. Murders (101)
"Accident" (173)
"The Actress" (173)
"The Adventure of Johnny Waverly" (173)
"The Adventure of the Cheap Flat" (173)
"The Adventure of the Clapham Cook" (173)
"The Adventure of the Egyptian Tomb" (173)
"The Adventure of the Italian Nobleman" (173)
"The Adventure of the Sinister Stranger" (174)
"The Adventure of the Western Star" (174)
Adventure with Crime (36)
"The Affair at the Victory Ball" (174)
"The Affair of the Pink Pearl" (174)
After the Funeral (144)
All Is Vanity (7)
"The Ambassador's Boots" (174)
And Then There Were None (116)
"The Apples of the Hesperides" (174)
Appointment with Death (161)
"The Arcadian Deer" (174)
At Bertram's Hotel (162)
"At the Bells and Motley" (174)
"The Augean Stable" (185)
The Big Four (81)
"The Bird with the Broken Wing" (175)
Black Coffee (191)
"Blindman's Bluff" (175)
"The Bloodstained Parchment" (175)
"The Blue Geranium" (175)
The Body in the Library (124)
Bones in the Barrow (19)
The Boomerang Clue (96)
By the Pricking of My Thumbs (165)
"The Call of Wings" (175)

"The Capture of Cerberus" (175)
Cards on the Table (105)
Caribbean Mystery (160)
"The Case of the Caretaker" (175)
"The Case of the Missing Lady" (175)
"The Case of the Missing Will" (176)
"The Case of the Perfect Maid" (176)
The Catalyst (43)
Cat Among the Pigeons (154)
The China Roundabout (25)
"The Chocolate Box" (176)
"The Clergyman's Daughter" (176)
The Clocks (158)
Closed Casket (199)
"The Coming of Mr. Quin" (176)
"The Companion" (176)
"The Cornish Mystery" (176)
"The Crackler" (176)
"The Cretan Bull" (176)
Crooked House (136)
Curtain (169)
Curtain Call for a Corpse (10)
"The Dead Harlequin" (177)
"Dead Man's Mirror" (177)
A Deadly Place to Stay (64)
"A Deadly Wedding Day" (196)
Dead Man's Folly (150)
"Dead Man's Mirror" (177)
Death at Half-Term (10)
Death at the Medical Board (12)
"Death by Drowning" (177)
Death Comes as the End (130)
Death in Clairvoyance (14)
Death in Retirement (23)
Death in the Air (99)
Death in the Clouds (99)
Death of a Con Man (44)
Death of a Poison-Tongue (53)
Death on the Borough Council (7)

MASTERS OF DETECTION

Death on the Nile (108)
Death on the Reserve (44)
Destination Unknown (147)
"The Disappearance" (197)
"The Disappearance of Mr Davenheim" (177)
Double Doom (27)
"The Dream" (177)
"The Dressmaker's Doll" (177)
Dumb Witness (106)
Easy Prey (32)
Easy to Kill (114)
"The Edge" (178)
Elephants Can Remember (169)
Endless Night (165)
"The Erymanthian Boar" (178)
"Evil in Small Places" (195)
Evil Under the Sun (12)
"The Face of Helen" (178)
"A Fairy in the Flat" (178)
Fall Over Cliff (7)
The Fennister Affair (46)
Fiasco in Fulham (37)
"Finessing the King" (178)
Fires at Fairlawn (21)
Five Little Pigs (125)
A Flat Tire in Fulham (37)
"The Flock of Geryon" (178)
"Four and Twenty Blackbirds" (178)
"The Four Suspects" (178)
"The Fourth Man" (178)
From Natural Causes (7)
"A Fruitful Sunday"(179)
Funerals Are Fatal (144)
"The Gentleman Dressed in Newspaper" (179)
"The Gipsy" (179)
"The Girdle of Hippolyta" (179)
"The Girl in the Train" (179)
"The Golden Ball" (179)
"Greenshaw's Folly" (179)

Hallowe'en Party (166)
"Harlequin's Lane" (179)
"The Harlequin Tea Set" (180)
"The Herb of Death" (180)
Hercule Poirot and the Greenshore Folly (150)
Hercule Poirot's Christmas (112)
Hercule Poirot's Silent Night (204)
Hickory Dickory Death (148)
Hickory Dickory Dock (148)
A Hole in the Ground (51)
A Holiday for Murder (112)
The Hollow (132)
"The Horse of Diomedes" (180)
"The Hound of Death" (180)
The House Above the River (30)
"The House of Dreams" (180)
"The House of Lurking Death" (180)
"How Does Your Garden Grow?" (180)
The Hunter and the Trapped (39)
A Hydra with Six Heads (50)
"The Idol House of Astarte" (180)
"In a Glass Darkly" (181)
The Innocent (64)
"The Jade Empress" (196)
"Jane in Search of a Job" (181)
"The Jewel Robbery at the Grand Metropolitan" (181)
"The Kidnapped Prime Minister" (181)
The Killings at Kingfisher Hall (202)
"The King of Clubs" (181)
"The Lamp" (181)
"The Last Séance" (181)
"The Lemesurier Inheritance" (181)
"The Lernean Hydra" (182)
"The Listerdale Mystery" (182)
"The Lonely God" (182)
Lord Edgware Dies (93)
"The Lost Mine" (182)
"The Love Detectives" (182)
"Magnolia Blossom" (182)

MASTERS OF DETECTION

"The Man from the Sea" ('81)
"The Manhood of Edward Robinson" (182)
The Man in the Brown Suit (73)
"The Man in the Mist" (183)
"The Man Who was No. 16" (183)
"Manx Gold" (183)
"The Market Basing Mystery" (183)
Marple (195)
"The Million Dollar Bond Robbery" (183)
The Mirror Crack'd (157)
The Mirror Crack'd from Side to Side (157)
"Miss Marple's Christmas" (196)
"Miss Marple Takes Manhattan" (195)
"Miss Marple Tells a Story" (183)
The Monogram Murders (197)
"Motive v. Opportunity" (183)
The Moving Finger (127)
Mrs McGinty's Dead (141)
Murder at Hazelmoor (88)
Murder at the Vicarage (86)
"Murder at the Villa Rosa" (196)
Murder for Christmas (112)
Murder in Hospital (7)
Murder in Mesopotamia (103)
Murder in Retrospect (125)
Murder in the Calais Coach (94)
"Murder in the Mews" (183)
Murder in Three Acts (98)
A Murder Is Announced (137)
Murder Is Easy (114)
The Murder of Roger Ackroyd (79)
Murder on the Links (70)
Murder on the Merry-Go-Round (25)
Murder on the Orient Express (94)
Murder with Mirrors (142)
"The Murdering Sort" (196)
The Mysterious Affair at Styles (65)
"The Mystery of Hunter's Lodge" (184)
"The Mystery of the Acid Soil" (196)

"The Mystery of the Bagdad Chest" (184)
"The Mystery of the Blue Jar" (184)
The Mystery of the Blue Train (82)
"The Mystery of the Spanish Chest" (184)
The Mystery of Three Quarters (202)
"The Nemean Lion" (184)
Nemesis (167)
New People at the Hollies (35)
"Next to a Dog" (184)
N or M? (23)
No Escape (41)
One, Two, Buckle My Shoe (119)
"The Open Mind" (196)
Ordeal by Innocense (153)
An Overdose of Death (119)
The Pale Horse (156)
Passenger to Frankfurt (167)
The Patriotic Murders (119)
Peril at End House (91)
"Philomel Cottage" (184)
A Pigeon Among the Cats (54)
"The Plymouth Express" (184)
A Pocket Full of Rye (146)
Poirot Loses a Client (106)
The Port of London Murders (9)
Postern of Fate (169)
"A Pot of Tea" (185)
"Problem at Pollensa Bay" (185)
"Problem at Sea" (185)
A Question of Inheritance (62)
"The Rajah's Emerald" (185)
"The Red House" (185)
"The Red Signal" (185)
"The Regatta Mystery" (185)
Remembered Death (130)
Room for a Body (37)
Sad Cypress (119)
"Sanctuary" (185)
"The Second Gong" (185)

"The Second Murder at the Vicarage" (195)
The Secret Adversary (68)
The Secret of Chimneys (77)
The Seeing Eye (29)
The Sevens Dials Mystery (84)
"The Shadow on the Glass" (186)
"The Sign in the Sky" (186)
The Sittaford Mystery (88)
Sleeping Murder (170)
So Many Steps to Death (147)
"SOS" (186)
"The Soul of the Croupier" (186)
Sparkling Cyanide (130)
Spider's Web (193)
"The Strange Case of Sir Andrew Carmichael" (186)
"Strange Jest" (186)
Stranger on a Cliff (18)
Stroke of Death (59)
"The Stymphalean Birds" (187)
"The Submarine Plans" (187)
Such a Nice Client (59)
The Summer School Mystery (16)
"The Sunningdale Mystery" (187)
"Swan Song" (187)
A Swan-Song Betrayed (60)
Taken at the Flood (133)
"Tape-Measure Murder" (187)
Ten Little Indians (116)
There Is a Tide (133)
They Came to Baghdad (139)
They Do It with Mirrors (142)
"The Third Floor Flat" (187)
Third Girl (163)
Thirteen at Dinner (93)
Three Act Tragedy (98)
"Three Blind Mice" (187)
"The Thumbmark of St Peter" (187)
To Let, Furnished (18)
Towards Zero (128)

"The Tragedy at Marsdon Manor" (188)
Treachery in Type (60)
"Triangle at Rhodes" (188)
The Trouble in Hunter Ward (57)
Trouble on Wrekin Farm (7)
"The Unbreakable Alibi" (188)
"The Under Dog" (188)
The Unexpected Guest (192)
"The Unraveling" (195)
The Upfold Witch (40)
"The Veiled Lady" (188)
Victim (56)
"The Voice in the Dark" (188)
A Well Known Face (33)
What Mrs. McGillicuddy Saw (151)
"Where There's a Will" (189)
"While the Light Lasts" (189)
Why Didn't They Ask Evans? (96)
The Wilberforce Legacy (48)
"The Wife of the Kenite" (189)
"Wireless" (189)
"Within a Wall" (189)
"The Witness for the Prosecution" (189)
Wolf! Wolf! (61)
"The World's End" (189)
"Yellow Iris" (189)

Made in the USA
Middletown, DE
31 May 2024